New Players, Different Game

New Players, Different Game

Understanding the Rise of For-Profit Colleges and Universities

WILLIAM G. TIERNEY

and

GUILBERT C. HENTSCHKE

The Johns Hopkins University Press
Baltimore

© 2007 The Johns Hopkins University Press

All rights reserved. Published 2007
Printed in the United States of America on acid-free paper
2 4 6 8 9 7 5 3 1

The Johns Hopkins University Press
2715 North Charles Street
Baltimore, Maryland 21218-4363
www.press.jhu.edu

Library of Congress Cataloging-in-Publication Data
Tierney, William G.
New players, different game : understanding the rise of
for-profit colleges and universities / William G. Tierney
and Guilbert C. Hentschke.
p. cm.
Includes bibliographical references and index.
ISBN-13: 978-0-8018-8657-7 (hardcover : alk. paper)
ISBN-10: 0-8018-8657-0 (hardcover : alk. paper)
1. Universities and colleges—United States. 2. Education, Higher—
Aims and objectives—United States. 3. Technical education—United
States. I. Hentschke, Guilbert C. II. Title.
LA227.4.T545 2007
378—dc22
2006037723

A catalog record for this book is available from the British Library.

*Special discounts are available for bulk purchases of this book. For more
information, please contact Special Sales at 410-516-6936 or
specialsales@press.jhu.edu.*

CONTENTS

ACKNOWLEDGMENTS

Any book is dependent upon many more individuals than those represented by the names on its cover. We began writing this book with support from Atlantic Philanthropies. Ted Hullar, Atlantic's program officer for higher education, was extremely helpful and supportive. More than one hundred individuals were kind enough to give us their time to be interviewed so we might gain their insights into the pros and cons of for-profit higher education. Several among these went way "above and beyond," sharing and discussing curricula, reports, and nonconfidential corporate memos and meeting with us multiple times over many hours. More than a dozen individuals read and commented on various versions of the book, and we are in their debt for their thoughtful (often wilting!) criticism. We wish to extend special thanks here to Phil Altbach, Mary Barry, Doug Becker, Goldie Blumenstyk, Jennifer Childe, Barry Currier, Mark DeFusco, Laura Rich Fine, Sean Gallagher, Nick Glakas, Sara Gubins, Ira Krinsky, Henry Levin, Brian Pusser, Elliot Sainer, Sally Stroup, and Marc Tucker.

Monica Raad and Diane Flores, in the Center for Higher Education Policy Analysis at the University of Southern California, were able to keep track of the multiple versions we kept producing; their support and goodwill made this undertaking much easier. Karri Holley, at the time a research assistant in the Center and now a faculty member at the University of Alabama, was a superb copy editor (and taskmaster).

Our editor, Jackie Wehmueller at the Johns Hopkins University Press, was ever so helpful in guiding our work and shepherding its journey through to completion. Peggy Hentschke and Barry Weiss had the good sense to encourage Gib to climb Mt. Kilimanjaro and Bill to climb Mt. Whitney, which may have slowed the writing a bit but also cleared our minds when we returned to the confines of our offices to rework the book.

We are deeply indebted to all of these good people. We also want to acknowledge and claim here that any and all errors of omission and/or commission contained within the book are ours alone.

New Players, Different Game

For-Profit Postsecondary Education

Lumpers or Splitters?

Throughout his teaching career, Stanford sociologist Richard Scott would begin his Sociology 101 courses with a sweeping characterization of all sociologists. Scott defined sociologists as either "lumpers" or "splitters." Such labels were a reference to tendency of sociologists either to examine a wide variety of phenomena and "lump" them together as variations on a fundamental theme or to examine one phenomenon, framing it as a fundamental "split" from other, similar phenomena. In their relatively short and recent history as a *new* type of higher education institution, for-profit colleges and universities (FPCUs) have been portrayed in two ways. They are either inevitable and incremental next steps in the evolution of American postsecondary education (Marchese 1998) or fundamental departures from what we have come to understand as postsecondary education (Heller 2003)—in other words, variations on the fundamental foundation of higher education or a division from expected postsecondary norms. In this book we examine FPCUs by way of a discussion about traditional colleges and universities (TCUs). The regulatory, cultural, and economic environments of for-profits are inevitably related to the history and current contexts of traditional institutions. The scaffolding we employ draws on both frameworks, but it begins and proceeds through most of the book with more of a splitter argument regarding for-profit colleges and universities—to wit, for-profit institutions represent a new, fundamentally distinct type of postsecondary education. As we look to the future in the conclusion, however, we are increasingly struck by the common forces acting on both types of institutions and the blurring of distinctions solely on the basis of economic sector—a lumper perspective.

Regardless of one's normative perspective regarding for-profit colleges and universities as good, bad, both, or neither, there is some sense that their existence and growth can be attributed to a combination of broad historical forces, including increased private as well as public benefits of additional postsecondary education; emergent governmental devolution and privatization of its historical functions; and a globalizing knowledge economy with requirements for a highly skilled work force. At the same time, FPCUs can be framed as representing (not exclusively) a fundamental shift in basic assumptions about higher education—a departure in public policy from exclusive reliance on public and private nonprofit institutions to produce the broad benefits of postsecondary education for society at large.

For-profit institutions certainly appear to be *different* from traditional colleges and universities for several reasons. Despite the long history of FPCUs in American education, such institutions differ in their rapid rise in scope, scale, and reach over the course of only a handful of decades; their distinctive corporate, for-profit structure and profit-seeking behavior; their minimalist, career-focused curricula; their unorthodox deployment of faculty; and their increasing penetration of traditional student aid resources, often redirecting them to new markets of heretofore non-college-bound students.

We are cognizant, however, that even if we portray FPCUs as splitters, they still exist in relation to traditional institutions. During the course of our research, we were aware of how much misunderstanding, even vitriol, exists between the various actors in the FPCU and TCU camps. Broadly stated, many who work in TCUs look on for-profits as charlatans out for nothing more than a quick buck; those who work in FPCUs regard the traditional postsecondary sector as antiquated and unwilling to compete. All too often, these perceptions have been formed anecdotally at best, with few data or little knowledge of what the other is doing. Although we understand the concerns of both sides, the goal of this book is to develop détente rather than disdain. The book is aimed neither as a polemic against FPCUs nor as a glowing tribute to a growing industry. Instead, we seek readers from both for-profit and traditional postsecondary education so that they might understand the inherent relationship between the two types of institutions.

Not all differences are equally important, by themselves or in conjunction with others. The sector difference among institutions—for-profit in contrast to public or private nonprofit—has existed since the founding of our country, but only recently have for-profit institutions increased rapidly in popularity. As we discuss, the private returns to postsecondary schooling have grown at a fast pace, fueling demand for schooling, followed closely by investor-backed leaders of for-profit institutions who seek to supply this demand with career-focused schooling services. Postsecondary education has now grown to such a level of economic importance that FPCUs constitute an important segment of the consumer retail industry whose economic performance is tracked continuously, not unlike the automobile and housing industries. FPCUs mean business.

From a perspective of traditional higher education, how might one view these new entities? Certainly one argument can be made that FPCUs are so *fundamentally* different that they cannot, or should not, be considered an integral part of what we have come to understand and accept as the higher education system, one made up solely of public and private nonprofit institutions. For-profit forms of organization may well be the ultimate source of wealth creation, which generate tax, gift, and investment revenues that are in turn reallocated as income to traditional education institutions. However, for-profit organizations that enter the business of postsecondary schooling should be allowed to operate only under uniquely crafted rules and policies. The very profit-seeking nature of these organizations requires special treatment, distinct from the manner in which public and private nonprofit colleges and universities are regulated. Or does it?

An alternative perspective of FPCUs is that they are best understood as a recent manifestation of the continuing proliferation of higher education institutions, building on a history of common varieties, each of which was in its own time a *recent manifestation*. Our oldest religiously affiliated, private nonprofit institutions such as William and Mary, Princeton, University of Pennsylvania, Luther College, and Mt. St. Mary's College were innovative enterprises in the seventeenth, eighteenth, and nineteenth centuries. Although each institution was unique on some level, all

of these TCUs shared roughly similar characteristics—the religiously related motivations of the founders, the sources of capital to start and operate, the underserved student market for which they were designed, and
the special character of the curriculum and the faculty they would employ.
One major motivation was the preparation of young men for the ministry;
this mission later included the provision of a proper religious orientation
to ongoing generations of students. The actors, their motivations, and the
means of these early religiously affiliated private institutions had much
in common even as they sought distinctiveness. Looking back, we can see
the founding of these institutions as reasonable responses to what some
today might call demands for human capital development by those individuals and organizations (religious groups) with the vision and means to
create and grow the enterprises.

Other kinds of institutions eventually emerged, not as replacements but
as supplements to the growing array of organizations. Each possessed its
own actors, motivations, and access to resources and, hence, had a distinct
character that set it apart from its older, well-established institutional
cousins. The large public land-grant universities of the nineteenth century
grew out of an entirely different set of circumstances with a unique set of
resources. These institutions even today are distinct from the religious
roots of the older private colleges. The availability of federal land, which
was granted to states to foster growth and development in the newly an-
nexed West, shaped TCUs such as Ohio State, Wisconsin, Missouri, and
Nebraska. In later stages and under different circumstances, the traditional institutions we know today as state college systems and community
college systems grew into prominence, each with its own leading actors
who responded to their versions of new demands for human capital development, and each with access to resources associated with their positions—largely state tax revenues for the state college systems and local
property taxes for the community college systems. In turn, each sought to
serve new categories of students, supported with resources available at the
time, and each took on a distinctive character that remains today. From this
simplified "last in" standpoint, FPCUs are not so different.

Indeed, from this perspective, the emergence of for-profit colleges and
universities over the past thirty years represents simply the most recent
arrival into postsecondary education of the next category of institution.

For-profit institutions in general represent, like their predecessors, new categories of actors. With access to new sources of start-up and operating capital, these new actors address new markets of student demand with new curricular and faculty role emphases. As these new entities arrive and take their place among the growing variety of higher education organizations, they require policy oversight and support in the public interest just as the more traditional colleges and universities have received and continue to receive.

Both perspectives are initially helpful and descriptive on one level, yet overly simplified on another. In the chapters that follow, we seek to unpack the primary presumptions about FPCUs, looking in detail at critical elements such as students, faculty, and programs. We also seek to understand the consequential ways in which FPCUs differ from TCUs, why they differ, and, ultimately what their combined impact might be for higher education in the United States. The purpose of the book, then, is to shed more light than heat on a rapidly changing industry. In order to discuss many of the central issues of for-profit institutions, we would be remiss if we did not also situate them in relation to traditional institutions. Those in the traditional sector can no longer simply ignore or dislike what is taking place in the for-profit world based on conjecture or whim. As we demonstrate, the growth of for-profit institutions is likely to continue, bringing consequences for all postsecondary colleges and universities. Similarly, those in the for-profit sector are mistaken if they believe that there is nothing to learn from how traditional institutions have functioned. The actors in both sectors can, and should, learn from one another, as they operate in quite different worlds. Accordingly, readers for this book, we hope, will come from both worlds and gain insight into the other. Eight interrelated issues consume our attention here, and they constitute the main chapters of the book.

In chapter 1 we use *innovation* to frame the arrival of FPCUs and to distinguish them from innovations over the years that have been pursued by traditional colleges and universities, both successfully and unsuccessfully. Many of the familiar innovations in traditional higher education, including the core curriculum, precept systems, variations in schedules and course calendars, are what Clayton Christensen calls "sustaining innovations"— in other words, measures that improve an existing service. FPCUs constitute organizations that employ "disruptive innovations." Such organizations redesign existing features in a way that initially captures new markets and ultimately moves into existing markets. Much of the "disruptiveness," we argue, comes from the fact that FPCUs operate out of a different economic sector, and hence operate within a radically different culture.

The second chapter, "New Forces in an Old Industry," examines changes in the social context that have shaped all higher education institutions in different ways but that have played well to the circumstances characteristic of FPCUs. Demand for more postsecondary schooling has been fueled by the combination of demographic growth, increasing intellectual content of work, and augmented returns to work resulting from increased schooling. FPCUs have aggressively responded to this demand by expanding capacity, while at the same time many TCUs have had difficulty maintaining the capacities that they had previously achieved. In addition, the changing nature of work and shifting subsidies for higher education have combined to draw large quantities of students into programs that promise wage premiums for graduates. Changes in student aid, tuition pricing, and the emergence of technology-related fields with worldwide demand favor new *job-relevant* training over traditional curricula at TCUs. As a consequence of these forces, several new forms of postsecondary schooling services are emerging. The most visible form is the for-profit college or university, due in large part to its rapid growth and widespread marketing.

What is the nature of these FPCUs that has enabled them to grow so rapidly? Chapter 3, "Growth of the For-Profits," asks two growth-related questions. First, what is the scope and scale of the growth in higher education, and specifically in for-profit institutions? What is the current share of the higher education market by for-profit institutions? How do FPCU growth rates compare with those of TCUs? How does growth in degrees compare to growth in certificates? What kinds of students have fueled FPCU growth?

Second, what are the ingredients of FPCU growth? Do they grow by enlarging campuses or by opening new campuses? How does the relative geographic immobility of TCUs factor into this? What role does program proliferation play in growth? Do FPCUs intentionally move up or down market in order to grow? That FPCUs have grown much more rapidly than TCUs is evident, and even some of the implicit tactics for growth can be discerned, such as rolling out the same program on multiple, small campuses. What is less clear is how and why the governance structures and incentive systems inside FPCUs align to focus heavily on growth. That is the goal of the next chapter.

In chapter 4, on finance and governance, we contrast the internal workings of for-profits, especially publicly traded corporations, with those of traditional colleges and universities, focusing particularly on differences in the decision rights and incentives of the major actors—governing boards, senior management, site or program management, and faculty. The attributes that lead investors to sink large amounts of money into an FPCU are also the attributes that focus the attention of those individuals at for-profit institutions with decision-making authority, such as governing boards and senior management. Because these individuals usually have a personal stake in the company, their incentives align (not always perfectly) with investors. At TCUs *shared governance* between faculty and management leads to different incentives and different behavior in pursuing revenues and in containing costs.

These differences in finance and governance, of course, carry over into differences in faculty and its work. In chapter 5, on faculty roles, the work of faculty at for-profits is dissected and compared with the work of faculty at traditional colleges and universities. The three-legged stool of research, teaching, and service found at many TCUs is instead a single pedestal of teaching at FPCUs. But even this generalization masks major differences in the roles that faculty members play in teaching-related matters (schedule, curriculum, specializations, etc.) at the two types of institutions. If the phrase "academic freedom" drives faculty work at TCUs, the FPCU analogue is more like "instructional effectiveness." Like TCUs, FPCUs rely on faculty expertise in the relevant field of instruction. While FPCUs pay for teaching services exclusively, such institutions differ from TCUs in that they do not support research and scholarly productivity. FPCUs rent faculty expertise for instruction but choose to let other institutions employ, monitor, exercise, and cultivate the professional expertise of their faculty. At the same time FPCUs separately employ multispecialty curriculum development teams as they create and roll out instructional materials, courses, and programs.

Differences in governance and the work environment of faculty set the stage to enable for-profits to pursue their special definition of success, ultimately in search of profitability, of which growth is a critical component. In chapter 6, "Defining Success at the For-Profits: Students, Programs, and Employers," we examine the FPCU core business of what might be termed *employment training*. Programs offered by FPCUs are directed toward employment markets; FPCUs are successful to the degree that they recruit, educate, graduate, and place students in positions that are promised. Pursuing this version of success requires much more intimate and sustained relationships with regional employers than is typical of multimission TCUs. Employer advisory boards, initially created as a component of federal school-to-work legislation during the 1990s, play an unusually large role in FPCU success. The programs of instruction at FPCUs require much more attention to skillful performance, above and beyond the mere acquisition of knowledge. Financial success (profitability at scale) hinges on the operational success that connects students to jobs through training.

The issues mentioned thus far—finance, incentives, curricula, faculty, and others—all point to the one topic that defines the entire field and encompasses all of the institutions in it: the student. As the individuals who are formally pursuing knowledge from a provider of education services, students provide higher education its reason for existence. In chapter 7, "Students and Other Priorities," we consider FPCUs and TCUs from a student's perspective. We compare the evolving concepts of a student, enumerate who constitutes today's postsecondary students, consider the needs of students from a societal perspective, and ask what students and curricula do public policy makers want to subsidize. In conclusion, we identify four perspectives from which to judge whether students are well served. We seek to use these perspectives to compare the quality of service of students at FPCUs with those at TCUs—a comparison that yields unclear outcomes.

In chapter 8, "Clashes of Cultures, Sectors, and Purposes," we seek at the same time to come full circle and address philosophical basics, addressing the salient and fundamental of differences between FPCUs and TCUs and then evaluating these differences in light of the historic purposes of higher education and the inextricably joint product they provide—public and private benefits to society and the individual student. Two recent highly publicized incidents illustrate what may be among the fundamental weaknesses or even failures of FPCUs and TCUs. If they are weaknesses or failures, what do they suggest for traditional and for-profit institutions and, indeed, for American higher education in the future?

Finally, in our concluding chapter we pull from all previous chapters to isolate five themes that, based on our study, appear likely to frame future discussions and thinking not only about FPCUs but about all of postsecondary education. In addressing these themes—environment, innovation, delivery, culture, and mission—we conclude that, over time and for numerous reasons, the distinctions between FPCUs and TCUs that we have examined will blur and blend. If we look from the present backward, FPCUs are understood to be a singular departure in higher education (the splitter argument). But in the view from the present forward, common, or at least increasingly overlapping, changes in both sectors will blur economic-sector distinctions among institutions of higher education. FPCUs and TCUs will increasingly be viewed as variations on a single theme (the lumper argument).

We have called upon various data sources to develop our argument. From 2002 to 2005, we were involved in a project that sought to understand emerging patterns of governance in postsecondary institutions. We interviewed approximately eighty-five individuals who were involved directly or indirectly with FPCUs. We also created focus groups of various players and called upon a good deal of federal, state, and business-related data to bolster our argument. As will become obvious, we did not entertain the more global aspects of for-profit education; our focus, instead, has been entirely on for-profit postsecondary education in the United States. We also want to underscore the dynamic nature of the for-profit sector. The "bust and boom" cycle of start-up companies such as the new for-profit postsecondary competitors defies a text that seeks to say, "This is how it is and will be." Instead, we focus on how the various sectors are changing, why they are changing, and where they might be heading. As with any new sector, there is very little previous research and a limited amount of data. Our goal is less to cheer for the changes or to denigrate the rise of FPCUs than it is to foster a useful, rational discussion about what one might expect from such a dynamic sector in the future.

CHAPTER ONE

The Innovators

New Services, New Sector

In their classic work on experimentation in higher education, Gerald Grant and David Riesman began by noting the challenge they faced: "We have attempted to assay as volatile a period of educational reform as America has ever experienced. . . . To understand what happened, it is necessary to go back nearly fifty years to see how contemporary reforms are related to and distinguished from earlier anti-university experiments, such as those at St. John's and Black Mountain" (1978, p. 1). Although the authors undoubtedly believed at the time that American higher education was undergoing a significant transformation, the assessment of that volatility would be decidedly different a quarter of a century later. Grant and Riesman defined "anti-university experiments" as efforts to move away from large institutions where research predominated. St. John's College, Black Mountain College, and Kresge College at the University of California at Santa Cruz are useful examples of institutions that rejected the ethos of a multiversity and embraced the ideals of a learner-centered curriculum.

Our comparison of more recent innovations at traditional colleges and universities with for-profit institutions suggests that the experimentation currently taking place in the postsecondary sector is unlike any that has been undertaken in more than a century. We analyze the transformations through four organizing questions: What are the drivers of change? Who champions the innovation? What are the innovations? How might the innovations be evaluated? Once we have answered these questions, we turn to a theory of change informed by the work of Clayton Christensen (1997; Christensen and Raynor 2003), which suggests that innovation in postsecondary education may be as much associated with the sector location of individual institutions as with their innovative behaviors.

Reform and Experimentation in the Traditional American College

For the past fifty years, the primary unit of analysis in American higher education has been the institution: the two- or four-year college or university. Many reforms to postsecondary education were instigated from outside the institution. Internal forces drove other changes. Affirmative action, for example, was fostered by a combination of social, legislative, judicial, and market mandates that forced institutions to change the way they hired faculty and admitted students. The passage of the Americans with Disabilities Act, federal concerns about human subjects' protection, and state and federal laws regarding age discrimination also prompted significant reform within academic organizations.

Systemwide changes also stimulated measures within individual organizations. Tenure became important to the academic profession, for example, and the result was that organizations were compelled to develop their own tenure-line policies. The doctorate has become the expected terminal degree for faculty because of a systemwide effort, just as research has become more important than teaching at a growing proportion of TCUs. Organizations have chosen to make internal modifications to maintain prestige and credibility within the larger system in which they find themselves.

Pass/fail grades, experimental colleges, and alternative living arrangements for undergraduates are examples of innovations that primarily originated from internal constituencies—faculty, student affairs administrators, or students—who worked to implement an idea that differed from the prevailing norm. Perennial debates about general education, as well as more recent academic changes such as writing across the curriculum and service learning, also reflect internal changes unique to an organization.

To be sure, most innovations require some external pressures for implementation. The introduction of pass/fail grades, a winter term, or a study abroad program does not occur through monastic conversation between individuals who are oblivious to what is taking place outside the institution. Such reforms, however, differ from changes that are mandated by external forces such as law or culture. An organization that does not adhere to civil rights legislation, for example, would face fiscal penalties; a university that does not have tenure would find itself outside of the academic mainstream and would have difficulty attracting faculty. Study abroad and other similar innovations, in contrast, are not mandates; they are changes that individuals within an organization decide would be beneficial for the college and university to implement.

Regardless of the impetus for the changes, however, the basic structure and culture of the academy were not brought into question. Consider, for example, the 1960s—a decade that many scholars believe to be among the most innovative periods in American higher education of the twentieth century. New institutions experimented with curricula, majors, and course offerings. Experimental colleges, or units within universities, catered to individuals and groups in unprecedented ways. The College of the Atlantic, Hampshire College, Evergreen State College, and the University of Wisconsin at Green Bay are all examples of institutions that attempted to break the academic mold. The College of the Atlantic developed a curriculum intensely focused on the environment. Evergreen State College assumed that co-teaching in an interdisciplinary manner was essential for a quality education.

By the end of the twentieth century, the experiments that had seemed so radical when they were first introduced had taken hold in only a handful of institutions. In most cases, the innovations had either been eliminated or had gradually regressed to the academic norm as a consequence of institutional change. Colleges and universities that experimented with pass/fail options, for example, had overwhelmingly returned to traditional letter grades. Indeed, given the litigious environment that exists today, many institutions have made explicit that an A means 95–100, and an A−, 90–94, and so on. Those institutions that had maintained pass/fail grades frequently allowed students the options of getting grades so that they would not be at a disadvantage in their opportunities for graduate school. Institutions that had eliminated a core curriculum returned to general education and distribution requirements. Standardized admission evaluations such as the Scholastic Aptitude Test (SAT) are currently as important as ever, despite (or because of) recent critiques and revisions.

Some new majors have taken hold, such as women's studies, African American studies, and regional or urban studies, but by and large such programs, though adopting the trappings of the standard curriculum, have remained small and underfunded. Their journals and conferences now exhibit the similar presentation and publication requirements as standard disciplines. Tenure and promotion committees expect the same type of professional profile from candidates in new fields as they have from everyone else. Accordingly, rather than change the academy, the experiments that survived are governed by traditional academic standards.

In hindsight, these innovations in postsecondary education were less revolutionary than they were modifications of an established structure. Although new majors such as cultural studies, Chicano studies, and biomedical engineering arrived, and new ways of grading and assessment such as narrative evaluations were developed, the overriding structure of American higher education remained remarkably intact. Tenure-track faculty offered classes to traditionally aged students in terms that covered an academic year. High school students applied to college in the fall of their senior year and admissions offices created an incoming class of new students based on set criteria a few months later. College life began for students in the fall when they arrived on campus. Students attended college for four years and, after they had taken a requisite number of course units, they were deemed eligible to graduate. Colleges and universities received accreditation from regional and professional associations. Not all of the experiments were failures, of course, but in terms of their deviation from the norm, they were modest and fell within preexisting academic structures.

To argue that experimentation within the postsecondary system has not occurred, or does not continue to occur, would be foolish. Yet innovation in higher education has remained within a socially constructed framework where the innovators have tended to accept the parameters of traditional higher education and have worked within them. How one defines the culture and structure of traditional higher education predetermines a great deal of what has been possible. Institutions acknowledge that they need accreditation and that there are standard sources of funding—primarily the state or tuition. Temporal and geographic aspects are also set. Classes occur on specific days over a set period of time; the term begins on a Monday at 4:00 p.m., for example, and concludes fifteen weeks later. Student learning is judged by credits; when a student accumulates a requisite number of units, as determined by seat-time in classes, the student may graduate. Students attend their classes on a campus. Individuals who are judged capable of instruction, and who have earned a degree in a particular subject area, teach students. These, and a host of other criteria, define the postsecondary universe.

As with all social constructions, deviations from these norms are relatively minor, in large part because those who participate in the construction have difficulty imagining ways much beyond the status quo. By making such an assertion, we are neither criticizing those who work in higher education nor suggesting that the structure that exists is somehow flawed or ineffective. Indeed, one reason why the postsecondary structure has remained stable is that during the past century American higher education rose to prominence throughout the world. If the structure is preeminent, then why opt for radical transformation? Instead, individuals have chosen to tinker around the edges.

Those in the traditional higher education realm recognize the need for innovation, but the types of changes they initiate tend not to deviate far from the norms. For example, some classes are offered in a more compact time period, such as on weekends, but the prevailing norm for classes is during the week. Funding sources remain tuition and state moneys, with an added contribution for some institutions from federal grants and private donations. Revenue is generally framed from a centralized model where the president and provost control funds and apportion it to the various deans and faculties, but institutions may also be revenue-centered, where each academic unit is a "tub on its own bottom" and responsible for generating and spending its resources.

Faculty credentials have overwhelmingly remained important, if not risen in importance, despite the fact that in some areas individuals may be hired to teach without a doctorate. Credit hours continue to be the standard by which student assessment exists, although some institutions have introduced exit exams. One change, however, is that the typical degree may now take considerably longer or slightly less than the standard two-

or four-year curriculum. Regional accreditation remains the most valued asset for all institutions that make a claim to legitimacy—although regional professional accreditation has weakened slightly in some professions.

Some innovations, of course, have taken hold. Technology, for example, represents a systemic innovation that has altered the postsecondary universe. The Internet, Web sites, and electronic technologies have transformed the way work is done within academia, as it has throughout society. A "library," no longer just a repository of paper, now can refer to paperless resources that can be accessed not only within a "library building" but also from one's home or office portal. Indeed, what is arguably the most significant change in postsecondary education in a generation is the way we define "information" and how we obtain it. Students may now visit a campus without ever having set foot on it; they may apply to a school on line; and they may learn if they have been accepted or rejected not by opening a thick or thin envelope but by checking their message box on the Internet.

Of equal interest are experiments in postsecondary education that have neither been attempted nor implemented. Until recently, those in traditional institutions, both private and public, have not examined their status or posited different ways to budget their moneys. Although there has been a significant rise in non-tenure-track and part-time faculty, few within traditional institutions have argued to abolish tenure or question the necessity of full-time faculty if the budget allows for them. Institutions have not suggested doing away with academic terms, credits, or degree requirements. Accreditation and professional affiliations have been updated and bolstered, with little hesitation regarding the value of such credentials. The academy still maintains that someone from inside the academic profession is usually best to run the organization and that the traditional ethos and culture of the academy are the most effective ways of providing a postsecondary education.

One of the more ironic observations about academic organizations is that evaluation has never been their strong suit. One might assume that in organizations where critique is part of the raison d'être, ongoing assessment and evaluation of activities would be required. Of course, that is not the case. Innovations have been implemented without rigorous evaluation. Some innovations are mandates, where there is no alternative; others, such as technology, are part of a large-scale societal transformation. However, innovations that are derived from internal forces often lack evaluative measures beyond the changing preferences of decision makers. If they fail, it is not because the innovation did not meet a particular criterion. Rather, changes fail or regress to the norm because they do not fit the overriding culture and ethos of the organization.

Regardless of whether the impetus for particular changes has come from outside the organization or from individuals within, those responsible for orchestrating and carrying out the innovations have been administrators and faculty. There is little wonder that individuals who are socialized to the mores of academic life will carry out experiments in predictable ways. The result is an adherence to the status quo and a system whose fundamentals today differ little from what they were a century ago. Some will quarrel with such an assertion and point to considerable changes in the manner in which academics do their work. We do not wish to suggest that the academy has not changed at all. It has. Yet, as we shall discuss, the types of changes that have taken place are what may be defined as "sustainable"—they have preserved the basic structure of the organization. If physicians or electricians from the early twentieth century were to walk into their respective places of work today, they would be unable to participate with their twenty-first-century confreres. In contrast, academics of the early twentieth century might be a bit confused by the Internet, but they would feel right at home in the classroom, on faculty committees, at commencement, and in interpreting the manner in which the institution conducts its business.

For-Profit Reform and Experimentation

Although for-profit postsecondary institutions have been in existence for well over a century, they have only begun to gain momentum in the past twenty years. What once had been a system populated by evening courses for working-class vocations such as beauticians and welders has blossomed into a full-service industry that is expanding in numerous directions. Given that such institutions have not been encumbered by a restrictive academic culture, for-profits have managed to undertake experiments that have been markedly different from the attempts of the traditional institutions that we have just described. Relatively few full-time faculty members are employed at for-profit institutions, and tenure is virtually nonexistent. "Faculty governance," a much-discussed issue among traditional institutions, is not even a topic, let alone an issue, among for-profits. Semesters, quarters, or academic terms in large part have given way to courses that begin and end based on the completion of core course requirements or the passing of a competency exam. Students have a wide array of options for when they begin and complete courses. The institutions still provide traditional seat-time programs leading to degrees, but the fastest growing segment of higher education is online programming with certificate-based as well as degree-based coursework that has been powered by for-profit and corporate universities. Adelman (2000), for example, has estimated that close to 2 million certificates were granted over a recent ten-year period.

Students generally are admitted the day they apply or make their enrollment deposit. The age of the student is irrelevant. For-profits are also more diverse than most traditional institutions; half of their students are minorities, half are women, all age groups are represented, and there is a mixture of full- and part-time constituencies. Students are as likely to take courses in an office building or in cyberspace as they are on a campus. Accreditation remains important, especially as eligibility for student loan funds depends on it. But accreditation is not essential for every institution and may be more associated with national occupational specialties than with regional efforts. For-profits have questioned the importance of accreditation and have suggested an alternative means of organizational certification that would be attached to program specializations rather than geographic regions of the country.

Again, we make no claim to the quality of such experiments, but when compared to those of the 1960s, the organizational changes taking place at for-profit colleges and universities appear to be quite far-reaching. These changes, in turn, may have significant implications for traditional postsecondary providers. Indeed, the impact already has begun to be felt. The usage of terms such as *marketplace, consumers,* or *providers* would have seemed strange if not anathema even a decade ago. Today such words are commonplace at traditional institutions and have come into the vernacular largely because of these new entrants.

As we discuss in chapter 4, the method of financing and governing for-profit institutions also stands in contrast to that of traditional colleges and universities. Research and alumni support at for-profits is virtually nonexistent. While tuition accounts for a significant portion of institutional revenue, investment capital also provides a major infusion of funding and is most often used to grow the company. Indeed, compared to TCUs, for-profits tend to invest more *new* funding into programs than into owning land and buildings. Most traditional colleges and universities have little idea of the costs associated with teaching, research, and service. FPCUs are the opposite. They understand the contribution, financial and otherwise, that all activities make to the organization; and if a course, program, or campus is not making a reasonable contribution to the organization, then it will be canceled or closed. For-profits' concentration on costs and benefits, coupled with tightened budgets among traditional institutions, has led to greater awareness of the price, cost, and margins of different activities such as graduate education.

The organizational forms and affiliations of for-profits also are at variance with traditional institutions. Professional associations such as the American Council on Education, National Association of State Universities and Land Grant Colleges, and the American Association of Universities have long played an important role for traditional institutions, yet hold little relevance for for-profits. Similarly the National Association for College Admission Counseling, National Association of Student Personnel Administrators, National Association of College and University Business Officers, and others have been commonplace organizations for professionals who work in traditional colleges and universities to join, but not always for those individuals employed by for-profit institutions.

As opposed to the internal and external demands on traditional institutions that have prompted experiments, the growth of for-profits has followed a fairly typical business model. FPCUs function in a manner that contrasts heavily with traditional higher education. An examination of educational demographics suggests that the student population will grow by an estimated 3 million students in the near future, and for-profit investors speculate that the traditional sector will not be able to absorb all of these students. Actual enrollments are running well ahead of earlier projections. In a knowledge economy, education is a growth industry, but the traditional segments of that industry, according to the for-profits, are neither able nor inclined to handle the increase in demand. Further, most colleges and universities are set up to serve traditionally aged clientele, while adults older than age 25 represent more than 50% of the potential postsecondary population. Whereas traditional institutions still assume that students want a typical college experience, including dorms, a campus, and extracurricular activities, for-profits assume that members of a significant sector care little about such activities and simply want a customer-focused curricula that will enable them to quickly receive job training and requisite skills.

Thus, there is a growing supply of potential customers whose demand cannot be met by the current providers. At the same time, technology has made it possible to reach the market in unprecedented ways. Because the structure of for-profits is not limited by a traditional culture, administrators at FPCUs do not see any problem with whole-scale utilization of electronic technologies; the only constraints are the current limitations of the technology itself.

Unlike most traditional institutions, which tend to demarcate their clientele by geography or constituency (California public institutions cater to Californians, women's colleges are for women), for-profits recognize that globalization and technology suggest a limitless reach. Market "niches" and "segments" do not imply local or regional reach. The use of typical business strategies such as branding and consolidation suggest that for-profit institutions will define themselves for a particular clientele and will merge and consolidate small companies into larger ones that have a more significant reach.

The traditional constraints of tenure or the desire for a full-time faculty are absent in for-profit companies. Instead, they seek to attract talent without future obligation and are inclined to outsource work that can be done more efficiently by other providers. The result is that the agents of change will almost never be "the faculty" because such a cadre of people does not exist, certainly not in "governance" roles. Those who drive the change are strategic agents within the organization ("senior management") who outline a plan based on market analyses and then hire the necessary personnel to undertake the plan.

For-profit institutions have focused primarily on developing course offerings that are individually convenient and collectively coherent in multiple ways. Without the traditional cultural mind-set regarding how courses should be constructed, FPCUs are not constrained by semesters and academic years. They have surveyed their potential markets and developed courses at times and in places that are easy to access; rather than require that the consumer come to the campus, the company has gone to the consumer. While tuition fees are rising among traditional public institutions, for-profit tuition prices generally run less than those of private nonprofits and are, thus, increasingly competitive. Aggressive corporate oversight keeps course and program costs generally below the prices charged to students. Plus, financial aid officers work extensively with the student to tap into as many possible revenue streams as possible.

Feedback is important to for-profits; when systems do not work, the organization will respond and change them. Finally, the curricula are stripped down, prepackaged into program specializations, and directed to the explicit needs of consumers (students) and employers who are anxious to hire program graduates. Rather than have a faculty decide what courses and programs should be offered, the company itself decides what it must offer for the client to gain requisite skills and compete successfully for specific jobs. The determination of whether the company is succeeding is twofold: the company needs to turn a profit; and standard benchmarks, such as job placement and enrollment growth, are used as indicators of the company's success.

As with the discussion of traditional postsecondary institutions, our purpose here is not to celebrate or criticize the way for-profits see the educational world or how they have responded. Instead, we outline these trends to demonstrate the dramatic difference between the two sectors with regard to innovation and change.

In summary, in traditional higher education, the impetus for change has come from external mandates such as government legislation and state policies, from systemic thrusts such as higher degree attainment for the faculty, or from internal champions of ideas such as professors who seek to create a new course or major. Pursuit of "prestige" rather than "profit" characterizes the behavior of faculty and administrators at traditional institutions. Their innovations are modifications to a preexisting cultural framework that defines what a "college" or "university" is. Innovation is often departmental rather than corporate, tactical rather than strategic. Evaluation is modest, at best. Changes that deviate significantly from the norm are eliminated or weakened. The result is that the reforms in traditional postsecondary education over the past generation have been minor changes to core functions, rather than dramatic reconfigurations. Most individuals who work in academia would likely agree with such an assessment and would argue that the overall structure of higher education is sound and that no "academic revolution," to use Jencks and Riesman's (1968) phrase, is necessary. Despite a steady flow of critical appraisals of higher education, such as Smith's *Killing the Spirit* (1990) and Readings's *The University in Ruins* (1997), numerous surveys point out that those within and outside of academia are relatively content with the services that are provided.

For-profit higher education has a different perspective. Changes at such institutions derive from neither legislative mandates nor internal agents of change. Instead, entrepreneurs have seen possibilities for change not by working within a set framework of traditional public and private nonprofit institutions of higher education but by setting the framework aside and building an altogether new model within a different economic sector. The entrepreneurs are the agents of change and are unencumbered by a culture that maintains "how things are done around here." Instead, they rely on an alternative culture that is much more familiar to them—the for-profit business world. In the past when they have encountered systemic roadblocks such as federal legislation or regional and professional accrediting associations, FPCUs have tried to change the legislation and associations rather than submit to them. We discuss this trend more in chapter 8. Summative evaluation is tied to growth and profit—"the bottom line." In for-profit institutions, formative evaluations are related to customer satisfaction as defined by job placement, employer satisfaction, and other factors.

In some respects, then, two different models exist. One form of innovation pertains to changes within an existing structure, and the other implies changes created by building new structures. The more modest innovations are framed by an assumption that tinkering around the edges is sufficient insofar as the structure itself is sound. The more dramatic innovations, in contrast, stem from an understanding of the vast potential that exists and that traditionalists have overlooked. To be sure, both forms of change are viable. But we suggest that with regard to the level and significance of innovation, a comparison of both models reveals that FPCUs are engaged in more substantial reform. In what follows, we place these changes first within a framework largely developed by Clayton Christensen and then within the framework of contemporary business.

Theorizing Experimentation and Innovation

In *The Innovator's Dilemma* (1997), Christensen posits that two forms of change occur with regard to technology: "sustaining" and "disruptive." Sustaining technologies are numerous and ongoing; they make current tasks more efficient. The change, for example, from a manual to electronic typewriter or from a dial-up modem to DSL enabled individuals to increase the output of their current activities. Laptops initially weighed thirty pounds and were the size of a suitcase; the speaking device of a phone was connected by a wire to the phone itself; garage doors had to be manually opened; car windows were rolled up and down. Eventually, the size and weight of laptops diminished, phones became cordless, an electronic device opened garage doors, and the push of a button rolled down the car window. All of these improvements sustained the technology; typewriters, laptops, telephones, garage doors, and cars all performed more efficiently, but they were not revolutionized by the innovations. Such changes generally decrease cost for those in a company who utilize the innovation, while they also appeal to the consumer. As such innovations lose their novelty, they become absorbed into the infrastructure of the company that adopts them.

The reform and experiment in traditional higher education that we previously outlined are examples of changes that sustained colleges and universities. Just as a fitness center updates its bicycles and treadmills, so too has higher education updated its curricula, developed new living arrangements, and improved the library. Faculty members no longer need to go to the library to check out books—they can now see if a book is available on line and have it delivered to their offices. Students do not have to wait in interminable lines to register for class; they too can do it on line. Still other experiments have been less "technological" in the sense of infrastructure and more in the way Cohen and March (1974) used the term, as the ideas and manners for carrying out and accomplishing organizational work. Offices have more open space, decision making is less hierarchical, and teamwork is frequently employed. These kinds of technologies have also sustained the organization rather than transformed it. The point is not that these changes are negative or useless, but that they enable the organization to do its current work more efficiently and effectively without changing the underlying structure.

Christensen posits that an alternative kind of technology is that which does not sustain an industry, but disrupts or revolutionizes it. Computer technology is the most obvious example of disruptive technology. Whereas the movement from manual to electronic typewriters increased the efficiency of a particular technology, the introduction of computers led to a fundamentally different situation. Computers did not sustain a technology but instead created a new technology that killed a related one: typewriters. Christensen maintains that it is not by chance that disruptive technologies emerge from new companies. Computers are attached to names such as "Apple" and "Microsoft," which did not exist fifty years ago.

Innovations that sustain and maintain work performance also attract the support of consumers. New, disruptive technologies are difficult to produce within a traditional organization because consumers have not expressed a demand for them. Customers may have wanted a typewriter that did not necessitate changing a ribbon, but no one envisioned a computer. Customers desired a telephone that did not tie them to one place, but no one anticipated that messages could be sent instantaneously on the Internet.

When technology is entirely new, it frequently fails or is cumbersome to use. A generation ago, computers were primarily used by academics and were linked to a mainframe. Computers often failed, and disks were regularly ruined. The cost of new technologies also is not price-sensitive for consumers. If the innovations do not perform well initially, why experiment with a new technology when the old one is sufficient? Why spend more on a risky experiment when the cost of the current product is cheaper and when the product reflects what today's customer wants? Most organizations, even "well-run" ones, are, in effect, a captive of their current customer base. They focus attention on what customers want and need. This, more than any other force, keeps organizations on the track of sustainable, rather than disruptive, technologies. Rather than waste time and money on innovations for nonexistent customers who might value the innovation, companies develop innovations that the current customer base will clearly value.

Disruptive technologies are generally simpler, smaller, and easier to implement; the company is often new and small and has no history of how to accomplish its tasks. Disruptive technologies, when developed, initially tend to cultivate new markets of consumers rather than compete directly with the existing consumer base. New technologies demand that multiple groups rethink the way they have created and delivered goods and services. In traditional organizations, a bureaucracy typically enables tasks to be accomplished in a standard manner. This standardization allows a traditional organization to reach the goals it has set for itself in as efficient a manner as possible. Inefficiencies are detected and corrected.

We are not proposing a crude interpretation of traditional companies as widget manufacturers where employees are little more than cogs in a wheel; such an interpretation would be incorrect. Companies aim to reduce inefficiency, and more recently such attempts have led not to factory-like changes but to changes that demand teamwork and creativity. Nevertheless, their aim is to maintain routinization toward the production of a particular goal. A disruptive technology, in contrast, demands that individuals not think and act in traditional ways. In an organization that has a highly routinized procedure for accomplishing its tasks, such experimentation appears to be difficult. Experimentation that will not serve the current customer base can, in effect, constitute a "bad" business decision.

Thus, insofar as the technology is unclear and the payoff uncertain, a traditional organization has little incentive to experiment by creating a new product. The result is that when innovators are able to refine a disruptive technology, it creates an industrial tsunami. An old technology such as a typewriter dies, and with it the organization that supported it. A new organization is born. Ironically, this new organization then sets about creating a standardized way of accomplishing its tasks, which in turns makes it incapable of creating the next disruptive technology—it too has become a traditional company.

In some respects, the traditional organization finds itself in a classic catch-22 situation: "The very processes and values that constitute an organization's capabilities in one context, define its disabilities in another context" (Christensen 1997, p. xxii). Thus, if an organization does what it is supposed to do (meet consumer demand), it ends up going out of business. An organization is incapable of doing what it needs to do to stay in business because of its success.

Of course, not every technology that aims to be disruptive actually meets its mark. Sometimes, by definition, experiments fail. Although we could take up a discussion about what traditional institutions might do to maintain their competitive edge, our purpose here is not to develop an innovator's cookbook. Rather, we wish to suggest that for-profit higher education has many of the markings of a disruptive technology—new products and services generating new demands from new consumers. As Robert Birnbaum (2005, p. 82) notes, "The possibility that traditional education may be challenged, or even eventually replaced by virtual education cannot be dismissed as idle speculation. Virtual enrollments are growing particularly in the proprietary sector."

For-profit institutions have not tried to develop within traditional organizations. The result is that they have not been encumbered by traditional notions of how to conduct business, especially vis-à-vis the traditional customer base. The manner in which they have defined delivery of services, cost, and personnel all point to dramatically different configurations that would be virtually impossible within traditional organizations, which in this case are public and private nonprofit organizations. For-profit colleges and universities have challenged the notion that education is a public good that can only be delivered by an institution in the public or nonprofit sector and instead have introduced business measures to gauge success. What frameworks help us to explain this disruptive technology in higher education?

The distinction between disruptive and sustainable technologies per se does not provide any explanatory power. Nor does the question of whether individual organizations are innovative. Rather, we make the simpler argument that structural distinctions among sectors—public or governmental, private nonprofit or charitable, and private for-profit or business—provide the greatest explanatory power. The behavior of for-profit higher education organizations is most clearly understood by their for-profit structure, and the differences in behavior between these organizations and traditional academia is best understood by *their* nonprofit or public structures.

While Christensen's ground-breaking analyses of innovation focused on sustaining versus disruptive technologies, all of his work at the time and since then has examined firms in the for-profit sector (Christensen and Raynor 2003), where innovation in the marketplace is extremely valued and consequential. There has been no focus on organizations in the other two economic sectors presumably because the rules of the game in these sectors are so different, and there was arguably much less innovation within them to study. It happens that the history of higher education in the United States is largely the history of private, nonprofit organizations, followed by public organizations and, more recently, for-profit organizations. Our analysis of for-profit higher education, then, is as much an examination of the role of an economic sector as it is an examination of individual firms within that sector.

The process of comparing and contrasting the organizational behavior of similar organizations in different economic sectors is not new. Perhaps the most widely recognized intersector comparative analyses have been conducted by Osborne and Gaebler (1992), who argued not only that there is a "sector-effect" in organizational behavior but that individual organizations within a specific sector enjoyed specific comparative advantages over similar organizations within other sectors.

According to Osborne and Gaebler, each of the three economic sectors—nonprofit, for-profit, and public—possesses distinct strengths compared to the other sectors. Organizations in the *nonprofit sector,* for example, are generally focused on "moral codes and individual responsibility for behavior" and are strong in areas that require "compassion and commitment to individuals" (Osborne and Gaebler 1992, p. 46). They are generally successful at meeting clients' needs and working in areas that "require extensive trust" or need "hands-on personal attention (such as daycare, counseling, and services to the handicapped or ill)" (p. 46). Organizations in the for-profit sector are particularly effective at innovating, adapting to rapid change, and performing technical tasks (p. 47). Furthermore, the for-profit sector brings access to finance and capital, managerial effectiveness and efficiency, and entrepreneurship (Rosenau 2000). Finally, organizations in the *public sector* are focused on the public interest and bring an understanding of policy management and regulations. Public organizations are usually effective at ensuring equity as well as continuity and stability of public services (Osborne and Gaebler 1992). Much of what we have come to recognize as differences among higher education organizations are explained at least in part by sector location.

While we do not intend to seek to "prove" the sector influence in higher education, we can understand for-profit postsecondary institutions first and foremost as for-profit businesses. At the same time, we also recognize that traditional (public and private nonprofit) academic organizations are not necessarily the same as for-profit businesses. Different "customers" have different expectations. The financial "bottom line" is not the only indication of quality. Social and symbolic interaction is at the core of academic life with beliefs such as academic freedom and shared governance as driving forces. The question, then, is not simply whether for-profits are at work inventing and implementing disruptive technologies, but how these technologies will be manipulated and used in advancing a postsecondary education.

Our contention is that for-profits have embarked on an innovation that is unprecedented. Rather than merely creating technologies that fundamentally alter and potentially improve upon a preexisting structure, FPCUs are engaged in an invention that could remake the postsecondary landscape, if they continue as they have. The implications for traditional higher education, of course, are significant. But our purpose here is to delineate the efforts underway in the for-profit sector so that we might better understand these changes and evaluate the attempts as FPCUs inaugurate new ways of conceiving of and delivering postsecondary education to emerging markets at home and abroad.

CHAPTER TWO

New Forces in an Old Industry

Although for-profit colleges and universities have a long history in American higher education, their rapid growth in recent decades can be interpreted as a response to several changes occurring in society at the same time, which, together, greatly increased the demand for postsecondary education and training. Increased numbers of eligible students, all facing employment prospects that increasingly required and rewarded technical training, have certainly contributed, along with shifts in college-attending financial aid toward the *consumer* (student). While the resulting increase in supply of education and training offerings can be seen across the range of for-profit, private nonprofit, and public sectors, for-profits have grown fastest by far, largely due to their access to rapid infusions of investment capital and, for the publicly held for-profit colleges and universities, their priority of growth. In addition to the FPCUs described in this book, at least four other forms of for-profit education and training have arisen alongside them, all in response to the greatly increased demands for schooling beyond high school.

The Demand Context of FPCUs
Demographics / Job Content / Wage Differentials

The demand for schooling is fueled foremost by the interaction of growing numbers of adults, the expanding knowledge content of jobs, and increasing real wages attributable to higher levels of schooling.

DEMOGRAPHICS

Enrollment in postsecondary degree-granting institutions has grown from about 7 million in the mid-1960s, to more than 15 million in 2001–

2 (Silber 2004, p. 60).This trend is expected to continue at about 1.3% a year over the next decade and to result in more than 20 million students in postsecondary institutions. Growing enrollments are attributable to overall population growth as well as greater rates of participation in college. Among the U.S. population, people between the ages of 25 and 29 who held a bachelor's degree increased from about 13% in the mid-1960s to almost 30% in 2003, indicating both greater participation in postsecondary education in the present than in the past. The potential exists for continued growth of participation rates into the foreseeable future (p. 60).

Greater college participation rates are themselves fueled more by the so-called nontraditional adult population (those who are 25 years old and older) than by the traditional 18- to 24-year-olds, as illustrated by enrollment trends between 1985 and 1992. During that time, the number of 18- to 24-year-olds decreased by about 11%, while overall postsecondary enrollment increased by more than 18%. College-going rates among high school students, on the other hand, have been fixed on average, hovering around 60% after peaking in 1997 (Silber 2004, p. 64).

The demographic trend fueling postsecondary demand is that of the older student. The nontraditional student is now in the majority and has thus become the new traditional higher education student. Between 1987 and 2000, the number of 25- to 44-year-old postsecondary students grew nearly 23% (from 4.9 million to 6 million), outpacing the approximately 20% growth in the total number of students over that time (Silber, p. 65). The National Center for Education Statistics (2003a) estimates that more than 8% of all 25- to 44-year-olds will likely be enrolled in postsecondary institutions by 2013, up from about 7% currently.

TECHNOLOGY AND THE CHANGING NATURE OF WORK

Although analysts differ on the social implications of changes in the nature of work, there appears to be consensus on the overall growth of the "knowledge content" in work, spawning shorthand sound bites like "information age," "knowledge economy," "knowledge capitalism," and "knowledge worker" (Burton-Jones 1999). The rapid growth of information technology (IT) is discernibly different from the growing knowledge content of work. The task of information management is increasingly incorporated into jobs in *all* employment sectors, not just within IT industries.

Beyond specific advances across a variety of IT fronts, such as falling costs of processing power and wide varieties of applications associated with communications, computer hardware, and software, IT is changing the way virtually all work is conducted and organized. While IT is an expanding field with its own demands for an increasingly knowledgeable and skilled work force, its growth has also greatly sped up the knowledge content of many other fields.

As noted in figure 2.1, widely diverse industries are investing heavily in IT, regardless of their overall characterization as high or low technology. These dual growth trends—IT and knowledge content in work—act as mutually reinforcing motivations of increased demand for schooling, both in IT-related fields and in many nominally unrelated fields such as manufacturing and services.

The content of work is also changing in more subtle ways. Indeed, cash registers at local fast-food franchises are now IT-enhanced with pictures instead of numbers, illustrating that IT can be associated with decreased as well as increased skill requirements. Overall, however, the result of increased IT activity has been to enhance the skill requirements of work. In fact, "the overwhelming evidence is that on balance, recent technological advances favor more-skilled workers, a phenomenon known as *skill-biased technical change*" (Autor, Levy, and Murnane 2001, p. 109).

Autor, Levy, and Murnane initiated perhaps the most formal analysis of changes in work content and in the process clarified and categorized what most of us intuitively, albeit vaguely, believe to be true. In their analysis of economy-wide trends in the average skill content of jobs over the past four decades, they evaluated five categories of skill content based on whether the job involved routine or nonroutine tasks and cognitive or manual skills. Each of these five categories was indexed to zero (no change) in 1959.

As portrayed in figure 2.2, there has been a steady rise, especially during the 1980s and 1990s, in the share of jobs that require nonroutine cognitive analytic (problem-solving) and interactive (communication) skills. The share of jobs requiring routine cognitive and manual skills, after rising during the 1960s, fell steadily afterward.

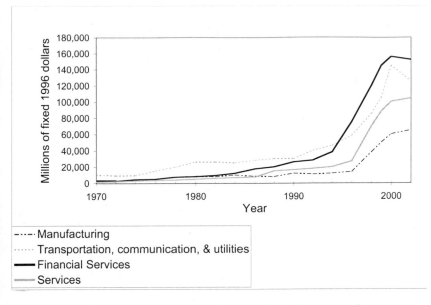

Figure 2.1. Real Costs Investments in Information Technology across Four Industries. *Source:* Karoly and Panis 2004, p. 87

The use of manual skills (both routine and nonroutine) fell less than routine cognitive skills, given the relative ease of computerizing routine cognitive skills. Considered alongside other studies (such as Bresnahan, Brynjolfsson, and Hitt 2000), we conclude roughly what Karoly and Panis (2004, p. 111) argued: "The evidence points to the growing importance of cognitive skills in the workplace, whether in the manufacturing sector, where production employees now program and repair complex machine tools, or in the services-producing sector, where workers increasingly are responsible for managing, interpreting, validating, transforming, communicating, and acting on information generated by new technologies." Higher proportions of workers are now required to go beyond simply providing information. They are also responsible for generating and conveying knowledge needed for decision making. This kind of knowledge is acquired through schooling.

Not only are jobs shifting toward greater intellectual content, but they are also beginning to shift from more permanent positions toward less permanent ones (Autor 2001; Neumark and Reed 2002). In the future,

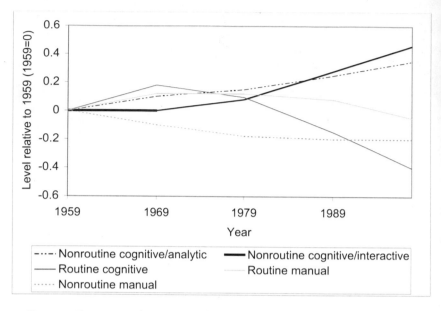

Figure 2.2. Economy-wide Measures of Occupational Task Input, 1959–1989.
Source: Reprinted by permission of David Autor, from *The Skill Content of Recent Technological Change* (MIT, Department of Economics)

the nature of work will require that individuals are increasingly able to retrain themselves and adapt to new or changing employment circumstances. "Workforce education and training in the future will involve continuous learning throughout the working life, involving training and retraining that continues well past initial entry into the labor market" (Karoly and Panis 2004, p. xxxvi).

Well-trained knowledge workers are those who have invested time and other resources in learning more skills. Those skills command some level of wage premiums in the marketplace, the exact amount of which depends on a host of local factors, such as employment opportunities and personal qualities.

INCREASING PRIVATE (AND PUBLIC)
RETURNS TO EDUCATION

As the world evolves into an information age or knowledge society, the value of human capital escalates. If we assume other factors are held con-

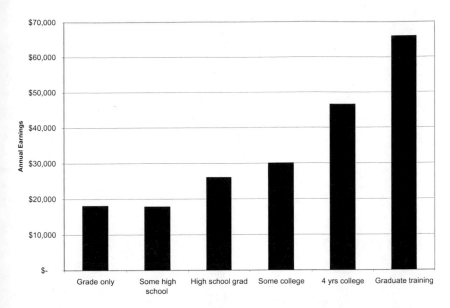

Figure 2.3. "The more you learn, the more you earn . . ." Annual Earnings of U.S. Workers by Education, 1998. *Source:* U.S. Census Bureau 2000

stant, this trend means the more knowledge is gained, the more financial rewards are earned (figure 2.3). This equation holds true for individuals and societies.* Although this has been accepted wisdom for several decades, we now realize that the connection is more pronounced than was previously believed (figure 2.4). Education is an even more dependable way to climb upward to a better financial life.

Correspondingly, greater and greater proportions of job holders have completed some level of college, regardless of field. As shown in figure 2.5, between 1973 and 2001 proportions have significantly increased, not only in technology and white-collar jobs but also in education, health care, and factory jobs.

The bad news is that the ladder is less available, especially to people

---

* Economist Gary Becker, the Nobel laureate who pioneered the study of human capital, estimates that the financial value of the average American is somewhere between $500,000 and $5 million. If we assume the low end of this range, the value of human, social, and other nonfinancial capital in our country is roughly $137 trillion (1999), or about three times greater than more traditional forms of financial capital ($43 trillion) (www.knowledgeu.com/capital _graph.html).

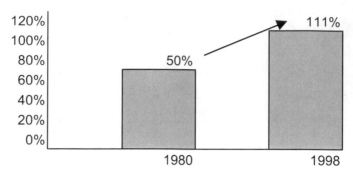

Figure 2.4. Widening Pay Gap between High School and College Graduates.
Source: U.S. Census Bureau 1980

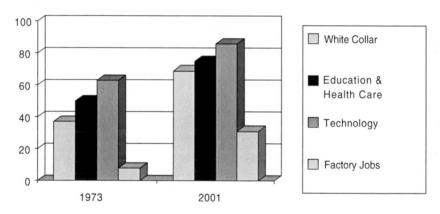

Figure 2.5. Increasing Percentage of Job Holders by Field with Some College Upskilling.

who are not far up that ladder at least by the time they reach the middle of their working life. Those consistently and pervasively near the bottom of the learning hierarchy are falling farther behind those near the top. Those with more education, both relatively and absolutely, are the most likely to invest in further education over the course of their working lives. As a result, education increasingly is a winner-take-all game. Although some of this game is due to an actual decline in earnings of high school graduates and those with less education, the fine distinction is difficult for most of us to discern.

Such a game suggests that, across the entire array of possible school-

ing levels, there is an average level of education above which earnings continue to improve over time as demand increases. Below that level, earnings do not necessarily improve over time, and may in fact decline in real
terms as relative demand for low-skill jobs decreases. As portrayed in Figure 2.6, that breakpoint is somewhere near the education level of *some college*. Demand and wage premiums tend to increase over time above that
breakpoint and to decrease in real terms below.

Of course, students attend postsecondary education for many reasons
other than to earn more money. The education that students receive generally includes much more than learning that is directly applicable to post-
graduation employment. The benefits of an education can and should be
measured in ways other than or at least in addition to wage premiums.
After all, the strong association of education with earnings does not directly or automatically suggest, per se, that students actually decide to go
to school to earn more. Yet, in a recent survey conducted for the *Chronicle of Higher Education*, respondents picked "prepare its undergraduate
students for a career" as the top priority for colleges for a second year in
a row (Silber 2004, p. 70). This was also the only answer that at least 70%
of the parents identified as very important.

Inequality, Competition for a Skilled Work Force, and the Public Good

To the extent that schooling increasingly affects lifetime income, we
can expect to see growing inequality in household incomes that are closely
associated with differentials in education levels. At the risk of overstating
the argument, there is little middle ground between households spiraling
upward through a *virtuous* cycle (more learning leading to more earning,
leading to investment in more learning, and so on) and those spiraling
downward through a *vicious* cycle (less education leading to less earning,
leading to increasingly obsolete education generating less earning, and so
on).

Up to this point, we have treated the learning-leads-to-earning connection as applied only to individuals, but the connection also holds for
groups of individuals—those in different communities, counties, states,
countries, and even regions of the world. Governments do not just decide

Figure 2.6. Real Median Hourly Wage by Education Level, 1973–2003. *Source:* Permission granted by the publisher, from L. Mishel et al., *Working America, 2002/2003;* Economic Policy Institute (www.epi.org)

to provide subsidies for schooling simply because education is inherently worthy. Government officials are aware that developing and retaining a more highly educated work force is increasingly the greatest guarantee of a positive social future through increases in tax revenues, increased individual lifetime earnings, and public goods such as greater civic participation. Hence, after more pressing short-term priorities have been met (including sizable budget deficits, prisons, roads, and K–2 education), state governments seek to support (subsidize) postsecondary schooling within their borders, primarily through appropriations to their public higher education institutions. State governments also seek to add to the supply of *seats* and provide increases in student financial aid, thereby seeking to intensify the demand for seats. In general, governmental jurisdictions want more educational opportunities for their citizens, just as citizens themselves want.

Governments are not unlike businesses, nonprofits, and households in that they must devote a large share of their attention to raising revenues, largely through systems of taxation. As with other social organizations, while the government's attention is directed to the visible specifics of the spending side, this spending is ultimately constrained by what revenues can be generated. As knowledge enterprises develop more taxable wealth and income, governments are increasingly forced to concentrate on overall levels of educational attainment by citizens within their jurisdictional borders. Aggregate human capital within their borders shapes the potential for economic development and access to tax revenues.

The same is true for cities, states, nations, and continents. The skill level of the work force varies greatly in these places. Those areas with a relatively highly educated work force are also characterized as generating jobs with relatively high levels of skill content and will likely generate relatively higher per capita taxes. Cities, for example, with a comparatively high ratio of college graduates to high school dropouts attract more knowledge industries than those with low ratios (see table 2.1). Arguably each factor affects the other; cities with more knowledge industries also attract more knowledge workers. Minneapolis–St. Paul represents a fundamentally different kind of work force than Las Vegas, and the work force closely characterizes the overall content of employment in the city. Average salaries are higher in Minneapolis–St. Paul.

TABLE 2.1
*"Brain to brawn" ratios: U.S. ratios of college
graduates to high school dropouts*

High	
3.53	Minneapolis–St. Paul
	Seattle–Tacoma
	Raleigh–Durham
	Denver–Boulder
	Washington–Baltimore
	Austin–San Marcos
	San Francisco–San Jose
	Houston–Galveston
	Greensboro–Winston-Salem
	New Orleans
	San Antonio
	Los Angeles–Riverside
	Miami–Ft. Lauderdale
0.79	Las Vegas
Low	

SOURCE: Milken Institute 2004, sec. V-14.

The primary providers of postsecondary education have been and will continue to be public community colleges, state colleges and universities, and, to a lesser extent, private nonprofit universities. But the ability of governments (especially state governments) to provide significant increases in subsidies to public educational institutions is constrained by their lack of political authority to raise taxes and also by other responsibilities that make an even higher claim on tax revenues. Most governments have great difficulty shifting significant proportions of tax revenues to education from other competing government services, such as health care, infrastructure, criminal justice, and transportation. This is even more the case for higher education than for K–12 education. In addition, many individuals are willing to pay higher tuition and fees knowing they can be recouped through higher earnings.

States, the traditional providers of subsidies to their own public postsecondary institutions, now compete among one another to provide quality education services even to those living outside their formal jurisdictions. Individuals (households) increasingly flow across governmental boundaries to find a better quality of life, including the best possible education, much like the free flow of financial capital in search of more productive investments. Governments worry about the possibility of a brain drain from their jurisdictions (see, for example, Pak 2005, and Cervantes and Guellec 2002).

Governments subsidize postsecondary education in two different ways. First, by subsidizing some institutions directly, governments seek to reduce the price charged to the students. Second, by subsidizing some individual students directly, governments hope to reduce the effective price at the institution that the student chooses to attend. Through its subsidization of education costs to individuals, the federal government facilitates the flow of students not just into higher education but also into those institutions that are most attractive to students. With the growing social and economic value of a more highly educated citizenry, governments and households find mutual interest in collaborating on educational matters. Private individuals, through a variety of means, shoulder more responsibility for schooling at all levels. Governments are taking note and are looking for ways to facilitate (not oppose) the process.

Because the cost of going to college outpaces inflation, it is increasingly difficult to afford. Escalating inequalities in private income and wealth, especially in countries like the United States, exacerbate the disparity between rich and poor households. Lower-income households find it increasingly difficult to pursue an advanced education, especially in traditional, prestige-driven institutions. Within this environment, for-profit universities, more so than public and nonprofit private institutions of higher education, have flourished as evidenced by the disproportionate growth of FPCUs.

Shifting Financial Resources into and within Postsecondary Education

The higher education system in the United States has been greatly affected by these financial forces. As a partial response, the flow of resources has shifted, affecting demand for education negatively as well as positively. Shifts in one part of the system constitute external forces on other parts of the system; FPCUs have tended to benefit from these developments relative to TCUs. The three most visible and relevant shifts for this analysis are those in sources of expenditures for higher education, in governmental subsidies for higher education, and in institutional subsidies for higher education.

SHIFTS IN EXPENDITURES FOR HIGHER EDUCATION FROM GOVERNMENTS AND INSTITUTIONS TO HOUSEHOLDS

A large proportion of expenditures for higher education derives from governments, particularly state governments, in the forms of appropriations to public institutions and financial aid to students. When those governments face revenue shortfalls and have to make budget-balancing cuts across competing services, higher education generally absorbs larger cuts than other sectors such as K–12 schools, welfare, and Medicaid (Callan 2002, p. iv). To illustrate this tendency, consider the changes in the relative proportions allocated by state governments to Medicaid and higher education in the past twenty years. In 1987 Medicaid received slightly more than 10% of state spending, and higher education received slightly more than 12%. By 1990 spending for Medicaid had slightly exceeded that for higher education. By 1995 Medicaid's share had grown to more than 19%, whereas higher education's share was just over 10% (p. 3). The reasons behind higher education's comparative disadvantage are numerous (see, for example, Callan, p. 6), but the effects are all essentially in the same direction.

State governments and institutions are likely to transfer these shortfalls in expenditures to students and their families by raising tuition, but without corresponding increases in student financial aid (Callan 2002, p. iv). The degree of this shift from governments to households varies from state to state, and even from institution to institution, but the trend is generally in one direction. By way of illustration, in New York State between 1990 and 1995, tuition increased from 4.2% of the median household income to 7.7%. In California, the increase during this same period was from 1.7% to 3.1% (Halstead 1998, pp. 11, 67). In 2000 all but the wealthiest families (defined as the top income quintile) paid more of their income to go to college than they did in 1980. The poorest Americans (bottom income quintile) paid 13% of their annual family income to attend public four-year colleges in 1980; in 2000 they paid 27% of their annual income to attend (National Center for Public Policy and Higher Education 2003, p. 55).

As the demand increases for households to shoulder a larger proportion of the expenditures for higher education, households respond accordingly. Some simply pay the difference; others postpone attendance or elect a less expensive option (community college instead of a four-year college); and some choose options other than college. Regardless of individual decisions, households are increasingly sensitive to the growing costs (and growing benefits) of schooling. Their decisions regarding schooling are increasingly influenced by circumstances associated with their ability to pay for schooling.

SHIFTS IN GOVERNMENT SUBSIDIES FOR HIGHER EDUCATION FROM INSTITUTIONS TO INDIVIDUALS

In an attempt to counteract the uncertainties of government appropriations to institutions, governments have sought to increase student financial aid through loans. The argument favoring direct student support over institutional subsidies takes several forms. First, if the goal is to increase student participation in higher education, studies show that a dollar allocated to student financial aid has a greater effect on enrollment increases than a dollar appropriated to the general support of institutions (Morgan, Kickman, and LaPlant 2001). Second, student aid can be targeted to those most in need and least able to afford tuition prices.

The shift in subsidies to households has been accelerated by the advent of tuition tax credits. The federal version of this policy benefits families with taxable annual incomes of between $40,000 and $90,000, especially those with students at colleges with high tuition rates. Only households that owe taxes are eligible, so lower-income households are excluded (Callan 2002, p. 19). Furthermore, over the past thirty years, much of federal student financial aid has gone from grants to loans, thereby raising the effective cost of schooling for households.

Government funds are not the only subsidies available to many households. In addition to traditional (government and institutional) providers of financial aid, postsecondary education subsidies to households increasingly come from employers. Employers make substantial investments in training their work forces, whether through on-the-job training or formal training via in-house or outsourced programs. One recent survey indicated that 80% of employers provide some type of formal training (Karoly and Panis 2004, p. 206) either directly or through subsidies to other providers.

With a greater proportion of subsidies allocated directly to students, students encounter—at least theoretically—a broader array of higher education options. Within the context of overall affordability, households (individual students) are increasingly able (or required) to choose among institutions and apply subsidies to the institution that is best suited to their needs.

SHIFTS IN STATE AND INSTITUTIONAL SUBSIDIES
TO HOUSEHOLDS FROM NEED- TO MERIT-BASED
SCHOLARSHIPS AMONG TRADITIONAL INSTITUTIONS

Simultaneous with the shifts in expenditures and subsidies to households, the criterion for aid has shifted (at the margin) from financial need to merit. State governments and individual institutions are increasingly concerned with maintaining and increasing the quality of their postsecondary students, a concern translated to the systematic funding of merit-based aid. States worry about possible brain drain, or the migration of high-achieving high school graduates to out-of-state colleges (Callan 2002, p. 18).

The net effect of governmental merit-based aid has been to distribute dollars to students who were already the most likely to attend college—and who could afford to pay—and to institutions that already receive the largest public subsidies (Finney and Kelly 2004, p. 55). On the positive side, the advent of merit-based financial aid increases incentives for improved student performance in high school (Henry and Rubenstein 2002). On a less positive note, however, this shift exacerbates the proverbial winner-take-all scenario among the more competitive TCUs, but does little to aid less wealthy TCUs or FPCUs that serve middle- and lower-income students.

The crosscurrents of shifting expenditures, costs, prices, and subsidies within postsecondary education do not uniformly impact FPCUs. As a whole, students are increasingly taking advantage of available subsidies only after consideration of the value to them of further education. For many, the premium for education is rising along with expected rewards. For a growing proportion of the potential postsecondary market, FPCUs represent a viable postsecondary option.

The Supply Context of FPCUs

All of higher education is affected to varying degrees by the contextual forces that drive demand for postsecondary schooling—especially demand by prospective students and employers. The recent rapid growth of FPCUs is understood in part by looking first at these forces, although FPCUs are not their only by-product. Others include, for example, the growth at TCUs of vocationally oriented, preprofessional, and career awareness programs, plus the growth at TCUs of IT-enhanced distance-learning offerings.

In the last chapter of this book, we explicitly examine the impact of these forces on TCUs and FPCUS and their contrasting responses. The differences between the two types of organizations help us to understand the differences and similarities we identified in the previous chapter. To imply here, however, that FPCUs and TCUs are the only two responses to these forces is misleading and serves to inaccurately diminish the power of the demand forces. While FPCUs tend to be less visible than TCUs, other suppliers of postsecondary education and training exist that are even less visible and less understood than FPCUs.

These least visible suppliers are also responding to new demands of postsecondary schooling. While these institutions are difficult to examine, do not categorize easily, and are often inextricably interdependent, together they make up much of the rest of what is new in postsecondary education—somewhat separate from TCUs and FPCUs. We have sorted these responses into four broad categories: workplace training, including workplace universities; IT education providers; distance-delivered education; and short-course training organizations. Although we treat these four types of supply responses here as categories distinct from TCUs and FPCUs, they are also increasingly found within (or closely associated with) TCUs and FPCUs.

Workplace Training and "Universities"

The workplace is increasingly serving as an educational provider for its employees. Workplace or corporate "universities" are administratively distinct educational entities embedded within larger corporations; their primary mission is not to provide direct education services (in contrast to FPCUs, whose primary mission is to provide education services). Today, there are approximately 2,000 corporate universities, most of which provide formal and informal training opportunities for acquiring job-specific skills. Some of the more easily recognized of these corporate universities include AT&T School of Business and Technology, Charles Schwab University, Disney Institute, MasterCard University, and Motorola University. Corporate universities tend to be less likely to invest in the general skills of their workers to the extent that those skills are more readily transferable to another employer (Becker 1975).

The curriculum within these entities ranges broadly across business topics such as customer relations, new product and service protocols, corporate strategies and cultures, and field-specific issues. Corporate universities are direct providers of education, but they also outsource, jointly produce, and otherwise partner with other providers. FPCUs are among the providers that offer educational services in partnership with corporate universities and through human resource departments of firms without distinct corporate universities. Overall, corporations spend between $50 billion and $75 billion on training their work force, depending on the specific year and whether government spending is factored in (Silber 2004, p. 135).

Part of this spending is flowing to FPCUs. Although student tuition is the primary source of revenue for FPCUs, a growing proportion of that tuition is provided by employers (in the form of student reimbursement for satisfactorily completing courses or as an interorganizational contract). This tuition is subsidized by government loans and grants. Due to the wide variety of content and arrangements among corporate universities, FPCUs can be viewed as competitors, substitutes, or partners, depending on individual circumstances.

Technology Education Providers

Information technology is driving changes in all fields as well as constituting a growing field in its own right. This development has fostered its own system of IT postsecondary education above and beyond the effects on the education offerings of TCUs and FPCUs. The new system is sufficiently different from the workplace university setting. Technology education is replete with content-specific, performance-oriented certificates such as MCSE and Cisco certification; content and performance standards (de facto accrediting functions); wide varieties of providers and standardized curricula; and a growing recognition globally across a wide variety of firms (Adelman 2000).

In early 2000 approximately 1.6 million individuals worldwide earned approximately 2.4 million certifications in information technology. Almost half of these individuals were from the United States. A sampler of some of the major certifications is portrayed in table 2.2. More than fifty major corporate vendors, IT industry associations, and larger intermediary training partners such as Learning Tree (which reports serving 113,000 information technology students) have formally established criterion-referenced standards for optimal performance levels in various parts of the IT-related world (Adelman 2000, p. 23). Indeed, many FPCUs

TABLE 2.2
*Sampler of major information technology certifications
as of 2000*

Microsoft Certified Professional (MAP)
Microsoft Certified Solutions Developer (MACS)
Microsoft Certified Systems Engineer (MCSE)
Certified Cisco Design Associate (CCDA)
Certified Cisco Internetworking Expert (CUIE)
Certified Novell Engineer (CANE)
Certified Novell Administrator (CAN)
Oracle [multiple certifications]
Citrix Certified Associate (COCA)
Certified Info Systems Security Professional (CISSP)
A+ [Computer Technology Industry Association]
Red Hat Certified Engineer (RHCE)
Accredited Systems Engineer (Compaq)
Certified Lotus Professional Application Developer (CLP)

SOURCE: Adelman 2000, p. 9.

(and some TCUs) function as training partners in this parallel universe and may benefit from growth as much as their competitors.

Online Learning

Advances in information technology have fueled demands for more skilled labor and provided more efficient and effective platforms for delivering education and training. Technology-mediated learning, or the use of computers and other information technologies as an integral part of the learning process, is increasing in popularity through such applications as computer-based instruction, Internet-based instruction, and other methods for customized learning (Karoly and Panis 2004, p. 121). IT changes foster access to instructional materials at any time and at greatly reduced costs because there is no need to bring instructors and students to a central location.

The variety and degree of IT course enhancement can be enormous. Fully online learning, as we use the term here, is limited to courses where more than 80% of the content is delivered on line and no face-to-face meetings take place (see Allen and Seaman 2004, p. 4, for taxonomy of courses where less than 80% of the content is delivered on line). About 1.6 million students took at least one fully online course in fall 2002, and nearly 2 million in fall 2003, with future estimated growth rates higher than implied by these figures (p. 4). Most of these course are offered by public postsecondary institutions (nearly 83% in 2003), followed by private nonprofit institutions.

The largest growth in the offering of online courses, however, is among private for-profit institutions, including FPCUs. The number of public institutions offering at least one online course has remained constant—about 90% over the past two survey years. During the same period, private nonprofits offering at least one online course dropped very slightly (54.5% to 52.6%). Private for-profit participation rates increased significantly over the same period (44.9% to 88.6%). Trends in distance learning will be significantly influenced by any changes in the "50% rule," which presently prohibits institutions from having more than 50% of their students enrolled in distance-education programs or offering more than 50% of their courses via distance education.

TABLE 2.3
Largest corporate training providers
(2003 revenues in millions of dollars)

Top 10 Companies	Ticker	Training as Primary Service	2001 Revenues ($)	2001 Market Share (%)	2002 Revenues ($)	2002 Market Share (%)	2003 Revenues ($)	2003 Market Share (%)	CAGR, 2001–3 (%)
New Horizons	NEWH	Yes	512	2.7	499	2.8	550	3.2	3.7
Institute for International Research (IIR)	Privately held	Yes	390	2.1	400	2.3	400	2.3	1.3
Thomson Learning	TOC	No	230	1.2	258	1.5	283	1.6	11.0
Global Knowledge Network	Privately held	Yes	346	1.8	228	1.3	249	1.4	−15.2
Skillsoft	SKIL	Yes	44	0.2	102	0.6	190	1.1	107.1
Learning Tree International	LTRE	Yes	207	1.1	171	1.0	168	1.0	−9.9
ExecuTrain	Privately held	Yes	133	0.7	133	0.8	141	0.8	3.0
American Management Association (AMA)	Privately held	No	208	1.1	135	0.8	135	0.8	−19.4
Franklin Covey	FC	No	165	0.9	124	0.7	131	0.7	−11.0
Element K	Privately held	Yes	91	0.5	95	0.5	105	0.6	7.0
Total market			2,326	12.40	2,145	12.20	2,352	13.5	0.5

SOURCE: Silber 2004, p. 136.
NOTE: As Simba defines the market differently than IDC, its total market revenue estimates vary. CAGR = compound annual growth rate.

IT-enhanced distance-delivered schooling, incorporated into FPCUs, TCUs, and other providers, is also growing rapidly. Corporation-based distance learning, for example, was a $1.2 billion business in 2000 and is growing at a rate of 80% per year (Karoly and Panis 2004, p. 121). Future applications of IT innovations to distance learning, such as standardized specifications that foster interoperability, accessibility, and worldwide reusability, plus wireless and PDA-based training, assessment, and tracking of online learning activities, all suggest that these growth rates will not diminish anytime soon (p. 122). FPCUs constitute an important part, but by no means the bulk, of the rapidly growing online learning boom. The degree to which FPCUs are competitors, collaborators, or complimentary providers depends on specific circumstances.

Short-Course and Training Providers to Corporations

Although corporations outsource or reimburse employees for the education provided by FPCUs, organizations other than FPCUs also provide similar services for corporations. Of the $50 billion to $70 billion in annual corporate expenditures for training and education, less than $20 billion is spent on outsourced services (Silber 2004, p. 136). As portrayed in table 2.3, short-course providers, like FPCUs, tend to be publicly traded and privately held for-profit entities. Unlike FPCUs, such providers largely tend to offer short, stand-alone courses rather than prespecified bundles of courses in (longer) certificate and degree programs.

FPCUs exist as a major entity within this relatively new demand-and-supply context of postsecondary education. Current demands for increased schooling across an employee's work life are expressed by individuals, businesses, and governments alike. Subsidies to support traditional suppliers of postsecondary schooling have not kept up, but new revenue sources are surfacing in sufficient quantity to support the creation and growth of new kinds of postsecondary schooling suppliers. Of those nontraditional suppliers, FPCUs represent arguably the largest, fastest-growing, and most TCU-like institutions that follow the ideas we outlined in chapter 1. What they look like in broad outline is the subject of the next chapter.

CHAPTER THREE

Growth of the For-Profits

Education is a small but growing part of our life, at least as measured by share of the U.S. gross domestic product (GDP). Education's share has climbed steadily over time, increasing 23% between 1986 and 2003 (2.6% to 3.2%). Similarly, for-profit colleges and universities represent a small fraction (single-digit percentages depending on what is counted) of postsecondary education in the United States, whether measured in dollars or enrollments, but they are growing especially fast. Postsecondary education in the United States generated about $291 billion in revenue in 2001–2 (National Center for Education Statistics 2005), or about 2.8% of GDP that year. The 2.6% annual growth rate in postsecondary spending in 2002, however, was much slower than the 8% average annual growth rate for postsecondary education over the prior three decades and slower than the growth rates of FPCUs especially during the past decade.

FPCUs have recently attracted interest and concern more for their high rates of growth than for their overall size or increased penetration of the postsecondary marketplace. In this chapter, we outline the basic characteristics of today's FPCUs, including their numbers, niches, and sizes. We seek to understand the factors that motivate their growth and the major mechanisms for achieving growth, such as mergers, acquisitions, and organic (or same-store) growth. The rapid increase in for-profit enrollment, at least as compared to that of TCUs, is due to a combination of factors: their focus on programs for which demonstrable employment demand and promising economic returns exist; their unique access to investment capital; their discipline in containing the operational costs of programs within the limits of earned revenue; their basic business model of small, distributed campuses with convenient locations; their operating flexibility and adaptability to changes in labor markets; and their ability to capitalize on productivity-enhancing technologies. Growth, however, is not an end in itself; growth is a means to profitability.

Of the 9,485 postsecondary institutions in the United States today, about 47% are organized as for-profit institutions. FPCUs tend to be less visible than their nearly 50% share suggests, for at least three reasons: for-profit institutions are relatively new despite their long history as a type; they still enroll a small share (less than 5%) of the postsecondary enrollment market; and their campuses tend to be small in size, often embedded within shopping malls and business office parks.

At the same time, FPCUs are also the fastest-growing segment of the postsecondary education market. Between 1998 and 2003, for-profit enrollment increased 80% in less-than four-year programs and 91% in degree-granting institutions (National Center for Education Statistics 2005, pp. 5, 6). The fact that FPCUs have increasingly gained visibility is perhaps attributable to the ubiquity of television commercials and freeway off-ramp signage promoting the large, nationally focused, publicly traded for-profits like University of Phoenix, Corinthian Colleges, Education Management Corporation, DeVry, ITT, and others. As evident in the levels of enrollment, revenue, and numbers of campuses, FPCUs are characterized by rapid growth. Certainly this growth is fueled by many of the theoretical and contextual factors discussed in previous chapters that are affecting all of postsecondary education (such as new technologies and increased demand). But factors inherent to FPCUs further contribute to their patterns of unusually rapid growth.

We look directly here at FPCUs—their characteristics, how they operate, and, in particular, why many of them are capable of accelerated growth. First, we look at growth in three areas: enrollments; institutions and campuses; and programs, certificates, and degrees. Second, we look at the growth strategies of several of the more visible publicly traded FPCUs. We demonstrate how each institution relies on common tactics, such as investment infusions, mergers, acquisitions, and program development, to pursue unique pathways and to distinguish itself from its competitors. The final component driving FPCU expansion is marketing, which also sets FPCUs apart from TCUs. A key objective and result of

FPCU operations is growth. Growth leads to scale; conversely, profitability at scale is possible, but not guaranteed, through growth. Despite our attention to factors that promote FPCU growth, we recognize that the ultimate FPCU objective is profitability.

Growth of FPCUs: Enrollments, Institutions, and Programs
Growth in Enrollments

Over the past three decades, for-profit enrollments (as measured in degree-granting programs) have increased at about seven times the rate of the entire postsecondary sector, or at a rate of 10.4% versus 1.4% for TCUs. With this differential rate of growth, FPCUs have increased their penetration of the postsecondary degree-seeking enrollment market by a factor of about seven, from 0.4% to about 3.4% in 2001–2 (Silber 2004, p. 73). Although FPCUs offer a wide array of programs leading to *certifications* in various occupational fields, they compete most directly with TCUs in the offering and awarding of *degrees*. Since the late 1970s, FPCU enrollments in degree programs have grown from less than 100,000 to nearly 600,000 students.

Enrollments vary by the size of the for-profit. FPCUs fall into three broad categories that are roughly analogous to the size of the institutions: the first comprises fewer than a dozen large publicly traded institutions that have top-line operating revenues in excess of $100 million; the second numbers perhaps twenty privately held institutions that have revenues between $50 million and $100 million and are large enough to entertain the possibility of going public at some time; and the third category includes the vast majority of firms that operate at less than $50 million per year. While enrollment data are treated as proprietary information by most privately held FPCUs, reporting requirements for publicly traded FPCUs provide another glimpse into both the scale and the enrollment growth of these super systems. Over a recent two-year period, enrollments at the eleven publicly traded FPCUs increased from 424,000 to 686,000, or by about 62%. Near the beginning of that period, median total annual growth across each of these FPCUs was about 20% (adjusted quarterly).

TABLE 3.1
Eleven publicly traded FPCUs: Enrollment and year-over-year growth, second quarter 2004

	Enrollment	Growth (%)
Apollo Group (APOL)	239,000	28
Career Education (CECO)	81,000	31
Concorde (CCDC)	6,000	3
Corinthian (COCO)	65,000	50
DeVry (DV)	41,000	−5
Education Management (EDMC)	53,000	33
EVCI Career Colleges (EVCI)	2,000	83
ITT Educational Services (ESI)	39,000	16
Laureate Education (LAUR)	131,000	55
Strayer Education (STRA)	17,000	22
Universal Technical Institute (UTI)	13,000	21

SOURCE: Silber 2004 and company reports.

Near the end of this period, median year-over-year total growth was about 27% (adjusted quarterly) (Silber 2004, p. 77).

Although large, publicly traded FPCUs grow faster than average FPCUs, it is by no means uniform among them. As shown in table 3.1, some are relatively large and growing at a relatively fast rate (e.g., Apollo Group and Laureate). Others are relatively small but are growing rapidly (e.g., EVCI). Still others of varying size are growing at slower rates (e.g., Concord and DeVry).

Enrollment growth at FPCUs occurs in two different forms. "Same school" growth describes enrollments on one for-profit campus between two points in time. This measure analyzes the degree to which FPCUs are increasing enrollments at an existing site as opposed to increasing enrollments by adding campuses. Near the beginning of this same two-year period, these FPCUs were adding enrollments to existing campuses at a rate of about 20% per year (adjusted quarterly); near the end of the two-year period, enrollment growth at existing campuses dropped to about 15% per year (adjusted quarterly) (Silber 2004, p. 77).

During that same period, as suggested by these rate changes, these FPCUs increasingly relied on acquisitions of additional campuses to buttress enrollment growth. Near the beginning of this period, median enrollment growth attributable to students at newly acquired campuses was about 16% per year (adjusted quarterly) and grew to around 22% per year (adjusted quarterly) near the end of the period. Both venues (through same-school growth and acquisitions) describe the connections between campuses and enrollments that fuel FPCU growth.

These growth rates do not speak solely to the demographic characteristics of the added enrollments, nor do they reveal how FPCUs are able to grow so rapidly. Where do FPCU students come from? Are they recruited away from TCUs, or do they represent a new market to postsecondary education? We will examine FPCU students in greater detail in chapter 7. We briefly summarize the demographics here. Based on some characteristics, these students tend to be those who have not actively participated in postsecondary education previous to FPCU enrollment.

Some have called these students the "other three-fourths," referring to the fraction of the adult population in society that may have participated in higher education but do not hold a bachelor's degree. When compared to TCU students, FPCU students tend to come from lower-income families, tend to be on their own rather than dependents supported by their parents, are generally older, and are more likely to be African American and Hispanic American. Over the past three decades, FPCUs have also tended to serve greater proportions of older students, who themselves have dependents, and students who are single parents. Besides the apparent conclusion that FPCUs tend to attract more underserved student populations, we can infer that FPCUs are tapping into new postsecondary student markets more than competing for existing ones.

Growth in Number and Types of Institutions

Compared to most TCUs, the average FPCU tends to enroll small numbers of students and offer a narrow range of programs. Of the 9,485 postsecondary institutions in the United States, 6,779 participate in Title IV programs, making their students eligible for federal financial aid (Career College Association 2003, p. 1). FPCU campuses actually constitute about 47% of all postsecondary institutions, but only about 38% of the institutions eligible to offer Title IV financial aid are FPCUs. (Apparent differences in enrollment data on FPCUs are sometimes due to whether all or just Title IV eligible FPCUs are included.) Among public and private nonprofit institutions that also offer Title IV financial aid, the aver-

TABLE 3.2
For-profit as percentage of total institutions and enrollment, 2001–2002

Institutions	Institutions		Students		
	No.	%	No.	%	Average Size
Public	2,099	33	12,370,000	76	5,893
Private nonprofit	1,941	30	3,198,000	19	1,648
Private for-profit	2,418	37	766,000	5	317
Total	6,458	100	16,334,000	100	2,529

SOURCE: Silber 2004 and company reports.

TABLE 3.3
Total number of private, for-profit Title IV institutions in the United States by level of institution and degree-granting status, 2002–2003

Level of Institution	Degree-Granting Institutions	Non-Degree-Granting Institutions	Total
At least 4 years	297	3	300
At least 2 but less than 4 years	494	270	794
Less than 2 years	NA	1,318	1,318
Total	791	1,591	2,382

SOURCE: Silber 2004 and company reports.

age enrollments are approximately 5,900 and 1,600, respectively, in contrast to slightly more than 300 at FPCUs (see table 3.2).

FPCUs vary not only by their Title IV eligibility but also by whether they award degrees (rather than certificates) and by the length of their programs. Most Title IV FPCUs offer relatively short programs (less than two years) resulting in certificates rather than degrees (see table 3.3). Their highly variable nature makes it difficult to generate unambiguous data from FPCUs. Any fixed and mutually exclusive categories that might be used to count FPCUs, such as Title IV eligibility, highest degree granted, and terminal degree or certificate offered, in fact are either not mutually exclusive or significantly out of date by the time they are reported. The counting and categorization problem is especially pervasive as the corporate universities, virtual universities, and other hybrids evolve (Kinser 2006). While the counting and comparing problem is vexing and will remain so for sometime, the general orders or magnitude and overall growth rates of individual institutions provide at least some context.

Considered as a single characteristic, small campus size is not remarkable. However, when considered in conjunction with many multiple campuses, such as is characteristic of larger FPCUs, and with larger FPCUs' inclination to migrate successful programs to other campuses, a growth strategy for FPCUs emerges. By having many small campuses instead of a few (or one) large campuses, FPCUs can locate programs closer to student markets. Among FPCUs, campuses vary significantly in size between those that primarily offer degrees and those that offer diplomas and/or certificates. About two-thirds of all FPCU campuses offer primarily diploma programs, and the average enrollment on these campuses is just under 150 students, in contrast to just over 650 students at degree-granting FPCU campuses (see table 3.4).

FPCUs are characterized as having roughly a direct relationship between the level of schooling and the number of students served. Most students enrolled are in schools that offer four or more years of postsecondary schooling, and the fewest students are in schools that offer less than two years of postsecondary schooling. At the same time, the reverse is true for the number of institutions; a majority of the FPCU campuses offer less than two years of postsecondary schooling and enroll the fewest number of students on each campus (see table 3.5).

Although generalizations about the nature of FPCU growth must be assembled from a wide variety of data, for-profits appear to be "growing upward." For example, more growth is taking the form of longer programs with higher levels of degrees and certificates on larger campuses

TABLE 3.4
For-profit institutions and enrollment by degree type, 2000–2002

	Institutions		Students		
	No.	%	No.	%	Average Size
Degree-granting	808	33	528,000	69	653
Diploma-granting	1,610	67	238,000	31	148
Total	2,418	100	766,000	100	317

SOURCE: Silber 2004 and company reports.

TABLE 3.5
For-profit institutions and enrollment by school type, 2001–2002

| | Institutions | | Students | | |
	No.	%	No.	%	Average Size
At least 4 years	324	13	321,000	42	992
At least 2 but less than 4 years	779	32	242,000	32	310
Less than 2 years	1,315	55	203,000	26	154
Total	2,418	100	767,000	100	317

SOURCE: Silber 2004 and company reports.

as opposed to short courses on small campuses. Historically, FPCUs offer programs to students at the early stages of postsecondary education. For example, of all students enrolled annually at less-than-two-year institutions, 66% were enrolled at FPCUs, whereas FPCU students were only 5% of all students enrolled at greater-than-two-year and less-than-four-year institutions. The "growing upward" story becomes more apparent at FPCU institutions with programs of four years or more. While currently only 7% of all students at baccalaureate (four-year or more) institutions are FPCU students, these constitute the majority of FPCU students, and enrollment at these FPCU institutions increased 106% between fall 1998 and fall 2003 (Career College Association 2003, p. 5). FPCUs are continuing to gain enrollment shares over TCUs among four-year institutions. However, like private nonprofit TCUs, they are losing enrollment shares to public two-year TCUs (see figure 3.1).

Growth in Programs, Certificates, Degrees, and Venues

The different dimensions of FPCU growth—enrollments, campuses, and programs—act as interdependent contributors to growth. As a group, FPCUs are continuing to diversify into additional curricular areas, with more FPCUs offering programs from the associate to the doctoral levels, and in fields as diverse as culinary arts, psychology, and teacher education (Gallagher and Bassett 2004, p. 13). Some FPCUs diversified in 2001 after a severe downturn in the IT credentials market drove them into other fields such as allied health, criminal justice, and business.

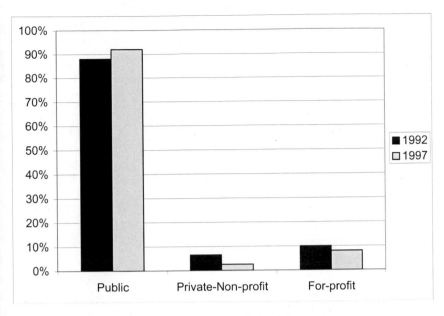

Figure 3.1. Enrollment Share at Two-Year Institutions by Sector

Enrollments continue to grow in part because new student markets are being tapped. They also grow as campuses are opened in new locations and programs are offered in new labor markets. The fastest growing cities are relatively concentrated in about a half dozen states, and tend to be popular states for FPCUs to open new campuses (Gubins et al. 2005, p. 51). Many FPCUs are growing online capability as a complementary channel through which to drive their programs, and a few are branching into international markets (through distance-learning and additional campuses) with programs that evidence demand. We discuss FPCU programs extensively in chapter 6 but emphasize here two program characteristics that contribute directly to revenue growth: scalability and profitability.

Each program designed and offered by an FPCU on one of its campuses can be replicated on other campuses. While also true (in principle) at TCUs, most traditional institutions are single campus entities. As the scale and reach of a program expands, the unit development and marketing costs shrink. Because it is unlikely that *any* program will be developed in which the costs associated with producing and operating it are higher than the revenues that can be generated through tuition charges, virtually all FPCU programs generate some level of earnings. Programs that have high fixed production costs require larger scales to break even. Because some FPCUs can spread program development costs across a number of campuses, they can elect to enter fields where program development costs are relatively high.

Profit margins are roughly the difference between all costs associated with providing a program and the tuition revenues generated by that program. Margins are determined by the interaction of costs and prices. FPCUs seek to control costs and raise prices as much as feasible in order to increase these margins. To the extent that a program is in high demand, a for-profit can increase tuition and, consequently, profitability. Beyond unit profitability, popular programs will multiply and be offered at several sites; programs in less demand will only be offered at those sites that are located in specific labor markets with a high demand for graduates. Such a *distributed campus,* in which each site has its own particular bundle of program offerings, is its own profit center. Campus-level management, then, determines the best mix of programs for an individual site.

The governance of multicampus FPCUs typically can be traced from corporate headquarters down through each family of programs (such as business or nursing), and through each degree or certificate awarded, all in a direct line to each campus. Primary accountability is between each campus and corporate headquarters, and despite many contributing factors, growth is typically a campus-by-campus pursuit. Growth in enrollments, campuses, and programs serves as the means for generating growth in revenues and earnings. Gross revenues are important, but revenues net of operating costs (earnings) constitute the primary focus of FPCUs.

Despite the appearance of commonly adopted strategies and tactics in the pursuit of earnings (including growth through initial public offerings, mergers, and acquisitions), each FPCU actively seeks to differentiate itself from its competitors. Apollo Group, for example, is primarily focused on serving working adults in the market for bachelor's-degree level work in business, technology, and education but is seeking to move into the 18- to 22-year-old market. Education Management Corporation, on the other hand, focuses on art and design, culinary arts, social sciences, health sciences, business, education, and technology. Most of the offerings of Corinthian Colleges are relatively short-term programs, such as diplomas and associates degrees in allied health, business, IT, trades, and criminal justice. Corinthian has recently expanded into auto repair and aviation. Kaplan Higher Education has the only accredited institution that offers a law degree purely online—Concord University School of Law. Universal Technical Institute is known for the close employer affiliations developed with corporations like Audi, BMW, Harley-Davidson, and NASCAR. Universal provides manufacturer-specific programs in automotive repair and diesel, collision repair, and marine technician training. Laureate Education is seeking a leadership position among American FPCUs in global markets through a network of international universities built through acquisitions. Several FPCUs are exclusively on line, including Capella, Jones International, Walden, Canter, and NTU (Gubins et al. 2005, p. 69). All strategies of differentiation are not equally successful. For example, DeVry's nearly exclusive IT focus earlier in this decade was a primary reason behind its undergraduate enrollment losses (see table 3.1).

These and other corporate strategies are each fueled by combinations of investor-leveraged initial public offerings; multiple rounds of investment, mergers, and acquisitions; and aggressive growth on existing campuses. Lincoln Educational Services Corporation went public in June 2005, offering 4 million shares at $20 per share. UTI sought growth through its initial public offering in late 2003. Career Education's growth has been driven by its acquisition (for nearly $270 million) of another publicly traded FPCU—Whitman Education, an allied health–focused company. Corinthian's growth has been more acquisitions-driven than almost any other FPCU. DeVry was able to become a provider of doctor of medicine (M.D.) and veterinary degrees through its purchase of Ross University for more than $300 million. EVCI Career Colleges began as a publicly traded educational videoconference firm that transitioned to a for-profit college model through the purchase of an accredited, degree-granting institution. Privately held FPCUs, as well as publicly held FPCUs, also grow through acquisitions as well as same-store growth. Examples include U.S. Education Corporation and High-Tech Institute.

Among the various growth strategies utilized by individual FPCUs, acquisition is the one strategy that reflects both the long-run consolidation among FPCUs and the scale of financial means available to the larger FPCUs. To some extent, the already large (publicly traded) FPCUs are in the strongest position to make significant acquisitions. Between 1999 and 2004, thirty-three FPCU acquisitions were made in which each was valued at more than $10 million. All but one of these was made by publicly traded FPCUs (Gubins et al. 2005, p. 63). Postsecondary education is growing faster than other markets in the education industry (Silber 2004, p. 11). FPCUs are growing faster than firms providing other postsecondary goods and services, and publicly traded FPCUs are outperforming the average of all FPCUs. Indeed, publicly traded FPCUs are becoming the most prominent among FPCUs, accounting for approximately one-half of all FPCU revenues in 2004, up from about 30% in 2000.

These publicly traded FPCUs are taking the lead in what might be termed *internationalization*. FPCUs that have gone international are motivated at least as much by traditional issues such as strategic fit, new markets, and new capacities as they are by the prospect of a presence in a particular country. The large FPCUs are internationalizing because they are growing rather than the reverse. Brief illustrations from five of the largest FPCUs are instructive of this expansion.

Apollo International's joint venture in Brazil (Pitagoras Apollo International) with the Pitagoras group will enable Apollo to migrate many of its existing programs to the new campuses.* Through its University of Phoenix campus in Rotterdam, the Netherlands, students can obtain a U.S. accredited M.B.A degree. Modi Apollo International Institute will expand both its campus sites and online education delivery system through a joint venture with one of India's largest industrial conglomerates and transfer the most viable of its current programs there. Similar initiatives are being developed in Mexico, Chile, and China.

Laureate, perhaps more than any other FPCU, is pursuing a growth path that capitalizes on its presence in a variety of different countries, rather than merely cultivating new markets for its services. Its presence

* Acquisitions associated directly with the Apollo Group (including University of Phoenix) are actually distinct and separable because Apollo International, Inc., was originally founded as an independent, privately held company by the Apollo Group.

in twelve countries serving more than 165,000 students features a component of network programming (e.g., study abroad programs, dual- and joint-degree programs, shared content and courseware among the universities, and international online education programs). In this instance, country presence matters to students in other countries. Even so, many of Laureate's acquisitions were also acquired in order to transfer specialty programs, such as hospitality management and sports, to other campuses. Acquisitions of online delivery firms extend Laureate's online capability and its reach beyond campuses and into non-U.S. markets.

Corinthian's acquisitions of forty-five colleges and fifteen corporate training centers in Canada was a natural extension into new locations for its programs and for importing new curricula into its campuses, providing, to quote founder David Moore, "an excellent platform for cross-pollination with Corinthian's curricula" (Corinthian Colleges 2003). De-Vry's acquisition of Caribbean-based Ross University was largely for its curriculum (medical and veterinary schools) and not for its locale (Blumenstyk 2003). Career Education Corporation's purchase in 2003 of the nine campuses of the French INSEEC Group had less to do with the fact that the group was French than that it represented a "chance to acquire an 'undermanaged' collection of properties for a relatively low cost," about $20 million (Blumenstyk 2003).

Growth through Marketing

Marketing efforts are critical to the growth of FPCUs, but such efforts are so fundamental that they might be overlooked as a distinct motivator of growth. The largest publicly traded FPCUs spend hundreds of millions of dollars on sales and marketing, and combined FPCUs spend billions of dollars (Gallagher and Poroy 2005, p. 3). The best available estimates suggest that the average FPCU spends about 15% of its revenues on sales and marketing. Of this total, about half is spent on promotions (e.g., advertising) and half on a mix of enrollment management, marketing, and direct-sales expenses. This is roughly similar to what is spent by firms in other direct-to-consumer markets (Gallagher and Poroy 2005).

Sales and marketing budgets are expected to grow faster than enrollment growth due in large part to increased competition. Leads from different media outlets vary among FPCUs, but averages of data from three large FPCUs (Career Education, Corinthian, and Education Management) are at least illustrative. The Internet generated 28% of new student enrollment leads for these three FPCUs; broadcast and print media, 25%; referrals, 26%; high schools, 7%; direct mail, 5%; and other, 10% (Gallagher and Poroy 2005, p. 8).

Leads are connected to FPCUs through the work of recruiting staff (including enrollment advisers, recruiters, and admissions counselors). Converting leads to enrollments is critical to growth and, hence, profitability. The typical recruiting staff person in an FPCU engages between 500 and 1,500 leads annually, seeking to convert about 10–15% of these to enrollments (perhaps redefining the traditional TCU concept of *selectivity*). The largest FPCUs are each handling millions of leads and looking to convert tens of thousands of prospects into paying students. Large numbers of enrollment service providers are part of each FPCU: more than 3,000 at University of Phoenix Online; 2,200 at Career Education; and 900 at ITT. One of the top regulatory issues revolves around potentially improper sales pressure. This issue is not expected to decrease over time, given the inherent challenges of creating access for underserved populations of students and the inherent profitability of successful enrollments.

Growth of FPCUs: Gross Revenues and Earnings

As a small part of the postsecondary education sector, FPCUs are aided in part by factors that motivate the growth of the entire sector (see table 3.6). But conditions associated uniquely with FPCUs (e.g., access to capital, corporate structure) help explain why for-profits constitute the fastest-growth segment in postsecondary education, growing slightly more than 14% from 2003 to 2004 to achieve revenues of more than $15 billion. The large, publicly traded FPCUs are becoming more prominent parts of this segment (reflecting both growth and consolidation). Revenues at these companies grew about 30% per year from 2001 to 2003, for reasons discussed earlier.

For-profit postsecondary schools generated approximately $13.2 billion in revenues in 2003 (Gallagher and Basset 2004, p. 3), or only 4.1% of the

TABLE 3.6
The financial size of U.S. education
(in billions of dollars)

	Total Expenditures, 2003	For-Profit Sector Revenues, 2003	For-Profit Revenues, 2008 (estimate)	Compound Annual Growth Rate, 2003–8 (estimate) (%)
Pre-K	52	13.8	16.2	3.2
K–12	486.5	36.3	49.8	6.6
Postsecondary	321.6	25.4	42.2	10.6
Corporate	51.2	17.4	23.7	6.4
Total	911.3	93	132	7.3

SOURCE: Silber 2004 and company reports.

TABLE 3.7
Publicly held for-profit postsecondary school providers:
Components of growth expectations

Item	New Annual Growth Expectations (%)
Same school enrollment growth	6–8
New campus openings, relocations	2–4
Facility expansions, relocations	1–2
Subtotal (enrollment growth)	10–14
Tuition increase	3–5
Subtotal (revenue growth)	13–19
Operating margin expansion	1–2
Total (earnings growth)	15–20

SOURCE: Silber 2004 and company reports.

estimated $322 billion spent on postsecondary education in that year. Although this percentage appears small, it should be noted again that for-profit postsecondary revenues have increased nearly fourfold since 1996, when only $3.5 billion (or 1.7% of the total) were generated.

The rapid financial growth of FPCUs is attributable to three bundles of factors: enrollment growth, revenue growth, and growth in profitability or earnings. Although each FPCU has a unique history in these areas, each tends to contribute to the "FPCU industry average" in predictable proportions. Based on estimates of some industry watchers, FPCU earnings growth is not likely to increase as fast as it has previously; the growth will likely slow down to somewhere between 15% and 20% per year (table 3.7).

Notice that about two-thirds of this earnings growth is attributable to enrollment growth. Less than a quarter of earnings growth is attributed to price (tuition) increases, and slightly less than 10% to increased profitability. Enrollments are the major growth driver. The growth of FPCUs is neither mysterious nor unduly difficult to understand. Access to investment capital deployed to grow enrollments, campuses, programs, and ultimately profitability tends to yield growth. Through similar reasoning, one could ascertain why many TCUs are not growing as rapidly as others or how they are pursuing distinct objectives. To say that TCUs serve the *public good* while FPCUs are responsive to *market forces* is to mask the similarities and differences between them to some degree.

The differences between FPCUs and TCUs can in part be attributed to characteristics of the economic sectors within which FPCUs (private for-profits) and TCUs (pubic and private nonprofits) operate. The *sector effect* influences growth rates. To the extent that this is the case, it is likely that the internal operations of FPCUs also differ from those of TCUs. After all, the people in FPCUs behave in particular ways that cause growth. The ways in which those people are organized and governed must somehow be associated with their behavior. Although it is difficult to prove (but easier to argue logically and to demonstrate empirically) that the sector effect shapes internal governance—the roles of governing boards, senior management, campus or program management, and faculty—we seek to do just that in the next chapter. How does the *corporate governance* of FPCUs appear to differ from the *shared governance* of TCUs, both of which offer education services?

CHAPTER FOUR

Finance and Governance

Not all of the growth of for-profit colleges and universities can be attributed solely to external demands for schooling and to the growing willingness of students to fulfill those demands at FPCUs. The fact that FPCUs are for-profit enterprises per se does not explain rapid growth rates in the past several decades. For-profit colleges and universities have been around for a long time. Further, traditional colleges and universities, both nonprofit private and public, have been pursuing net revenues (a form of profits) for years. The corporate form of for-profit higher education business, however, does seem to contribute to the recent growth of FPCUs, because much of that growth has been concentrated in the large, publicly traded corporations that have entered the field.

The internal governance and finance of FPCUs, especially those structured as publicly traded corporations, distinguish FPCUs from TCUs. As for-profit entities, FPCUs frame their organizations as investable propositions, and as publicly traded corporations, they provide a ready means for accessing investment capital to grow, provided that they can prove their potential. Despite the wide variations among TCUs and among FPCUs, the institutional finance and governance of each group are distinctively different.

The For-Profit Form: As Much about Raising Capital as Pursuing Net Revenues

The association between private, for-profit business and making money is inherent. Taxonomic distinctions between TCUs and FPCUs, even relatively comprehensive ones represented in table 4.1, imply that

TABLE 4.1
Distinctions between nonprofit TCUs and FPCUs

Nonprofit TCUs	FPCUs
Tax-exempt	Tax-paying
Donors	Investors
Endowment	Private investment capital
Stakeholders	Stockholders
Shared governance	Traditional management
Prestige motive	Profit motive
Cultivation of knowledge	Application of learning
Discipline-driven	Market-driven
Quality of inputs	Quality of outcome
Faculty power	Customer power

SOURCE: Ruch 2001.

making money is the distinguishing feature, driven by the reinforcing characteristics of investors, the profit motive, market-driven forces, and other similar factors.

One problem with this facile association of for-profits and revenue is that it masks two fundamental distinctions. First, it implies incorrectly that TCUs, as nonprofit institutions, do not seek to generate revenue. Yet the most successful private, nonprofit TCUs have done very well financially, although they follow a fundamentally different model of finance and governance. The Association of American Universities institutions, which possess billion-plus-dollar endowments and annual operating budgets, increased revenues from research contracts and grants, and growing royalty streams from licensing of intellectual property, are pursuing net revenues just as aggressively as FPCUs. What really separates FPCUs from these TCUs is the nondistribution constraint. Individual decision makers at TCUs cannot share personally in the distribution of net revenues through buying or selling of organizational shares. Even though they cannot literally buy or sell shares, senior management and faculty at more successful TCUs can certainly command greater wage premiums than those at less financially successful TCUs. Furthermore, senior faculty and staff at more successful TCUs enjoy more favorable working conditions, such as lower teaching loads and higher levels of staff support, not to mention increased satisfaction from the association with a more prestigious institution.

Second, the making-money distinction masks other differences associated with profit seeking. The possibility of future profitability attracts investors and stockholders along with their private investment capital. FPCU senior management and governing board members are usually stockholders; they have a large personal stake in long-term profitability (overall size as well as margins) and act accordingly. Faculty members at FPCUs, unlike their TCU counterparts, have much less voice in most organizational decisions. Their preferences and opinions are not factored into the decision equation. Even decisions such as whether a particular discipline or program should be cultivated, maintained, or eliminated are outside their purview.

Because customers have a great influence on services at FPCUs, changes in market demand for different FPCU programs shape the decisions of FPCU management. In contrast, at TCUs, faculty-driven attention is focused on issues such as disciplinary knowledge, departmental faculty hiring, support for research, admissions decisions, and the quality of student inputs, such as Scholastic Aptitude Test and Graduate Record Examination scores. Think of these governance differences as reflecting different sets of rules that specify what organizational actors can, must, should, and cannot do.

The distinctions between TCUs and FPCUs listed in table 4.1 are then somewhat a blend of these rules as well as a result of the rules. An additional distinction defines the rules of the game: whether or not individuals can own and trade shares of the organization (stockholders vs. shareholders). The first three distinctions indicate the major potential source of financial capital (investments vs. gifts); the motives of the individuals controlling those sources (investors vs. donors); and the tax consequences of success (tax exempt vs. tax paying). This additional distinction applies less directly to the donors and investors in that the former receive a tax deduction for their gifts and any earnings accrued by the latter are subject to taxation.

The fifth through tenth distinctions listed in table 4.1 are manifestations of the basic differences between FPCUs and TCUs as opposed to definitions of the difference. Ownership (or lack thereof) influences governance, which in turn shapes organizational behavior. But what distinguishes the shared governance at TCUs from the traditional management of FPCUs? Decisions, and who makes them, represent one approach to understanding the distinction.

Governance distinctions can be summarized across different types of decisions, where different sets of actors either have a voice at the table or do not (a topic examined in greater detail later in this chapter). Among the most visible actors at both TCUs and FPCUs are their governing bodies (boards), all of which, at least in theory, are responsible for the overall direction of their institutions. But the similarities between FPCU and TCU boards are more apparent than real. As Pusser and Turner (2004, p. 254) have noted, among private TCUs "governing boards are essentially self-perpetuating in the sense that current officers choose their successors, whereas for public TCUs "such decisions are either directly or indirectly a function of the state or local political process." In addition, FPCU boards typically have shareholder claims to their institutions, whereas boards of TCUs do not. "For-profit board members," according to Pusser and Turner, "have significant fiduciary interests in the success of the institutions they preside over, through stock holdings and stock options." Further, the backgrounds and expertise of FPCU board members shape their interests; they tend to be both more interested in, and qualified to evaluate, the financial performance of their organizations.

To put it more bluntly, FPCU board members have a significant *personal* fiduciary interest in the organization. At a rhetorical level, all board members of all higher education institutions have some level of "significant fiduciary interests in the success of the institutions they preside over," but only at FPCUs are governing board interests personal, tangibly financial, and tradable.

The same personal stake in the organization is typically true of senior management at FPCUs. In contrast, senior management at TCUs, like their board members, has no personal financial equity in the organization (despite arguably large amounts of psychic equity). Finance and governance are particularly interdependent at FPCUs. The distinction between FPCUs and TCUs is twofold: people at the top of FPCUs have both the decision-making authority and the personal financial incentive to cause FPCUs to pursue profitability. For boards and senior management at TCUs, finance and governance are not so closely linked, and, not surprisingly, numerous priorities other than profitability (such as prestige, selectivity, or real estate) compete with profitability for priority.

This attribute of the FPCU governing board may be the most distinctive attribute of the for-profit form of governance: its facility for attracting and accommodating private investment by investing wisely and managing strategically. In effect, for-profits create incentives for senior management and governing board members to seek profits through growth. In short, FPCUs possess the ability to raise investment capital by selling shares of the organization and deploying those resources in pursuit of long-term profitability. With their legal authority to buy and sell shares of their organization, FPCUs are able to pursue capital to invest in profitable growth.

The subtext of the growth of the large, publicly traded FPCUs is the ability of successful firms to procure investment capital to acquire and create new campuses as well as to expand existing campuses. Nonprofit and public TCUs have to rely on other sources of capital (including bank loans, bonds, gifts, grants) and government sources to finance expenditures. Several of those alternatives are also available to FPCUs. But investors do not invest in TCUs because there is no possibility of return on their investment. What, then, motivates the investor to invest specifically in postsecondary education, and in a specific FPCU? And how much of a difference does this make in the behavior of FPCUs? These factors, rarely, if ever, applied to TCUs, are fundamentally important to the overall viability of FPCUs, collectively and individually.

Ten features (three sector-wide and seven firm-specific) illustrate the types of investor considerations associated with for-profit postsecondary education—considerations that sway decisions to invest (or to divest) large amounts of investment capital into (or out of) FPCUs. These factors change over time; reflect some FPCUs more accurately than others; may apply, more or less, to all of postsecondary education; and repel as well as attract some investors, depending on investors' risk aversion as well as their desired rates of return.

First, the overall postsecondary industry outlook, from an investor perspective, is generally favorable. This is in sharp contrast, for example, to the perspective of some TCU providers who are justifiably lamenting the drop-off in revenues—from state appropriations, for example. According to an analysis from Bear Stearns, one of the growing number of investment bankers specializing in the analysis of FPCUs, "The post-secondary industry . . . boasts enviable fundamentals, namely high barriers to entry, strong pricing power, favorable cash-flow dynamics, strong operating leverage, and very strong earnings visibility. . . . [D]emand for higher education among adults has never been stronger . . . [and is not even close to saturation] . . . [plus TCU circumstances, especially among publics, have caused them to] raise tuition dramatically, cut student services, and reduce class availability" (Childe and Newell 2004, pp. 4–5).

Second, the regulatory risk faced by FPCUs can mitigate some of the attractiveness of the for-profit postsecondary industry. In addition to the regulatory environment associated with credentialing, accreditation, and licensure that we discuss in more detail in chapter 8, FPCUs are subject to a wide variety of state and federal regulations and oversight that govern their operations, financial conditions, and provisions for student aid. Compliance measures include maintaining certain student-loan default rates below authorized maximums, ensuring that governmental financial aid funding does not exceed 90% of the company's total tuition revenue, and meeting specific financial performance and liquidity measures. Perceived changes in the regulatory environment (tightening vs. loosening) affect the investment viability of FPCUs. To the extent that regulatory changes are perceived as "bad for FPCUs," investors are reluctant to invest additional resources in for-profits.

A third sectorwide factor entails the murky world of investor psychology. Specifically, what is called *sector rotation* refers to the possibility that, as attractive as the postsecondary sector may look to investors today, some other sector with even better fundamentals may work its way into the minds of analysts and investors. This would cause them to move their money out of the sector into something more attractive or to pass on making an initial investment in for-profits, a circumstance more attributable to the for-profit K–12 education sector.

These three factors that can attract or repel investment capital apply to the entire for-profit postsecondary education sector. A larger number of firm-specific factors can have similar effects on investments in individual

FPCUs. Consider the following seven illustrations, most of which reflect more directly on the capability of FPCU senior management.

First, FPCUs that demonstrate the ability to grow enrollments consistently at individual campuses (organic growth rates) are seen as having capable senior management. Career Education Corporation, as an illustration, has delivered same-store enrollment growth averaging in the mid-20% area over twenty-two quarters (through the third quarter of 2003), although this pace has slowed subsequently. Career Education's ability to deliver consistently high same-store growth is seen by investors as a definite plus.

Second, strong senior management is evidenced in substantial and continuous overall growth in enrollments and top-line revenues. Whether through same-store growth or acquisitions, FPCUs that consistently grow enrollments demonstrate a capacity to continue to grow enrollments in the future. Along with same-store growth, Career Education Corporation has acquired twenty-seven smaller FPCUs since its inception and has grown its enrollments at a compound annual growth rate of 33%. With those acquisitions, plus same-store enrollment growth and tuition increases, its compound annual growth in revenue over a recent four-year period was more than 50% (Childe and Newell 2004, p. 4).

Third, growth and top-line revenues play an important supporting role to operating margins and returns on investment, which reflect the degree to which an FPCU is able to turn growth into profitability. In addition to continuously generating double-digit organic enrollment and revenue growth, Career Education Corporation is gradually improving its operating margins and return on investment capital. In the same twenty-two-quarter period already noted, it had never missed a positive quarter.

Fourth, the diversity of an individual FPCU is generally seen as a positive attribute, largely because it acts as a hedge against unexpected downturns in specific programs, among specific student demographics, or in specific local labor markets. An FPCU with more diversity along these dimensions is considered less susceptible to a cyclical downturn. At the same time, however, being in too many businesses that are too different (no synergies) is seen as a weakness, because the FPCU is forced to divide its attention among different sectors. Laureate's (Sylvan) decision to sell off its K–12 businesses and focus solely on postsecondary education was perceived as a move that strengthened the business, because it enabled senior management to focus greater attention on the higher-potential postsecondary sector.

Fifth, socioeconomic backgrounds of student markets, in the eyes of investors, are relevant insofar as they affect various performance metrics, such as loan default rates, completion rates, and job placement rates. If an individual FPCU caters extensively to students who, as a group, are particularly vulnerable to these problems, the investment is considered less secure. Unemployed students with low levels of education who are financing their own study are among the more vulnerable. Students who are relatively low risks include those who are already employed and those whose schooling is sponsored by their employer.

Sixth, programs with shorter durations and more frequent start times can be seen as positive differentiators among FPCUs. A counterargument, however, is that with longer programs, there is less frequent turnover of graduates and fewer new students that need to be recruited. These programs can be seen as less volatile. Programs that take less time to complete than comparable competitors put the student into the job market sooner and require less third-party tuition financing. Full-time programs get students through faster than comparable programs offered on a part-time basis. Shorter programs are usually associated with more scheduling options that enable the student to start or finish sooner.

Seventh, enterprise valuation of an FPCU can, by itself, affect the attractiveness of investment capital. This characteristic sometimes gets confused with size (the larger the institution, the greater its valuation), but it really involves the current value placed on any given FPCU by investors, independent of its size. How does this work? Shares of publicly traded FPCUs, along with changes in the number of shares outstanding and their current price, constitute a broadly accessible vehicle for investment capital in (and for) FPCUs. The market capitalization of a publicly traded FPCU plus its net debt provides one measure of the dollar value of the enterprise.

A more realistic measure of company worth is equity value, which is enterprise value less debt. If we use enterprise value as a crude proxy for its worth, some of the publicly traded FPCUs are worth more than a billion dollars (Career Education, Corinthian, DeVry, Education Management, ITT, Laureate, Strayer) with Apollo in a category by itself (near $15 billion). Their worth is not unrelated to their performance over time or to the current scale of operations, but the worth represents a distinctive attribute of an FPCU. These larger enterprises are able to capitalize on economies of scale in a wide variety of parts of the business, including program development, IT investment, lobbying and accreditation, responsiveness to regulatory oversight, personnel, marketing, and employer relations. Independent from advantages of size, an FPCU may be perceived as being over- or undervalued in the marketplace. Overvalued FPCUs are less likely to generate the returns that an undervalued FPCU might, if all else were equal.

To the extent that senior management, not faculty, is responsible for affecting these factors at FPCUs, it arguably plays a more consequential role at FPCUs than at TCUs. But these are not the only factors investors consider at FPCUs, or necessarily even the only important ones. The distinctiveness of these factors, however, lies in the degree to which they do *not* resemble the top factors considered by key actors at TCUs. The governance and finance of nonprofit TCUs (both public and private) call forth a wide variety of other factors—stewardship of gifts, prestige, selectivity, production of research, attractiveness of campuses, winning sports teams, alumni connections, comprehensive provision of the public good—but not so much the FPCU investment factors we have mentioned.

Investment factors apply in theory to all FPCUs but are more practically relevant among FPCUs that have elected to become publicly traded entities, thus enabling a vastly larger pool of investors to consider investing. The number of publicly held education companies has increased substantially in the past several decades. At the height of the dot.com heyday at the end of the twentieth century, eleven education companies went public, many of which specialized in e-learning. Similar to most sectors of the economy, the pace of public offerings had slowed until the end of 2003, when FPCU Universal Technical Institutes went public. By late 2006, Lincoln Education and Capella University also went public.

Privately held FPCUs must rely on private investment to grow. The falloff in initial public offerings in education since the turn of the century was accompanied by a similar falloff in private investment during the same period. Private investment in the education industry grew from $93 million in 1994 to a high of nearly $3 billion in 2000, but then fell in 2003 to $181 million, and since then has risen back up.

Legal access to investment capital clearly does not guarantee capital, as this recent history illustrates; the overall attractiveness of FPCUs depends on the overall availability of investment capital as well as the relative attractiveness to individuals with alternative investments. FPCUs compete for capital not only among themselves but across all other investment opportunities. While the number of publicly traded FPCUs has grown significantly in the past several decades, the number of multinational corporations has grown to a scale that is larger by a factor of at least 1,000 (Gabel and Bruner 2003). Because investment capital (across a multitude of large and small investors) finds its way to those enterprises with the perceived highest risk-adjusted return, FPCUs must perform in order to warrant investor interest and their capital.

We have focused our attention here on publicly traded FPCUs, but they do not represent all FPCUs. Large, publicly traded, multicampus FPCUs constitute less than one-half of the for-profit postsecondary campuses. About one-half of all FPCUs are made up of what some have called *enterprise colleges*, including those "mom and pop" trade schools with fewer than 500 students per campus and/or fewer than 3,000 students at multiple campuses. The average FPCU is small, enrolling slightly more than 300 students on average (Silber 2004, p. 67). Most of the arguments about for-profit scale economies tend not to apply to these FPCUs.

Internet institutions make up an additional small fraction of for-profit enrollments (about 10%), and the large publicly and privately traded FPCUs make up the rest. Due to ongoing mergers and acquisitions, along with the growth of online learning by "brick and mortar" providers, these numbers are approximate and changing. Our disproportionate interest in the larger, usually publicly traded FPCUs is twofold: first, they represent an increasing proportion of FPCUs over time due to mergers and acquisitions; and, second, with their scale economies, they can more readily capture the economic benefits of program innovation and growth—and, in general, they do.

Despite large variations among the eleven publicly traded domestic FPCUs, their average scale and levels of performance reflect above-average rates for the sector as a whole. As mentioned in the previous chapter, these FPCUs enroll on average about 53,000 students. Between the first quarter of 2002 and the second quarter of 2004, these for-profits have experienced an average year-to-year total enrollment growth rate of nearly 28% (Silber 2004, pp. 76–77). More than half of that average growth rate (15%) was achieved on existing campuses (same-store enrollment growth), with the remaining growth occurring on new campuses that were created or acquired.

Could this have been financed exclusively from operations? Most likely not, as additional investment capital was also required. Even so, it is likely that some of the net earnings from one year were reinvested into capital expenditures for the following year. Median gross revenue per student across these eleven FPCUs was $13,114, with median earnings before interest, depreciation, taxes, and amortization of $2,647 (Silber 2004, p. 101). This story of revenues, costs, and earnings is of interest in large part due to the rapid overall growth in enrollments. Profitability is a joint function of scale and margins. Stated another way, profitability achieved on a small and non-growing student body—without the promise of scale—is not interesting to most investors.

The concept of profits constituting a reward for risk taking is particularly apt when considering publicly traded FPCUs, which, in addition to the usual risks associated with a business, take on those associated with stockholder behavior. The ease with which shares can be acquired in rising markets equals the ease with which they can be disposed of in falling markets; the enterprise value of the FPCU fluctuates significantly as a result. All investments are not necessarily profitable, a truism that applies as much to FPCUs as to other investments.

Consider the market fortunes of DeVry University, one of the largest FPCUs. In 1988 Ronald Taylor and Dennis Keller bought the then eleven-campus system. They took it public in 1991, generating $10 million in working capital. DeVry grew aggressively between 1991 and 2002, when, due to a "perfect storm" of overall recession, the dot.com bubble burst, and DeVry's focus on high-tech preparation programs, the institution ran into a series of major problems. Enrollment dropped 15% and its job placement rates fell to 85% (Kirp 2003, p. 2). As a result of stock sell-offs, DeVry shares lost half of its value. Despite these misfortunes, DeVry has continued to increase its number of campuses and overall enrollment, and its short-term decline in market capitalization was disproportionate to its short-term decline in performance. More recently, DeVry has rebounded remarkably. In looking at the more successful (profitable) segment of FPCUs, we should at least acknowledge that performance can vary significantly over time. Some for-profits are less successful, and some of these have even ceased to exist.

FPCU Finance: Focus on Subsidized Sales of Instructional Programs

The for-profit form that distinguishes FPCUs from TCUs is reflected in greater detail in the accounting records of the two types of institutions. Despite the wide range of accounting issues that FPCUs must address, including those involving tax treatment, public reporting (for publicly traded enterprises), cost accounting, and earnings reporting, certain financial elements of FPCUs are actually simpler than those at TCUs.

As compared with TCUs, FPCUs are in fewer fundamentally different kinds of businesses. TCUs often disaggregate those businesses into separate entities called funds and, in effect, underreport the scale of those businesses in their main operating budget. For all practical purposes, FPCUs pursue tuition revenues to the exclusion of all other typical higher education revenue streams. As portrayed in figure 4.1, tuition and fees make up 87% of FPCU revenue, compared to 38% for private nonprofit TCUs and 18% for public TCUs. In contrast, FPCUs generate only about 4% of their revenues from sales and services (largely from textbook sales), whereas nonprofit and public TCUs generate 24% and 22% respectively. FPCUs generate less than 1% of their revenue from private gifts, grants, and contracts, in contrast to TCUs that generate 19% (private nonprofit) and 5% (public) respectively. Governmental subsidies to TCUs, especially publics, make up a vastly larger proportion of their revenues when compared to FPCU revenues.

The implications of this distinction for internal organizational management and governance are significant. If we think of every major stream of revenue in an organization as having unique customers and performance measures, then each requires separate services; serves indi-

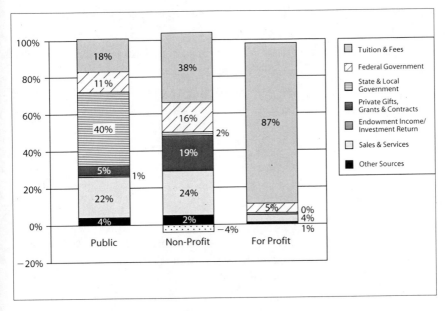

Figure 4.1. Revenue of Degree-Granting Institutions, 2000–2001.

vidual customers; has separate accounting and reporting; exhibits separate measures of performance; and requires expenditures to do what it takes to bring in those revenues. FPCUs' focus across different instructional programs constitutes *variations on a single theme* of instruction (and the revenues that come from selling instruction). TCUs, on the other hand, concentrate on enrollments, funded research, donations and donor relations, state appropriations, endowment performance, auxiliary services such as housing and food service, and intellectual property licensing. Each market requires resources, staffing, services, and oversight to earn revenue from these separate businesses. In contrast to FPCUs, TCUs pursue, in effect, *variations on multiple themes.*

The long-recognized revenue theory of management in higher education (management organized largely around major revenue sources) applies equally to FPCUs and TCUs, except that the mixture of funding within these two types of institutions differs radically. Simply put, all organizations organize around their important sources of revenue, so that appropriate managerial attention is devoted to maximizing the returns from each major revenue source. It is not surprising, then, that public TCUs are particularly attentive to state and local governmental relations or that well-endowed private TCUs devote extensive organizational attention to the cultivation of private gifts, grants, contracts, and endowment income. FPCUs get the vast majority of their revenues from tuition and fees.

The differing proportions of revenues among TCUs and FPCUs are indicative of more than simply *where* management focuses its attention, such as gift giving and endowment performance versus government appropriations. The very nature of the issues varies greatly. Almost by definition, FPCUs must focus on factors that influence tuition revenues, including program offerings, campus locations, marketing, and pricing. Public TCUs, on the other hand, depend heavily on government appropriations and must focus managerial attention on the conditions, or "strings," that accompany them.

Although all postsecondary institutions cannot fully control revenues from any particular source, this does not necessarily mean that all comparative advantages between FPCUs and TCUs are equal. For instance, there arguably may be more that FPCUs can do to impact their tuition revenue stream than public TCUs can do to impact their government appropriation revenue stream. Although difficult to prove one way or the other, we can assert that some revenue streams can be more easily grown than others.

While the revenue possibilities for two-year FPCUs are quite similar to those for four-year FPCUs, differences emerge when comparing two-year TCUs to four-year TCUs (see table 4.2.). Two-year public TCUs are significantly more dependent on government appropriations than their four-year public counterparts, and four-year nonprofit TCUs are more dependent on donations and government grants and contracts than their two-year nonprofit counterparts.

Although public TCUs enroll the largest proportions of students and charge the lowest tuitions, their price advantage is slowly being eroded over time, largely due to the states' difficulty in increasing appropriations to public TCUs on a predictable schedule from one year to the next. While overall revenues at TCUs are increasing, the share from state governments is steadily decreasing (figure 4.2), from about 45% to about 35% of

TABLE 4.2

Percentage of revenue for Title IV degree-granting institutions, by level and control of institution and source of funds, fiscal year 2000

Source of Funds	Public Institutions		Private Not-For-Profit Institutions		Private For-Profit Institutions	
	4-Year	2-Year	4-Year	2-Year	4-Year	2-Year
Tuition and fees	18.1	20.3	24.4	21.9	86.1	81
Government appropriations	32.2	56.6	0.6	0.7	6.0	6.2
Government grants and contracts	13.8	11.9	8.4	3.9	——	
Private gifts, grants, and contracts	5.6	1.1	12.9	4.7	—	0.1
Investment income	—	—	31.5	3.6	—	—
Investment income and investment gains (losses)	—	—	—	—	0.4	0.4
Endowment income	0.9	0.1	—	—	—	—
Sales and services of educational activities	3.6	0.8	2.4	1.5	1.4	1.8
Sales and services of auxiliary activities	10.5	5.6	6.9	3.1	4.3	2.6
Hospitals	10.8	0.0	6.0	49.1[a]	—	—
Independent operations	0.4	0.1	2.6	0.1	—	—
Other sources	4.0	3.5	4.3	11.5	1.7	7.9

SOURCE: Knapp et al. 2003.
[a]Of the approximately 140 Title IV private not-for-profit 2-year institutions, only 5 institutions reported hospital revenues; however, the hospital revenues account for 49.1% of the total.

total revenues over the past approximately twenty years. The bulk of this squeeze is showing up in tuition increases, which grew during the same period from about 13% to about 18% of all public TCU revenues. This overlap between the TCU and FPCU student markets could eventually pose a problem for TCUs. Currently, however, price differences between *public* TCUs and FPCUs tend to be relatively large.

Over the past three decades, tuition levels have grown on average between 7.2% and 8.2% annually across all of higher education. Tuition increases at FPCUs have run well below the overall average (about 5%), especially in recent years (Gubins et al. 2005, p. 28). The price advantage of public TCUs over FPCUs, while still large, is shrinking.

Like other institutions of higher learning, FPCUs are organized around their primary source(s) of income, and the lines of accountability and responsibility within the organization are associated with those revenues

	$43.2BN	$94.9BN	$176.6BN	
100%	2.4%	2.5%	3.7%	
90%		22.7%	21.7%	Other sources
80%	0.5% 19.6%	3.8% 0.8%	5.1%	Sales and services
70%	2.5%	0.5%	4.0%	Endowment
60%	3.6%	3.7%		Income/Investment Return
50%			35.60%	Private gifts, and contracts
40%	45.6%	40.3%		
30%	12.8%		11.2%	State & Local Government
20%		10.3%	18.1%	Federal Government
10%	12.9%	15.1%		Tuition and Fees
0%				

Figure 4.2. Revenue of Public Degree-Granting Institutions. BN = billion. *Source: National Center for Education Statistics 2003a*

and their associated expenditures. Unlike TCUs, FPCUs do not staff offices or departments of advancement and gifts, endowment management and payout, or local, state, and federal government relations.

They instead employ lobbyists to pressure Congress and state-governing bodies to pass legislation that will be favorable to their interests, such as additional forms of student aid. The only sales and services that FPCUs conduct is directly related to instruction—a bookstore, for example. They do, however, devote extraordinary attention to marketing, student advisement (beginning before admission through graduation and placement), and program development, and arguably more so than do TCUs due to the greater importance to FPCUs of tuition and fees.

As we elaborate in chapter 7 and elsewhere, the rhetoric of *student as customer* is sometimes applied to FPCUs to distinguish how their students are treated in comparison to those at TCUs. From a revenue-generating perspective, tuition-paying students at FPCUs are clearly the primary customer, whereas at TCUs they are a primary customer within one of about a half-dozen differing types of markets.

Because tuition is the center of FPCU financial life, two financial issues most closely associated with tuition are also of central importance—

issues relating to the differences between gross and net tuition (financial aid and support) and between prices (tuition) and costs. Although many students at FPCUs pay full retail prices, others pay discounted prices by virtue of the fact that their campus is eligible to receive federally sponsored grants and loans, primarily Title IV of the Higher Education Act, not unlike students at many TCUs.

Institutional eligibility that entitles students to access Title IV financial aid serves three significant purposes at FPCUs: the resulting aid can act to discount the high (relative to public TCUs) sticker price that students have to pay; official Title IV institutional eligibility provides a soft form of consumer protection guarantee in that minimum operating standards are required to earn it; and the threat of withdrawing institutional eligibility acts as a significant enforcement mechanism for regulators. With some exceptions, financial aid tends to flow disproportionately to students with greater financial need, and the aid arrives disproportionately at institutions with higher tuition prices. More two-year FPCUs and public TCUs are Title IV eligible than their four-year counterparts, whereas more four-year private TCUs are Title IV eligible than their two-year counterparts.

Title IV eligibility is a major vehicle for making FPCUs price competitive, a fact that contributes to the rancor of intersector competition, including consequential legislation such as the Higher Education Reauthorization Bill that we discuss in chapter 8. Price competitive does not mean least expensive. Rather, in this context, it provides sufficient perceived value per dollar charged to attract a satisfactory share of the market at prices that more than cover its costs. These twin factors—value for dollar and profitability—cause FPCUs to control costs, provide customer service, and, like TCUs, to *price discriminate,* or charge more to those willing to pay more and less to those who will, for whatever reason, buy only at a lower price. Increasingly, FPCUs are relying on a variety of revenue sources to reduce the sticker price for those students either unwilling or unable to pay full price.

Despite major price differences across sectors (figure 4.3), FPCUs are discounting tuition almost as heavily as public and private TCUs. They are achieving this in part by relying on a variety of revenue sources for financial aid to a growing proportion of students. Students attending less-than-four-year FPCUs are more likely to receive federal financial aid than

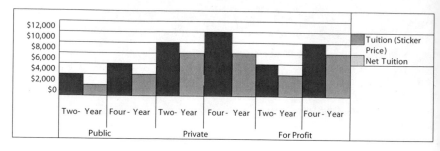

Figure 4.3. Sticker Price and Net Tuition by Institutional Type and Sector.
Source: Knapp et al. 2003

TABLE 4.3
Percentage of undergrads with aid from various
sources, enrolled at less-than-four-year FPCUs

Source	1992–93	1995–96
Federal aid	71	71
Nonfederal aid	12	27
State aid	5	11
Institutional aid	4	10
Institutional loan	1	5
State grants	3	9

SOURCE: Knapp et al. 2003.

students attending less-than-four-year TCUs. Part of the reason is due to different prices. Tuition at less-than-two-year and two-year FPCUs is higher than tuition charged at most public TCUs, but tuition at four-year-or-more for-profits is lower than the average tuition at comparable private, nonprofit TCUs. Higher proportions of FPCU students received federal financial aid (for the academic year 2003–4) than from state student aid appropriations and private endowment scholarships (Career College Association 2003, pp. 14–15).

FPCU students tend to shoulder a larger proportion of their cost of schooling, as reflected in table 4.3. Although the average federal grant amount per recipient was not significantly different between FPCU students and TCU students, the average federal loan amount for FPCU students was higher.

As we mentioned earlier, year-to-year changes in prices are reducing the sizes of the price gaps between FPCUs and TCUs. TCUs, especially public ones, are instituting double-digit tuition increases for each of a number of years running.

FPCU Governance for Profitability through Growth in Size and Margins

In examining the coin of profitability, price constitutes only one of two sides, the flip side being cost and its control. Comparing price and cost for FPCUs is relatively easy compared to doing so for TCUs. The business model of FPCUs is, relative to TCUs, pretty straightforward. Generally accepted accounting and financial reporting practices have yielded commonly accepted metrics for recognizing various forms of profits as well as revenues. According to group medians available from eleven publicly traded FPCUs, students pay on average $13,114 for a completed one-year full-time program of study, and from that generate $2,745 in earnings before interest, taxes, depreciation, and amortization (Silber 2004, p. 101). Of that amount, about $2,275 results in operating profit per student. Of that, some $1,598 is free cash flow per student, which is arguably the purest form of profit. (This is measured across all FPCUs' programs. Comparable data are not gathered routinely by or for TCUs. Presumably, however, some TCU courses and programs are at least this profitable, such as freshman English or M.B.A. courses, but many are not.)

Depending on the precise accounting metrics used to assign costs, it apparently costs these eleven FPCUs somewhere in the range of $10,000 to produce the average instructional program for its average student. As shown in figure 4.4, this amount is several thousand dollars more than the average cost for all FPCUs but, even so, is significantly less than the cost per student derived for TCUs, that is, if we merely divided total budgets by enrollments. But, does this make sense given that TCUs are in other *businesses* beyond direct instruction and that TCUs produce very little financial accounting and reporting of the costs directly or solely associated with instructional programs?

With this lack of data, is there any way to compare per pupil costs and prices between FPCUs and TCUs? Crude comparisons of costs and net prices between TCUs and FPCUs can be made, but they require a number of assumptions. While the cost per student is below net price for

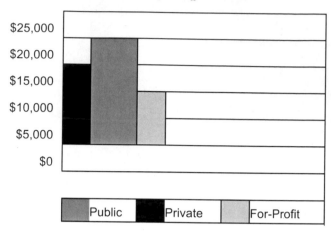

Figure 4.4. Cost to the Institution. *Source:* Ruch 2001, p. 87

FPCUs, it is not for either public or private TCUs. At TCUs, institutional subsidies (and cross-subsidies within TCUs) make it possible to set prices far below costs and to mask costs. So comparisons are difficult. TCU subsidies come from a variety of sources (such as endowment earnings and state appropriations) and serve a variety of purposes (such as affordability), but they do, in the end, suggest a more costly process for producing instruction and more services not directly related to instruction. Data from Ruch (2001) presume that instructional costs are computed by dividing total costs by enrollments, which requires us to assume that, like FPCUs, instruction is all that TCUs do. This may be largely true on some campuses, but there are many expenditures that may not be directly related to instruction. A direct comparison is difficult to make. TCU prices have outpaced inflation for many years, and the increased revenues are paying for something, including possibly reducing their discrepancy between cost and price.

Of course, both cost and price are confounded by public subsidies. How do subsidies between FPCUs and TCUs compare? Because community colleges are TCUs that most nearly resemble FPCUs, we can make a somewhat more defensible comparison by comparing public subsidies to them rather than to all TCUs. Using data from several sources, the Career College Association estimated that the total public subsidy per full-time equivalent student for two years of schools is $7,722. The equivalent public subsidy at a community college is estimated at $18,069 (Career College Association 2003, p. 26). More of these types of cost (and benefit) analysis are needed in order to get a clearer picture of similarities and differences.

Long-Term Differences between FPCUs and TCUs? Governance More Than Finance

In our quest to unravel finance and governance distinctions between FPCUs and TCUs, we have examined general sector location, governing board incentives, the impact of the investor, instructional sales, and incentives for controlling costs and growing margins. These factors no doubt illuminate FPCU and TCU differences, but they are more about whether and how they differ than why. Yes, FPCUs seem to focus more on cost, and in ways different from TCUs, for example, by enabling outdated and underenrolled programs a better chance of survival at a TCU than at an FPCU. But why is that so? The answer lies less in differences among the financial numbers than in differences in internal governance, such as the incentives and decision rights among actors at each type of institution.

Up to this point we have used the term *governance* to refer to the sector location of colleges and universities—in other words, to indicate that each is governed by the rules associated with the economic sector in which it resides. At this point, we use the term governance to describe the internal workings of colleges and universities; in particular, we seek to understand the decision rights of actors. Earlier, we alluded to *shared governance,* a widely recognized, if seldom specified, descriptor of the inner workings of most TCUs. In contrast to shared governance, FPCUs employ what Ruch (2001) describes as "traditional management," which we refer to here as *corporate governance.*

These descriptors beg a number of questions, such as what is shared, who shares it, what is corporate, and so on. The questions are sufficiently abstract to embrace a wide variety of situations, but, at the same time, suffer from a lack of specificity. We have tried to create some specificity without at the same time excluding large segments of institutions from

TABLE 4.4
Comparing FPCU corporate governance with TCU shared governance

Decisions	Boards of Governors	Senior/Central Management	Campus/ Program Management	Faculty
Businesses and services	FPCU	FPCU/TCU	TCU	TCU
Delivery of services	FPCU	FPCU/TCU	FPCU/TCU	TCU
Employment and compensation	FPCU	FPCU/TCU	FPCU/TCU	TCU
Customer service	FPCU	FPCU/TCU	FPCU/TCU	TCU
Revenues	FPCU	FPCU/TCU	FPCU	

NOTE: FPCU, for-profit colleges and universities; TCU, traditional colleges and universities.

both sectors. The result is a matrix of the major *actors* (four) in each post-secondary institution, arrayed by the major categories of *decisions* (five) that get made on behalf of the institution. The cells in the matrix portray (table 4.4) the typical decision rights of actors at FPCUs and TCUs.

The major categories of actors—boards of governors, senior/central management, campus/program management, and faculty—are relatively easy to identify. The categories of consequential decisions, on the other hand, are less obvious. We have adapted this taxonomy from work on other kinds of organizations for use here. Perhaps the most fundamental decisions are those involving the basic business to be in and the fundamental mix of services to provide. These decisions include whether to enter or leave that business, when to shift dramatically to an adjacent business, and when to spin off major parts of the business. Boards and senior management at FPCUs make more of these types of decisions than do their counterparts at TCUs. At TCUs, more of these types of decisions bubble up from committees of faculty, as articulated through central administration.

Another set of decisions routinely get made about how to organize service delivery, including hierarchical reporting, administrative and programmatic reporting relationships, the configuration of academic and support units, and how all units interface with students and with each other. Because of the implications for profitability, governing boards at FPCUs are much more involved in this level of decisions. Given the close association at TCUs with issues of faculty rights and responsibilities, faculty members there are much more involved in this level of decision. Representatives of both central and campus management from both types of institutions are engaged in these decisions, but at FPCUs they tend to make decisions with their governing boards. In comparison, at TCUs they tend to make these decisions with committees of faculty.

The same general differences apply to decisions about the types of labor to be employed and the manner in which individuals are compensated as well as which types of customers (students) will be served. Decisions about the types of revenue to pursue and with what degrees of intensity and what levels of investment are largely the province of boards and senior management at FPCUs, with involvement from campus management. At TCUs these kinds of decisions are largely the responsibility of senior or central management.

Individuals familiar with higher education may differ on the accuracy of including individual FPCUs and TCUs in the matrix in table 4.4. But overall, it is clear that many of the consequential decisions that guide FPCUs tend to include the governing board more heavily; at TCUs, the faculty are more heavily engaged in many of those decisions. The incentives, priorities, values, and decision rights of FPCU governing boards are fundamentally different from the incentives, priorities, values, and decision rights of TCU faculty. Even if we hold constant the orientations of those in the managerial ranks, the overall behavior of FPCUs should be different from the behavior of TCUs. Are these differences likely to grow or diminish over time?

TCUs, admittedly, do things other than provide focused instruction like FPCUs, and these activities may have major financial implications for TCUs. But are these differences between TCUs and FPCUs growing or shrinking? We know that price differences between TCUs and FPCUs seem to be converging, in part as a consequence of tuition increases at public TCUs to replace lost revenues from state appropriations.

> While the historical difference in revenue sources [between nonprofit and for-profit organizations] is unambiguous, there appears to be a contemporary convergence in revenue sources. . . . [T]he share of revenue coming from tuition charges as well as revenue coming from fee-for-service activi-

ties has risen at all three institutional types (public and private TCUs and FPCUs). . . . [I]t rose by approximately 47% [at public TCUs], 17% [at private TCUs] and 15.5% at FPCUs between 1980 and 1995. (Pusser and Turner 2004, p. 240)

The fact that TCUs are gradually approaching FPCUs in their reliance on tuition income may well suggest some incremental shift in the revenue theory of management, in that marginally more attention will be devoted to nurturing and protecting the tuition revenue stream. It is much less clear, however, how this might impact the governance and its sector-driven attributes. More specifically, the governance features that give incentive to FPCUs to seek profitability at scale do not appear to follow, ipso facto, from increased reliance on tuition revenue. Indeed, many tuition-dependent TCUs (such as open-enrollment institutions or small liberal arts colleges) have been in this condition for years without behaving (or sometimes even trying to behave) like FPCUs.

While TCUs and FPCUs may be inching toward financial convergence, the more fundamental similarity may be that institutions within both categories are increasingly differentiating themselves from others. At the gross level of analysis, TCUs include such diverse entities as community colleges, liberal arts colleges, and others up through the Carnegie classification system. Similarly, FPCUs are beginning to aggregate around differentiating factors, which include, but are not limited to, employment and labor specializations, program concentrations, certificates versus degrees, different levels of degrees, levels and types of students (age, employment status), and mode of instructional delivery, to name the more apparent early differentiators among FPCUs. The focus associated with for-profit enterprises in general, it seems, operates with regard to FPCUs in that individual businesses seek to differentiate their services from possible competitors.

A third possible long-term difference between TCUs and FPCUs (in addition to convergence on tuition revenue and differentiation within sectors) is direct competition by FPCUs with TCUs. This possible future, sketched by Kinser (2006, p. 62), suggests that FPCUs "are increasingly narrow competitors to [TCUs] in cash-cow fields rather than niche providers for students ill-served by [TCUs]. In a form of for-profit mission creep, [publicly traded FPCUs] have tended to develop new programs in high-demand fields regardless of their original mission and focus." If such a future were to play out over time, the contest between TCUs and FPCUs over lucrative programs will likely be a contest of organizational forms with the state-chartered public or private nonprofit institution facing off against larger, more aggressive multinational corporations with global access to investment capital. The likelihood of such a future is simply not known at this point.

CHAPTER FIVE

Faculty Roles

Academic work at for-profit colleges and universities differs from that at traditional institutions in the twenty-first century, as an overview of the curriculum at for-profit institutions suggests. After reviewing faculty roles at traditional institutions, we consider who populates faculty positions at the for-profits and discuss how they become socialized to the organization. In doing so, we will suggest not only what these portraits say about the goals of for-profit institutions but also what they imply for academic life in general.

Faculty Work at Traditional Institutions

Although there may be any number of starting points for determining how faculty roles have been configured in American higher education, most scholars point to the late nineteenth century, a time of significant change in what was expected of American colleges. The Morrill Act of 1862 created land-grant colleges, whose designated role was to educate a new group of students in the technical arts and sciences. With this development, college was opened up to more than just the wealthy. Higher learning no longer referred only to the study of classical disciplines and religion; the practical arts were also to be taught. Agriculture and science for the working classes demanded new kinds of institutions and, of consequence, a new kind of faculty.

Further, students who had been trained in Europe, primarily in Germany and England, returned to the United States with the idea that faculty work should be more than teaching. Philanthropists had the income to support such a desire. Thus, by the start of the twentieth century, a handful of colonial institutions and church-related colleges had experienced dramatic institutional makeovers, and newcomers had entered the academic ranks to allow current powerhouses like Johns Hopkins, Stanford, Vanderbilt, Duke, Cornell, and Chicago to come into their own. In 1900 the Association of American Universities was created and laid claim to institutional greatness for American research universities, not simply in the United States but throughout the world.

The growth of American higher education and the professionalization of the faculty had many results that few could have predicted. By the early years of the twentieth century, the size of the faculty had more than doubled. As institutions grew, the size of the administration increased as well. Having received their training, students returned from Europe with a desire for greater autonomy in their professional lives. The Germanic concept of *Lehrfreiheit* came with graduate student training in the disciplines, and American students learned their lessons well. The concept pertained to "the right of the university professor to freedom of inquiry and to freedom of teaching, the right to study and to report on his findings in an atmosphere of consent" (Rudolph 1962, p. 412). The desire for freedom of inquiry and teaching and the rise of professional associations were on a collision course with the manner in which colleges and universities were run. Faculty members no longer saw themselves as the equivalent of hired labor, but they had not yet determined what their new role would be. Conflict was bound to erupt.

In addition to the creation of disciplinary associations as a means to confront issues related to the infringement of academic freedom, faculty formed an association in 1915 that cut across disciplines and demanded professional rights. The American Association of University Professors (AAUP) chose John Dewey as its first president. Among its first tasks, the AAUP established a committee to conduct investigations and begin developing policies that protected academic freedom. During its first two years, the organization investigated more than thirty cases of infringements on academic freedom.

The result of these actions was fourfold. First, academic freedom became enshrined as a hallmark declaration for American higher education. In declaring that institutions of higher education were conducted for the common good, individuals agreed that the search for truth and its free exposition were essential. Second, to preserve academic freedom, a system of tenure came into existence that guaranteed college professors lifetime employment and protected them from being fired at will if they studied a topic that drew the ire of administrators or legislators. Third, in order for academic freedom to remain a hallmark of the institution, the concept of shared governance came into existence. Shared governance acknowledges the central role of the faculty in governing the internal affairs of the institution, such as the hiring, evaluation, and firing of faculty, the standards for admitting students, and the curricula. Fourth, the role of faculty was revised. Research, teaching, and service became the three primary functions of academic work. The assumption was that to be good teachers, the vast majority of the faculty needed to participate in research; for some professors, research would be their primary activity. If shared governance was essential, then service to the institution and the profession was also necessary.

Such a transformation did not occur overnight, but by the end of World War II most traditional colleges and universities more or less accepted these basic precepts. Although many individuals complained about one or another aspect, especially tenure, they also recognized that after tenure came into existence, shared governance became the norm, and the United States emerged as a global superpower, American higher education became the envy of the world.

This brief overview of faculty work in traditional organizations is obviously an idealized type. Although tenure remains a basic precept, the reality is that more part-time and non-tenure-track faculty are hired today than full-time tenure-track faculty. Similarly, shared governance is still said to be important and valued, but administrators have greater authority on campus today than a generation ago. Nevertheless, the norms remain in place and stand in contrast to the norms at for-profit colleges and universities.

Faculty Work at For-Profit Institutions

One may ask why it is necessary to understand the role of faculty in traditional organizations to discuss faculty at for-profit institutions. We do so because in one sense, the contrast is not very significant, and yet in another, the differences are vast. That is, at most traditional and for-profit institutions, faculty teach courses to students. However, to make such a facile comparison is a bit like implying that since a bicycle and an airplane are both means of transportation, they are quite similar. As we previously outlined, although faculty teach classes at traditional institutions, the impetus of the organization is quite different from a simple desire to offer courses, much less to make a profit.

In some respects, traditional colleges and universities have been arranged more to serve the needs of the faculty than to meet the needs of other constituencies. Some will argue that such a statement makes self-evident the criticism that traditional institutions ill-serve their various constituencies. We disagree. Traditional colleges and universities have had as their priority a concern for academic freedom and the search for truth. The assumption has been that such a search is not a self-encapsulated benefit to those who do the searching—the faculty. The argument has instead been made (and supported by the Supreme Court) that society gains when it provides faculty with the conditions for the unfettered search for truth. If tenure is nothing more than lifetime employment, then it is merely a sinecure for intellectuals. However, tenure came about to ensure academic freedom, and that protection has been supported time and again in the courts and in public opinion polls.

As we have noted, such a statement appeals to an ideal type with regard to organizational purpose. Clearly, not all professors lay claim to searching for truth every time they set foot in a classroom or research setting. The same may be said, however, about any overarching ideology. During the course of their lives, not all of America's citizens will need to call upon the First Amendment to support what they wish to express. Every time an individual opens his or her mouth, it is not a test of free speech. Nevertheless, the ideology frames how people define themselves as citizens of the United States. We suggest that the same may be said for faculty at traditional colleges and universities. In what follows, however, we point out that at for-profit colleges and universities, rather than a devotion to academic freedom, what determines academic work and faculty modalities is quite another goal altogether.

Curricula, Not Research, Drive Faculty Work

As we noted in chapter 4, one way to think about for-profit colleges and universities is in regard to their fiscal status. Some are publicly traded entities that are set up as corporations where shareholders own a portion of the company. Others are privately held companies where an investor, or group of investors, owns the institution. While the fiscal implications for profit sharing, ownership, strategic direction, and manner of corporate decision making are important, whether an institution is a publicly traded or privately held company does not appear to influence significantly the makeup, modalities, or work of the faculty.

Instead, faculty work is determined in large part by what we define as five curricular categories. Four functional categories pertain to what is taught; the fifth category refers to the structure and delivery mechanism of the curricula. In turn, these categories impact the expectations of professional and regional accreditation associations that also frame faculty work. We suggest, then, that just as a desire for academic freedom determined how faculty work was constructed at traditional institutions, the curriculum determines academic work at proprietary institutions.

VOCATIONAL CURRICULA

The most common for-profit colleges in the United States are less-than-two-year, non-degree-granting institutions (National Center for Education Statistics 2001). This type of college enrolls the largest proportion of students attending for-profit institutions. They offer a curriculum that traditionally has been associated with for-profit education. Barber colleges, court reporting schools, trade schools for welding and plumbing, and other similar programs are examples of stand-alone proprietary institutions that offer training usually in one or two locations. The courses are generally not applicable toward a degree; upon completion, the student receives a diploma that enables him or her to apply for work in a particular trade.

Bryman College, for example, offers programs in medical office management, massage therapy, and business administrative assistance. Students are provided with an education that emphasizes practical skills that lead to employment in a vocational area. Like many for-profit institutions that offer vocational training, Bryman is nationally accredited. National accrediting agencies such as the Accrediting Commission of Career Schools and Colleges of Technology, the Accrediting Council for Independent Colleges and Schools, and the Accrediting Council for Continuing Education and Training provide national accreditation to career colleges across the country.

CERTIFICATE CURRICULA

Because employers seek out individuals whose skill competencies are independently certified, for-profit institutions are catering to this new student market by offering courses that lead to certification. Certificate courses generally fall within two types: additional courses that are added to diploma programs to meet minimum standards set forth by a specific organization or agency, and stand-alone course sets that a student must complete to qualify for a specific job. The central difference between vocational and certificate curricula pertain to the certification of competencies by an independent group. Vocational curricula are courses that provide students with fundamental skills that are required for a given vocation. An administrative assistant program, for example, may provide students with basic clerical skills such as word processing, basic accounting, and Internet proficiency. When the student has completed the training, he or she qualifies for an entry-level position as an office assistant.

A certificate curriculum prepares students to take an examination that will certify that an individual has met or surpassed formally established measures of competency. Upon completion of a certificate curriculum, a student can take an exam that qualifies him or her for a job with an employer who seeks specialized training that goes beyond basic knowledge in a given area. The job is generally with a company where a specific skill set is required. The growing demand for information technology specialists, for example, spawned the tremendous growth of IT certification. CCDA (Certified Cisco Design Associate), MCSE (Microsoft Certified Software Engineer), CAN (Certified Novell Administrator), and other similar certificates are quickly becoming standard requirements for employment in the IT field. Whereas a vocational curriculum qualifies someone for a trade that might be used wherever the person finds employment, a certificate frequently leads to a specific job title. A computer technician qualifies to be a computer technician anywhere computers need to be repaired and maintained; an individual with MCSE certification qualifies for a position with an organization that utilizes the Microsoft Windows operating systems.

Although they prepare students for industry certification, for-profit colleges and universities do not directly offer IT certification. These providers "operate outside Title IV of the Higher Education Amendments and the Integrated Postsecondary Education Data System(IPEDS). That is, they do not participate in the federal student aid and reporting systems. We thus know little about their students" (Adelman 2000, pp. 24–25). The primary vendors, such as Microsoft, Novell, and Cisco as well as industry associations, establish the certification criteria.

UNDERGRADUATE CURRICULA

A third form of curricula offering pertains to coursework that leads to an associate or bachelor's degree. As we have discussed, most degrees offered by for-profits are practical majors that lead to specific jobs such as in business or engineering. Although an institution may offer general education requirements and a few electives, the central focus of the curriculum is on a specific number of established courses that a student must take to receive a professional degree. (Regulations prohibiting FPCUs from offering liberal arts degrees are discussed later.)

GRADUATE CURRICULA

Master's and doctoral degrees, though the least common curricula to be offered by proprietary institutions, are seen as an area with tremendous growth potential. As with undergraduate curricula, the focus is on degrees that are more professional in nature and do not require extensive laboratory work or primary research. Thus, one is likely to see coursework leading to a master's degree or doctorate in education, nursing, or business, but not in areas such as medicine, biochemistry, or philosophy.

Curricula Structures and Delivery Mechanisms

The final category, which has significant implications for faculty work, is how FPCUs arrange their courses and programs. One commonality among traditional institutions is the structural nature of what is meant by a course. A course is a discrete body of knowledge that a faculty member develops and offers over a set period of time for a specific number of units. When courses are combined with one another, they count toward a major and a degree; when a predetermined number of credits have been accumulated, the student receives the degree. Programs of study are made up of specified sets of courses and can lead to majors, degrees, and other certifications of successful completion of the set of courses.

Although some for-profit institutions mirror traditional notions of the structure of curricula and how a course should be delivered, there is also significant variation. Credit for work experience is much more common at for-profit institutions. Courses frequently begin and end irrespective of the start of a fall or spring semester or quarter. The mastery of a skill set, especially in certification courses, is much more important than the accumulation of credits. Students are more likely to utilize the Internet and Web-based learning than at traditional institutions. Indeed, the manner of delivery is a key decision at for-profit institutions, whereas at traditional institutions delivery is more a matter of matching specific instructors with particular courses at predetermined times.

In some respects, what we have outlined here is not so different from what exists in the traditional sector. Community colleges offer vocational courses; four-year institutions, provide undergraduate and graduate degrees. And although certificates are not in the mainstream of traditional institutions' course offerings, several continuing-education centers have begun to offer them. As we discuss more in chapters 6 and 7, there may be no single key factor that alone differentiates FPCUs from TCUs. Rather, a combination of incremental differences—including faculty roles, curricula, programs, instructional strategies and modalities, and locations—together differentiates for-profits from traditional institutions and helps to explain why someone would enroll in a for-profit program when a similar program might well be offered at a traditional institution.

If there were a key single factor, however, it would be profit maximization. At least, a major part of the differentiation lies in the fifth category—the structure and delivery mechanism of the for-profit institutions. For-profits in general do not necessarily offer curricula that cannot be found at some traditional institutions; indeed, most often, for-profit institutions have fewer course offerings and fewer individual choices. In some respects, unlike the innovations discussed in chapter 1, the product itself is not entirely new. But sometimes the technologies that deliver the product have unique potential to capture the imagination of consumers.

For the plan to work, however, for-profit colleges and universities must conform to the regulatory arrangements demanded by state, regional, and professional accrediting associations. To be sure, a college does not need to offer credit-bearing courses that have been approved by a particular accrediting agency. However, the absence of accreditation is a major hurdle with the potential to cripple an organization that seeks legitimacy. Without accreditation, an organization cannot receive federal funds. Students are generally unable to transfer credits to another institution, and employers may not recognize the degree. Thus, most current for-profit institutions, especially those that offer undergraduate and graduate degrees, have a desire to gain professional and regional accreditation—or, as we shall discuss, to change the rules that govern accreditation. *Regional* accreditation, the historic accrediting bodies of TCUs, seek oversight of all institutions in a geographic region, regardless of the program specialties at each institution. *National* accreditation, the major accrediting bodies of FPCUs, seek oversight of individual program specializations, regardless of the region of the country in which the FPCU is located. Both types of accrediting bodies have specific requirements pertaining to faculty, which returns us to a discussion of faculty work at for-profit institutions.

Profiling the Faculty

The hiring arrangements for faculty at for-profit institutions are designed in response to the demands by associations that were formed according to what constitutes faculty work at traditional organizations. That is, traditional colleges and universities framed faculty life as a way to ensure that academic freedom existed. To guarantee this freedom, professors were given considerable autonomy in their teaching and research; service to the profession and organization was also deemed important. Tenure and full-time status for faculty were assumed to be essential. Such assumptions, however, create inevitable tension for an organization that does not organize its activities around the same beliefs. Rather than preserve academic freedom, for-profit organizations seek to provide effective curricula in efficient time formats in order to turn a profit. The result is that what constitutes faculty work and who populates the role of the professorate differ dramatically from what is found at traditional institutions.

In some respects, due to accreditation requirements, those who populate faculty roles at FPCUs bear a resemblance to faculty at traditional institutions. Faculty who teach graduate classes are primarily individuals who hold terminal degrees; those who teach baccalaureate classes uniformly hold master's or doctoral degrees; and certificate-based and vocational instructors parallel faculty one might find at community colleges. Indeed, a significant percentage of faculty at FPCUs come from traditional higher education. Many of them have retired from teaching and no longer desire a full-time job, but are intrigued by the work of for-profits.

Some professors are the equivalent of "freeway flyers"; they teach multiple classes at numerous institutions because they cannot find full-time employment at a single institution. Others come from business and industry, have at least a bachelor's degree, and enjoy teaching a course. At institutions that rely on distance learning, many faculty members are intrigued by the new technology and are eager to experiment. One overlooked aspect of for-profit education is that the oft-commented convenience of courses extends not only to students, who are often working adults, but also to instructors. Many individuals who would like to teach a course are unable to do so when or where traditional campuses require. Of consequence, a ready labor force exists to meet the needs of for-profit teaching. Most of these instructors are technically qualified to teach the types of courses needed. Compared to that for TCUs, the labor pool for FPCUs may be much broader.

An anomaly exists insofar as instructors at for-profits are generally a bit older than their confreres at traditional institutions; they are also more diverse in terms of race and gender. That is, one might assume that if instructors are older, there would be more white men teaching classes.

However, the reverse is the case. While a significant percentage of faculty comes from the ranks of retirees with time on their hands, a similarly large number of faculty is concurrently employed in business and industry. Simply stated, the pool of women and people of color to choose from in business and industry is larger than that in the elite graduate programs that offer a Ph.D. The programs that for-profits offer also have larger numbers of people of color in them than the panoply of departments that require staffing at traditional institutions. There are more people of color and women, for example, in nursing, education, and business as opposed to biochemistry, electrical engineering, and classics.

If the individuals who work at for-profits are similar to those who work at traditional institutions, then what differentiates them? To answer this question, we return to our discussion in the first part of the chapter. As noted, one impetus for change at the turn of the twentieth century was the faculty itself. The pattern had been to hire full-time tenure-track staff, some of whom had returned from their European education with a desire to conduct research and have greater say in the affairs of the institution. At for-profit institutions, the pattern has been in large part not to hire full-time tenure-track faculty. Also, for the predominantly part-time faculty at FPCUs, research has never been a condition of academic work, whereas relevant successful employment and experience have been major components.

To be sure, some variation exists with regard to hiring patterns at FPCUs, although tenure is rare. (Tenure exists, for example, in several FPCU law schools.) At some institutions, such as DeVry University, about half of the faculty is full-time. Other institutions such as the University of Phoenix have what appear to be a number of full-time faculty, but they spend "the majority of their time doing administrative tasks" (Floyd 2005). Vocational institutions also may have full-time instructors, but they parallel their counterparts in a community college, albeit without tenure. A very few institutions also have long-term contracts, and faculty members at these institutions, such as Argosy University, claim that they have a great deal of input into the direction of the curriculum (Berg 2005, p. 225). The bottom line is that for-profits want their faculty to teach, and their assumption is that tenure is unnecessary at best, and a serious impediment at worst, for achieving the goals of the organization.

FPCUs may want their faculty to teach, but given accreditation requirements, they also recognize that faculty must be involved in the governance of the organization in some manner. It is not uncommon, for example, that a visiting accreditation team might comment that a for-profit college "exhibits a lack of mature faculty integration or a common faculty appreciation of the proper role of faculty governance. While faculty members have individual roles, as a whole, they lack a sense of a collective role." Such a statement highlights an inevitable tension. Members of accreditation teams overwhelmingly come from the ranks of traditional institutions. The idea of shared governance in business is a bizarre concept for those who work in companies whose purpose is to turn a profit. True, a minuscule percentage of organizations are actually worker run or owned, but the paradigm in place is one that rejects the idea of shared governance. Although hierarchical and linear decision making may be out of fashion, no one makes a serious argument that business and industry need to adopt the model that exists at traditional colleges and universities. Furthermore, with many employees owning shares of their FPCUs, corporate accountability to shareholders has no analogue in TCUs.

As a result, FPCUs face criticism from accrediting agencies for their lack of shared governance. Furthermore, when employees are part-timers, it is no easy task to incorporate them into a decision-making framework, especially when many are also employed elsewhere and seek part-time teaching for its prestige, fulfillment, or additional income. Indeed, traditional colleges and universities face the same conundrum. While standing governance committees already exist at postsecondary institutions, most of them do not accommodate part-time workers; as the percentage of part-time employees increases, colleges and universities struggle with how to incorporate part-timers into governance.

At FPCUs, however, the challenge is even more severe because frequently no governance structure exists for faculty. Consider, for example, how little we mentioned faculty in the previous chapter in our discussion of FPCU governance. The omission is not an oversight on our part but a comment on where faculty fit in the governance structure at FPCUs—nowhere. The result is that institutions construct a structure to alleviate the concerns of accrediting agencies, but the structure bears little resemblance to what currently exists at traditional institutions. Often, a structure will be put in place that might appear to have some decision-making authority, with faculty as participants, but those who are members of the decision-making group are closer to assistant deans than faculty. For-profits hire full-time individuals who manage the curriculum, hire faculty, set teaching times, evaluate teaching, and perform other similar duties; even though these individuals may bear the title of faculty, they operate more like department-level administrators at TCUs.

If we consider why shared governance arose in the first place, we can appreciate why it is so weak at for-profits. Shared governance, like tenure, came about to protect academic freedom. If academic freedom is not of concern at an institution, then why are cumbersome decision-making and employment structures necessary? The answer from those who work at FPCUs is that such structures impede their effectiveness. The answer from those who work at traditional institutions is that academic freedom is essential and profit ought not to be the overriding motive for offering a postsecondary education. Notice that each argument can be true and does not directly or completely address the other.

As opposed to traditional colleges and universities, for-profits also work from a sense that tight coupling is essential for creating an effective and efficient organization. Because individual, *interest-driven* research conducted by those who teach is irrelevant or nonexistent, tight coupling pertains to the curricula that get offered, taught, and evaluated. By and large, for-profit faculty are not free to teach whatever they desire in a manner of their choosing. In a multicampus system such as the University of California, while the same English course with the same title and same credits might be taught by instructors across the state, no one would ever try to implement a system where all the faculty would teach from the same syllabus; such a strategy would be seen as an infringement on academic freedom. At for-profits, the opposite is the case. DeVry University, for example, has numerous campuses and centers throughout the country, but, as Gary Berg (2005, p. 152) notes, the system seeks uniformity:

> They want a student who gets a degree at [DeVry's] Fremont, California cen-
> ter to get essentially the same education as someone who attends the North
> Brunswick, New Jersey campus. Faculty members are free to make their
> own assignments, choose textbooks, do what they want within the frame-

work of the course, but the structure of the course is established with terminal learning objectives that fit the preceding and successive courses.

At for-profits, part-time and full-time faculty generally receive manuals with predetermined curricula and learning objectives, or they are able to develop a course that meets the approval of the department chair or academic administrator. Course learning objectives are created centrally. Standardized course materials are the norm. They highlight an organization that is tightly coupled; if faculty do not use the materials or achieve the predetermined objectives, they will not be rehired.

Laura Palmer Noone and Craig Swenson (2001, p. 21) point out that, although faculty at traditional institutions may know a great deal about their subject matter, they have two "dirty little secrets"—they know very little about teaching and even less about learning. By contrast, Noone and Swenson, the highly experienced president and provost of the University of Phoenix, claim that FPCU part-time instructors can be just as effective as full-time faculty because of the rigorous training, evaluation, and assessment they go through, which allows them to build on the subject matter knowledge they bring with them to the job. The authors also emphasize that, by and large, the curricula offered at for-profits are in professional fields and that the instructors usually come from those fields. Indeed, at some institutions, it is mandatory that instructors have a full-time job in the relevant content area. Rather than a theoretical curriculum that may be interesting but have little real-world import, for-profits bring the external world into the classroom.

If teaching is important and for-profit institutions rely primarily on part-time faculty, then socialization and faculty development become essential. In a discussion about the University of Phoenix, for example, Gary Berg (2005, p. 221) points out that they are "serious about evaluating and training faculty members before they are hired. . . . Applicants are required to go through an intensive four-week training session." Training generally implies a specific approach to teaching, an overview of adult-learning theory, and specific policies and procedures. At some for-profits, dress codes are even put in place, and professors generally have little choice about the time and location of their classes. Further, at some institutions, such as the University of Phoenix, new faculty are assigned a mentor during their first course to discuss teaching strengths and weaknesses.

When distance learning is involved, a technology staff exists to train and support faculty. Although one might argue that the same kind of support exists at traditional institutions, the impetus is different. The authors of this text, for example, may decide to teach a course on line at the University of Southern California. If we made such a decision, we would need approval from our departmental colleagues, the School of Education's faculty curriculum committee, the dean, and, in our case, a faculty committee of the graduate school. All of these committees pertain to the idea of shared governance; input from one's faculty colleagues is expected. If the course were approved, we would then need to contact the instructional technology staff at the university and see if it would be willing to help us put the course on line. The course content and the manner in which we decided to offer the class, of course, would be up to us.

At Walden University, a for-profit institution, the entire graduate curriculum is delivered via distance learning. Although instructors express concerns about the ability of the technological staff to keep pace with changes, the role faculty play is considerably different. Faculty members do not decide whether the course they deliver will be on line or in class. The technological staff sets up the modules in predetermined ways; although an instructor may deviate a bit from the syllabus, the entire process is predetermined, including how and when the instructor interacts with students. What an instructor needs to know, then, is how to deliver the course. Training and development pertain not merely to technological know-how, but also to pedagogical instruction in how to be an effective online instructor.

Considering the Differences in Faculty Work

We have demonstrated here the differences in expectations of faculty roles and modalities between traditional and for-profit institutions and why these differences have developed. Although both sectors deliver a similar curricular *product*, what they expect from their *providers*—the faculty—is significantly different. From a traditionalist perspective, what the for-profits are doing is a violation of true academic life and, hence, a bastardization of the role of the faculty. The response from the FPCUs is that they are doing something quite different from traditional institutions; given their different purposes and markets, they should not be compared directly with TCUs. Indeed, critics of the traditional sector would suggest that many TCU faculty roles have become moribund and risk averse. For-profit institutions develop a business plan with the risk built in. They assume little risk from the faculty because they do not think of academic freedom and its accoutrements (tenure, shared governance, research, and service) as necessary for what they are attempting to do.

We have heard it said that when the film industry began, innovators such as Charlie Chaplin were a veritable one-man show: Chaplin wrote, produced, directed, and starred in his movies. Today, of course, the film industry has distinct individuals who write, produce, direct, and star in movies. It is rare indeed when an individual assumes more than one role in the development of a movie. The analogy is then made to teaching. At traditional institutions, both then and now, one finds the equivalent of multiple Charlie Chaplins. Faculty members do everything—develop the syllabus, determine when and where they will teach, decide who their students will be, and star in the show. The response by those at traditional institutions is that such an analogy is not apt. They argue that what is really intended by such analogies is for the capitalists at for-profits (and elsewhere) to claim the intellectual property of faculty and to reduce professors to little more than day laborers.

As the demand and supply of postsecondary education increase, possibilities of peaceful coexistence between FPCUs and TCUs may erode. Those at FPCUs are quite critical of ideas such as tenure and shared governance. Those at traditional colleges and universities find equally repugnant the notion that profit has replaced core values such as academic freedom. Perhaps such contradictory opinions pertain to our observations in chapter 1 about innovation and change. TCUs are comfortable with moderate, sustainable change, and FPCUs are fomenting disruptive technologies. Alternatively, we may be seeing the distinctions that occur when for-profit organizations produce services heretofore produced by public and nonprofit organizations.

Obviously, no one can predict the future with certainty. In a system as vast as postsecondary education in the United States, however, we wish to proffer a question. It appears self-evident that the postsecondary *industry* has two quite different notions of the role of faculty, just as one group accepts the notion of capitalism (being in business to make a profit) and the other views profit making in education with suspicion. Similarly, as we have noted previously, the idea that either traditional or for-profit institutions are going to go away seems far-fetched. One is a mature industry that undoubtedly will undergo transformation but is likely to remain more similar to what it is today than different. The other is a growth industry that will undergo changes, but the demand for its product exists and will no doubt increase in an age where knowledge and information are essential. Why, then, is it not possible for both sectors to define more clearly what they do and, of consequence, what they expect of faculty?

It is difficult to imagine that all of postsecondary education in the United States will adopt the for-profit faculty model. If academic freedom as a central precept were eliminated from all of postsecondary education, then the country would suffer in numerous ways—classroom dialogue would be cheapened, research would be circumscribed, and the country would lose a vital link to a value that it holds essential, free speech. However, it seems a very weak argument indeed to say that FPCUs, which claim a different undertaking, must adhere to the same beliefs and strategies of traditional institutions. Yet some might argue that a professor at a for-profit classroom should enjoy the same right of academic freedom that his or her colleagues enjoy at a small liberal arts college.

We acknowledge this point but are not convinced that every individual must march to the same configuration. Indeed, if we look hard enough, we can see configuration proliferation within TCUs. Although most individuals support some unions, for example, few individuals make the claim that every individual in America who works should be a member of a union. Rather, a common challenge appears to be how to ensure that both FPCUs and TCUs enable their respective faculties to perform to the best of their abilities.

CHAPTER SIX

Defining Success at the For-Profits

Students, Programs, and Employers

While professors constitute the fundamental ingredient of work at traditional and for-profit colleges and universities, they pursue different versions of success at the two types of institutions. The difference might be described as prestige at TCUs versus profitability at FPCUs. FPCU profitability depends on a variety of factors, but the most widely shared attribute of profitability among FPCUs derives from the successful recruitment and education of a student and then the placement of a student in a position requiring that education. Successful job placement not only reflects well on the graduate and the program (similar to a traditional institution), but it also sends positive signals to employers and prospective students—both of whom are greatly valued by FPCUs.

Students are *produced* (prepared with a set of marketable skills) for employers who seek students with those particular skills. In this sense, the employer is the client and the student is the happy and willing *product*. Students are willing in no small part because they enroll in FPCUs with the aim of gaining specific skills for specific jobs, or at least completing degrees in order to compete for those jobs. Not coincidentally, program-relevant job placement is largely what for-profits offer, and it is also what regulators seek to enforce. While the content of the programs certainly matters at FPCUs, simply providing job training is not enough. Operating success is often defined in terms of how well job placement is accomplished, something of marginal concern to TCUs. It follows, then, that local labor markets influence the chances for success for FPCUs more than they do for TCUs (table 6.1), especially if we factor in the value

TABLE 6.1
Influence of local labor market on school

	FPCU			TCU		
	Strong	Some	None	Strong	Some	None
Campus location	√					√
Majors/minors	√				√	
Faculty	√					√
Employees	√				√	

at FPCUs of the connections established between students and the instructors, who are often recruited from the ranks of potential employers.

Campus locations of FPCUs are more influenced by proximity to the labor markets they seek to serve than are TCU locations. Certainly TCUs may accidentally happen to be located in places where some graduates are locally employable, but FPCUs, especially the growing number of multicampus FPCUs, make campus location decisions based in part on the employability of their graduates. An even stronger difference applies at the program (majors/minors) level. FPCUs offer relatively few programs at each campus and those tend to be the ones most likely to capitalize on the local labor market. TCUs offer many more programmatic options, only a small fraction of which are directly aimed at the labor market in their region.

Faculty members at FPCUs are more intimately associated with local labor markets than TCU faculty in two interrelated ways. First, those hired as FPCU faculty tend to be drawn from the local labor market. The occupational programs at the FPCU are the occupations in which they are also employed. Second, through their personal involvement in that occupation, they are also connected to others in the same field who know about the latest job openings and evolving qualifications in those fields. Finally, local employers have a greater influence on FPCUs than on most TCUs. The success of FPCUs is closely associated with successful placement of graduates. FPCUs want employers to hire FPCU graduates, and thus, they exert no small amount of effort to ensure that the graduate has been well prepared—not just in general, but for specific occupational titles. Many FPCUs formalize employer input by creating local Employer Advisory Boards (EABs) to garner employer perspectives on curriculum, trends in the field, and the performance of recent graduates.

TCUs have typically included preparation for the working world among their stated missions but rarely provide programming for work. For-profits, on the other hand, pursue this goal in a manner that is more focused and jointly produced with regional employers. Regional employers influence a local FPCU's array of programs as well as the course content of each program. Joint production arises from joint dependency. Because it is important to FPCUs that their graduates be hired by firms into program-relevant positions, FPCUs actively seek input on curricula and instructional methods from boards or focus groups composed of employers and occupational specialists in the local markets. These groups serve a wide variety of functions beyond providing curricular advice on occupational programs, including offering feedback on program effectiveness, recruiting graduates from programs into employment, placing employees into programs (as students and teachers), and addressing employer-based human resource and training needs (Hughes, Bailey, and Mechur 2001).

Employee Advisory Boards grew in part out of federal legislation in 1994 (School-to-Work Opportunities Act), which called for their creation as a means to address issues of transitioning from (largely high) school to work. Although the legislation and the funding to support the program have not been renewed, EABs have continued to exist because of the mutual benefits experienced by both educators and business leaders during the 1990s. Today, some business and engineering schools at four-year TCUs, plus numerous individual programs at community colleges, employ them. Very few, if any, TCUs make Employer Advisory Boards an integral part of their *entire* curriculum, but FPCUs have adopted their use as a means to advancing their career-oriented programs. FPCUs want employers to depend on their services and products (students) for a large and growing fraction of their human resource development goals, just as they depend on those employers to aid them and their students. This joint dependency is characterized by a bundle of interorganizational relationships between FPCUs and employers that are at the same time formal and informal, structured and casual, organizational and personal.

The reliance of Career Education Corporation (CEC), a leading publicly

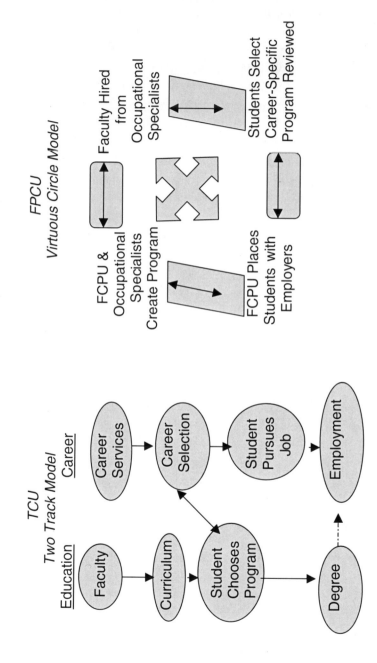

Figure 6.1. Interplay of Career and Education.

traded FPCU, on employer advisory boards is illustrative. CEC focuses on (only) five key employment fields in its programmatic offerings: visual communication and design technologies, information technology, business studies, culinary arts, and health education. It has established employer advisory boards focusing on these fields at all of its forty-two campuses "to keep academic programs current with workplace needs and strengthen relationships with prospective employers of CEC graduates" (www.careered.com/leaders.aspx.). All CEC schools are also aligned within six broad occupational divisions, which better enables it to build its brand name as a leader in that occupational field. These occupational fields (divisions) then enable CEC to bring new programs to individual campuses. In this instance, then, EABs are aligned with CEC's organizational structure and operational goals. Employers have an advisory but highly valued role in shaping the school's curriculum.

The stronger influence of the local labor market on FPCUs portrayed in table 6.1 is achieved through the mutually reinforcing processes characterized in figure 6.1. The broad-based, elective-oriented curricula at TCUs have relatively few structural or functional relationships between education and career. The student selects a course of study and then independently selects among available career options. The student's degree is not intentionally associated with specific occupational titles. At FPCUs, the education-to-career distinctions are not only blurred but are intentionally co-produced through several functional relationships. The curriculum is co-produced by FPCU and employer/occupational representatives. Instructors who teach in the programs are hired from those same employers and other occupational specialty groups. Students select career-specific programs designed with few, if any, electives. During the course of the program, students are often placed in externships that are made available by employers and occupational specialty groups. Subsequent to graduation, they often seek employment in those same firms. The employers, and the occupational specialty groups whom they employ, play an influential role in the operation and success of FPCUs, just as FPCUs and their faculty play an influential role in the successes of the employers. With traditional institutions, the assumption is that schools will independently prepare students for work and life. With FPCUs, the assumption is that schools will work together with employers to prepare students; students are the products of that interdependency.

The links among employability and employment, students, programs, instruction, and placement define the core services of most FPCUs. Their characteristics and interactions are the subject of the five remaining sections of this chapter. (1) For FPCUs, campus locations and program offerings are tactical responses to perceived local labor market demands. (2) The content of program offerings closely reflects the array of skills and aptitudes required for increasingly specialized workplaces. (3) Because the skill requirements are highly specified and specialized, programs have relatively few electives and courses do not easily transfer to other programs. (At the same time, it is generally easier for a student to transfer credits from a TCU to an FPCU than the reverse.) These conditions increase the importance of correct initial student placement into a program at an FPCU. (4) While programs at FPCUs may be distinguished from programs at traditional institutions along the lines of vocational versus liberal arts, it may be as accurate to argue that FPCUs currently emphasize more applied and formal knowledge than traditional institutions. (5) Placement metrics and behaviors at FPCUs are much more heavily emphasized than at TCUs, due in part to incentives created by the prospect of future enrollments and to the regulatory conditions imposed on FPCUs.

The For-Profit Focus: Workplace-Focused Programs for Students Requiring Some College-Level Preparation

The generalizations in chapter 2 (the more you learn, the more you earn . . . more and more) take on concrete meaning for FPCUs, their students, and the employers they serve. FPCUs tend to focus on programs that require some college, where additional learning makes the greatest relative differences in earnings. About a quarter of students who attend FPCUs enroll in short-term (less-than-two-year) programs, about one-third enroll in courses lasting from two to less than four years, and the rest attend programs lasting four or more years (Coombes 2003).

The United States is experiencing an increasing divide between individuals with skills at the level of "some college and above" and those with skills at the level of a high school diploma or less (Carnevale and Descrochers 2003, p. 7). It is at this juncture in the education spectrum where differences in the economic returns to schooling are greatest and are growing. The United States (having recently surpassed Great Britain) now has the widest income dispersion among the world's advanced economies (Carnevale and Descrochers 2003, p. 7). Currently, about 40% of American adults do not have skills typical of those with some college, but the fastest job growth will occur in those jobs in which incumbent workers currently have skill levels that reflect at least some postsecondary education or training.

Going forward, demand for college-educated workers will continue to grow along with the income divide between those who have some postsecondary education and those who do not (Carnevale and Descrochers 2003, p. 7). Put more starkly, college-level wages are rising, and the wages of those with a high school diploma or less are declining. Most FPCUs focus their programs between the bookends of high school graduation and a bachelor's degree. The greatest growth of FPCUs has paralleled the relatively recent, three-decade growth in the demand for a more highly skilled work force.

Evolution toward a global knowledge economy has been gradual, taking place over a number of decades. Our education and work force preparation systems have also evolved gradually and now total roughly $1 trillion annually. Until the 1970s, "people who would become managers and professionals received a broader education [at TCUs], but those who would eventually work down the line got very little education or formal skills training" anywhere (Carnevale and Descrochers 2003, p. 9). The same global knowledge economy is also increasing new kinds of value in the workplace. "Traditional competition based on the ability to mass produce standardized goods and services and sell them at low cost has been gradually displaced by a competition based on a diverse mix of requirements and new kinds of value added" (p. 11) (by those workers heretofore "down the line").

These changes in what the employment market values, briefly noted in earlier chapters, have led to two major shifts in the labor markets: a shift in job creation toward occupations that tend to require at least some college; and increasing postsecondary skill requirements in all jobs, many of which formerly required only a high school education or less. The largest share (about 72%) of the increases in postsecondary education requirements comes from *upskilling,* or providing the higher skills demanded by employers for jobs that previously did not require any college (as portrayed in table 6.3). A significant but smaller share (about 28%) comes from occupational shifts toward jobs that have always required postsecondary education (Carnevale and Descrochers 2003, p. 19).

What are these jobs and what has happened to them? Six large bundles of jobs have changed significantly, but differentially: office jobs, education and health-care jobs, technology jobs, low-wage service jobs, factory jobs, and natural resource jobs. Office jobs account for the largest, fastest-growing, and generally best-paid group of employees. White-collar office jobs constitute 39% of all jobs today, up from just 30% in 1959 (Carnevale and Descrochers 2003, p. 19). In 1973 only 37% of office workers had some kind of postsecondary education, compared with 69% today. More people are working in education and health care jobs, up respectively since 1959 from 4% to 7% and 6% to 8% of all jobs. This growth is in large part because the new economy requires more education, the demand for health care grows with the aging population, and productivity is not rising as fast as in manufacturing. The proportion of these workers with some college grew from one-half in 1973 to three-quarters in 2001. Technology jobs (those with highly specialized expertise, education, or training in technology-related fields) have doubled since the late 1960s to about 7% of all jobs in the economy. In 1973, 63% of technology jobs required some college; now it is up to 86%. (More than 50% of these require at least a bachelor's degree.)

Low-wage service jobs are at the bottom of the earnings and skills hierarchy and have constituted about one-fifth of all jobs for nearly half a century. For some workers, such as students, some immigrant groups, part-time workers, and retirees, low wages may be less of a concern than for others. After they complete their education, many individuals below the age of 25 who work in this sector (about 36%) will probably move on to better-paying jobs. While low-wage services jobs are not growing as a proportion of all jobs, factory jobs are shrinking both proportionately and in absolute numbers, falling from 32% to 17% of all jobs between 1959 and 2001. In 1973 only 8% of workers in factory jobs had any college; by

2001 that proportion had increased to 31% (Carnevale and Descrochers 2003, p. 24). Like factory jobs, natural resource jobs (such as farming, fishing, forestry, and mining) are declining relatively and absolutely, down from 5% in 1959 to about 1.3% of all jobs in the economy today. High school dropouts held more than two-thirds of these jobs in 1973, down to 42% in 2001 when more than one-third were high school graduates, and workers with at least some college held 23% of these jobs.

Generally, those who hold bachelor's degrees or higher have clear and growing earnings advantages; those with a high school education or less have clear and growing earnings declines; those with some college experience growing earnings, but differences exist based on the nature of the student and the nature of the program or major. Average earnings by degree level mask wide intradegree variations. While those who hold associate degrees earn on average less than those who hold bachelor's degrees, fully 83% of workers with associate degrees earn the same as workers with bachelor's degrees (Carnevale and Descrochers 2003, p. 29). The differences in a program account for some of this variation. Still, some college is the cusp of the upward versus downward ladder for earnings both at present and into the future, because workers with more education are more likely to receive more training and skill-development opportunities at work. FPCUs work largely with students who are between high school graduation and a bachelor's degree (with some notable exceptions of programs for high school nongraduates and for college graduates), preparing them for positions in the workplace that require some college-level skills and abilities.

What Programs to Provide: The Role of Employers in Determining and Updating FPCU Program Offerings

Broad categories of work (such as office jobs) with vague requirements (such as some college) are much too abstract to be useful for FPCUs or employers for several reasons. For prospective students, broad generalizations about future positions would hardly allow them to differentiate between FPCUs and TCUs. Preparation for specific positions requires detailed curricula and program requirements. FPCUs develop programs in part through relationships with employers and employer advisory boards.

TABLE 6.2
Sampler of major FPCU program specializations
(From Peterson's list of 120)

Accounting	Information sciences & systems
Acupuncture/Oriental medicine	Insurance & risk management
Administrative assistant/secretarial	Marine maintenance & ship repair
science	Massage therapy
Adult & continuing teacher education	Mechanical engineering/Mechanical
Advertising	design
Air traffic controller	Medical assistant
Aircraft mechanic/technician, airframe	Medical laboratory technician
Alcohol/drug abuse counseling	Medical transcription
Animation/interactive technology/	Mental health counseling
video graphics	Nursing
Athletic training & sports medicine	Occupational therapy assistant
Automotive mechanic/technician	Ophthalmic medical technologist
Baker/pastry chef	Paralegal/legal assistant
Biomedical technology	Pharmacy technician/assistant
Business administration & management	Phlemotomy/phlebotomist
CAD/CADD drafting & design technology	Photography
Childcare services provider	Physical therapy assistant
Computer engineering	Plumbing technology/plumber
Computer programming	Real estate
Computer software engineering	Robotics technology/technician
Computer & information system security	Sports medicine
Computer technical support specialist	Surveying
Construction/building inspector	Taxation
Cosmetologist	Teacher training
Dental hygienist	Telecommunications
Emergency medical technician	Veterinarian assistant/animal health/
Graphic design	technician
Health services administration	Webmaster/multimedia management
Hospitality management	Word processing

SOURCE: Peterson 2006.

All parties share similar goals—to create a curriculum that adequately prepares students for specific positions.

FPCUs collectively offer a wide and complex array of program specialties, although the average campus of an average FPCU offers fewer than several dozen. In addition to the position-specific character of FPCU programs, the sampler of programs in table 6.2 suggests a wide array of program offerings among FPCUs as well as an implication of the importance of *laboratory, hands on,* or *workplace* practice within each program. Programs with diverse pedagogical demands such as marine maintenance, medical assistance, and veterinary assistance also suggest why individual FPCUs tend to cluster program offerings within broader occupational fields. For students and employers alike in each local labor market, some of these programs will be more attractive than others.

The major decisions of FPCUs involve determining which among their programs to offer students and employers, and in which local labor markets. They must also decide whether to create or acquire new campuses for the programs or to add programs to existing campuses. These FPCU decisions differ dramatically from those at TCUs regarding majors and new courses. At TCUs, new programs may be developed around federally sponsored research initiatives. Programs and individual courses are not necessarily developed in direct response to formally scrutinized local market demands. At FPCUs, decisions to offer new programs would be made only after an analysis of local market demand was conducted, which itself would be based on input from local employers, analyses of any other competing providers in the region, costs to start up and operate the programs, pricing possibilities, and a host of demographic intelligence.

At the individual course level, the differences between typical behavior at a TCU and FPCU are perhaps more dramatic. At a TCU, a faculty member may wish to create a course that closely aligns with her or his research interests, such as the changing portrayals of women in the Elizabethan novel, the impact of globalization on regional governments, or the evolutionary paths of ocean-born microbes. After preparing a sample course syllabus and, increasingly, a proposed new course form, the faculty member submits the documents to a departmental curriculum committee of peers for approval. Once the package works its way up the channels and gets listed in the course catalog, the faculty member can then offer and teach the course as part of his or her formal teaching responsibilities. Often the faculty member owns this course, because the syllabus reflects his or her (unique) special interests and expertise.

This process would typically not exist at FPCUs for several interlocking reasons. Individual courses that have no connection to a program are seldom considered at FPCUs because there is no way to link them to a *sales channel*. Faculty members do not take the initiative in creating new courses, because their primary role is to teach courses that have already been developed for fully designed programs. (New courses at both TCUs and FPCUs are often offered once or twice as prototype or trial versions before becoming permanent.) Finally, while FPCU instructors usually have the right to make a yes or no decision regarding whether they will teach a particular course, they never own a course, that is, have the right to decide whether anyone else may teach the course.

These differences are also more consequential at multiple-campus FPCUs. While there are still many FPCUs with only one or a few campuses, the average number of campuses per FPCU and multicampus FPCUs is growing due to mergers, acquisitions, and the creation of branch campuses. In comparison to single-campus TCUs, multicampus FPCUs face somewhat lower costs per new program, per campus and somewhat less uncertainly in rolling out new programs to additional campuses.

Consider as an illustration the Program of Computer Engineering Technology/ technician (CET/T). In Florida, fifteen of these programs are offered by FPCUs throughout the state, and eleven of these fifteen are offered by FPCUs that have multiple campuses in Florida: Remington College (two programs), Florida Technical College (four), and ITT Technical Institute (five). Each of the FPCUs, whether it is a one-campus operation or a large corporation, has to decide whether to offer a CET/T program. ITT Technical Institute offers this program on five Florida campuses, which indicates that Computer Engineering Technology is an important program for ITT. Even so, it currently does not offer this program on eight of its other campuses.

A number of factors have gone into the ITT decision to locate its program of CET/T on some of its campuses but not on others. ITT has already incurred the developmental costs of the program, and therefore the costs of introducing it to an additional campus is much less than if it had to be developed from scratch. Based on its experience with CET/T on five of its campuses, ITT is in a much better position to assess the likelihood of its success on other campuses (and in other labor markets). In ITT's decision to add CET/T to any other campuses or to eliminate it from a campus, local labor market demand can be a large factor, but so can facility constraints, the opportunity costs of alternative programs, the presence or absence of competitive programs, the overall population around the campuses, and other local, contextual factors.

More than TCUs, FPCUs tend to look more outwardly to local market conditions in deciding which programs to offer. The presence and absence of multiple campuses influence the access students and employers have to programs. FPCUs, especially the growing number of multicampus ones, are structurally positioned to gather, evaluate, and respond to the differing labor market demands of the areas in which their campuses are located.

New programs are offered in communities where sufficient demand (student and employer) is present; correspondingly, programs are dropped if demand withers. As portrayed earlier in table 6.2, FPCU administrators at the campus level, including program admissions officers, placement services providers, and senior campus management, scan the local labor market through individual employers, faculty drawn from these employers, and employer advisory boards. Through this examination of local conditions, campus managers make decisions about specific programs. In a particular region, for example, cosmetology may be evolving into a program with many small private competitors and large, low-priced public competitors. It may offer relatively low-wage prospects upon graduation, which might lead to a growing perception among prospective students that it has less advancement potential than other, newer programs. As a result, it could be a candidate for elimination.

Large FPCUs with multiple campuses are in a position to evaluate employment trends across an array of local labor markets and to create and locate new programs that have the highest demand. (In addition to high demand, FPCUs also are likely to be more inclined to consider programs closer to their historic mission, those that pay relatively well and cost less to offer.) Apollo's campuses, for example, are located in thirty-two of the top fifty largest metropolitan markets in the United States (Silber 2004, p. 9). Based on employer insights from these thirty-two labor markets, coupled with their capacities for growth (both in campus locations and in distance learning), Apollo senior management believes that it can extend its program offerings into "more than 100 new markets" (p. 19).

Large multicampus FPCUs face issues and opportunities on a different order of magnitude than single-campus institutions. An air traffic controller program may work in Chicago but not in Des Moines; advertising in New York but not in Washington, D.C.; massage therapy in Los Angeles but not in Salt Lake City; hospitality management in Las Vegas but not in Seattle; insurance and risk management in Hartford but not in Cleveland. Because the large FPCUs operate with more campuses in more cities, they have more options for targeting programs to markets. Just as financial capital flows more freely in today's economy, so do human capital and human capital development.

Unlike FPCUs, TCUs are typically one-campus entities with less organizational connectedness with local employers. Most often the link is provided between the career planning and placement office of a TCU and the various firms that seek to recruit future employees from the institution. Those student affairs functions are rarely connected managerially, let alone strategically, to the faculty-led majors and minors that students enroll in at the TCU. (Graduate professional programs at traditional universities are a possible exception to this.)

For FPCUs the employment connection is made through two relatively independent means—the employer advisory boards, and faculty from the ranks of local employers. Employer advisory boards are creatures of individual FPCU campuses, composed of local employers who represent the program specialties of the FPCU in that particular labor market. The self-interested function of EABs is twofold: to provide the FPCU with estimates of employment demand across program specialties and to provide it with evaluative comments on the quality of individual programs (and the preparedness of its graduates). Such boards then help to inform FPCUs of which programs are likely to succeed in their local labor markets.

Employer advisory boards are an integral part, but only one part, of the program review and development process of FPCUs. Consider how the campus and local employers are integrated in program development at one FPCU:

> Ongoing evaluation of existing programs and input on the new program development agenda is provided by individual schools' Employee Advisory Boards composed of working professionals, educators, government leaders, and other representatives appropriate to the community. Program revisions are a result of feedback from that group, as well as from faculty, students, administration, accrediting and regulatory agencies. Revisions may be initiated by changes in technology, job scope requirements, changes in the law, student performance or other classroom dynamics and new or emerging skill-based needs of employers. (Corinthian Colleges, personal communication, September 21, 2004)

Multicampus FPCUs harvest this intelligence from their individual campuses (and labor markets) and complement it with information generated at corporate headquarters to determine which programs to create and where to offer them. Corporate departments produce program data on student retention and completion, student satisfaction, graduate placement, and feedback. All of these data are reviewed by program directors and school-based department chairs who participate in formal annual curriculum institutes that are conducted for each program.

Developing the curriculum of individual programs tends to be a centralized function at most FPCUs, regardless of the number of campuses. Although many faculty and staff from individual campuses are involved in curriculum development, leadership and direction are provided from headquarters. Only in this way can the benefits of potential *scalability* be possible. For similar reasons, multicampus FPCUs tend to manage centrally other key functions besides curriculum development, such as financial aid, information technology, treasury, accounting, marketing and advertising, purchasing, human resources, payroll, leads management, staff training and development, internal audit, facilities, and support for online learning. These centralized functions are brought into play when the FPCU considers entering a new labor market or expanding its array of programs within an existing labor market. Growth in existing markets, for example, often requires more facilities, and such developments are addressed centrally. Over a recent four-year period, Corinthian Colleges, for example, chose to relocate about 27% of its campuses and expand or remodel another 55% of campuses to respond to growth (Corinthian Colleges 2005).

FPCUs seek to create employer-relevant programs that are scalable across multiple campuses for a variety of interrelated reasons. Program-specific quality control and standardization greatly simplifies marketing, career placement, and program accreditation. From that programmatic base, financial scale economies in program development, recruiting, marketing, assessment, and job placement are possible. Overall quality of service is then made possible, especially for geographically mobile students and multisite employers. Closely related to scalability is the portability of credit among campuses of an FPCU, which is made much more feasible through the vertical and horizontal articulation of program components.

Program or course A on any one campus equals course A in any other campus. If A is a prerequisite for course B in a program on one campus, all As can be counted as prerequisites for course B on any campus.

Through the dual processes of assessing local labor market demand and developing programs, FPCUs determine which labor markets will be served with which career programs. This process of program redesign is repeated across FPCUs in varying forms and timelines, resulting in continuously evolving curricula offerings from campus to campus. According to a survey of 1,200 FPCUs, the following ten programs were those most added by FPCUs nationwide in 2003 (Coombes 2003):

1. Massage therapy
2. Medical assisting/medical secretary
3. Criminal justice/law enforcement
4. Computer technology
5. Computer network management
6. Medical office computer assistance
7. Medical insurance specialist
8. Medical insurance coding specialist
9. E-commerce
10. Pharmacy assistant

All the rest of the literally hundreds of other programs grew at lower rates or actually shrank. Arguably, program evolution, program offering, program locations, and program discontinuance at for-profits move along more rapidly than is the case at many TCUs.

Recruiting Students through Programs: The Initial Match Is Important

Unlike at TCUs, where enrolled students are encouraged to explore a variety of topics, subjects, and even majors, FPCUs push all student curricular decisions to the front end. The biggest decision, and the one for which the most deliberation and supportive counseling is applied, is whether to enroll in a particular program. The enrollment stakes for the student and for the FPCU are high, beyond the usual sense of loss associated with a student not successfully completing a course of study. As we discuss in chapter 8, federal and state legislation governing FPCUs has created a formal, enforceable set of performance parameters that reinforce incentives for FPCUs to admit students who are most likely to complete the programs in which they enroll. Commitment to a program comes early for the student. Altering this commitment comes at a cost to the student *and* the program.

Some decades ago a number of FPCUs engaged in practices that yielded excessive numbers of dropouts. The increased regulation that followed led to a debate at the federal level about the appropriate level of consumer protection oversight required of FPCUs. These fraud and abuse concerns occur on the state level as well. The motivation of state and federal governing bodies to create performance parameters is illustrated in California Education Code, Sections 94850–82, known as the Maxine Waters School Reform and Student Protection Act, 1989:

> The Legislature finds and declares that students have been substantially harmed and the public perception of reputable institutions has been damaged because of the fraudulent, deceptive, and unfair conduct of some institutions that offer courses of instruction for a term of two years or less that are supposed to prepare students for employment in various occupations. . . . Some students have been enrolled who do not have the ability to benefit from the instruction. . . . Students who leave schools before the completion of instruction, often because of misrepresentations and inadequate instruction, do not receive adequate refunds of tuition for the instruction not received. . . . [T]he state and federal governments spend many millions of dollars annually to satisfy loan guarantees for often inadequate and misrepresented vocational school courses. . . . [T]he tuition refund policies of institutions often encourage unfair practices by creating a financial benefit to the institution if a student drops out, and do not encourage institutions to provide adequate counseling or to adopt policies designed to curb student dropouts. (Maxine Waters School Reform and Student Protection Act 1989, 94850–51)

The regulations imposed on FPCUs resulting from this perspective include minimum program completion rates as well as minimum subsequent employment rates, plus numerous other FPCU performance stipulations. According to this California legislation, at least 60% of the students who began an FPCU program must complete it during the specified duration of the program. (Sixty percent is about the average attrition rate for all TCUs as a group.) In addition, at least 70% who completed the program within the specified duration period of the program must be employed within six months in a position to which the program was designed to lead (California Education Code 94854 2000). These standards are then enforced through specified requirements for monitoring FPCU enrollments by external bodies. When and if FPCU performance measures fall below the required percentages, individual FPCUs are then subject to an array of sanctions, including limitations on enrollments, revisions of admissions policies, and increased and improved academic counseling, student support, curricula, facilities, equipment, faculty (quality and quantity), and job placement services. In these cases, a compliance report by an independent certified public accountant may also be required.

If these regulations were to be applied to some TCUs, such as public community colleges in California, it is likely that many of them would not be in compliance. These regulations are not applicable to TCUs in large part because traditional universities have never been subject to the systemic scandals that were associated with FPCUs in the 1970s and 1980s. Because of their for-profit status, however, FPCUs are regulated much like businesses and are subject to related consumer protection policies, rules, and regulations. Investigations and lawsuits against FPCUs can (and do) emanate from a variety of sources, including federal agencies (such as the Department of Justice, Securities and Exchange Commission, and Department of Education), state attorneys general, accrediting bodies, and class-action lawsuits from disgruntled employees and/or students.

Although instances of civil or criminal pursuit of individual FPCUs can be based on a wide variety of regulations and motivations, the major performance metrics of program completion rates and successful placement rates generally align with the internal operating incentives of FPCUs. High program completion rates and subsequent employment rates are positive indicators for a for-profit organization. Problems arose with organizations that simply sought to utilize federal moneys (Title IV) to secure profit and cared little about program completion or employability.

Within the regulatory parameters outlined here, FPCUs seek (1) to get the *right* students, (2) into the *right* programs, (3) through those programs, and (4) into high-paying program-relevant employment. To increase the odds that all these goals are met, student advising encompasses much more than ascertaining an alignment of student interests and program content. Additional issues that conceivably frustrate students in their journey to successful employment include those associated with self-awareness, classroom learning skills, time and money management, workplace behavior, dress, interpersonal skills, resume preparation, and job interviewing.

As with TCUs, the variety of support services available to students at FPCUs is only as effective as the organizational arrangements to provide those services. At most TCUs, many of the functions and services listed in the preceding paragraph are handled by a variety of different, often un-related, offices, such as recruitment, admissions, financial aid, academic departments, student services, and career planning and placement. At many FPCUs, admissions counselors play a variety of roles, acting as the student's first point of contact and continuing with the student, in some cases up to graduation, thus improving intra-organizational accountability for a successful journey from initial contact to job placement. Here is how Corinthian Colleges describes the process on its campuses:

> An admissions representative will help the prospective student determine their [sic] interest and readiness for a particular career program by conducting a personal interview. Once the admissions representative and the prospective student are satisfied that the chosen career program will help the student to achieve desired goals and that the student is properly prepared to meet the challenges of school, the representative will become a personal guide through the admissions process. The representative coordinates entrance testing, financial aid appointments, and the gathering of other required documentation. *The admissions representative will maintain contact with the students as a partner/mentor until successful completion of the program.* (Corinthian Colleges 2004, p. xv; emphasis added)

Regardless of how deep or productive the contact is at Corinthian, or at other FPCUs, the claim functions both as a selling point and as a mechanism of governance that aligns responsibility for successful throughput from recruitment to graduation—an alignment that does not exist at most TCUs.

Once the student is enrolled in a program, there is little room for her or him to wander among elective courses or majors. Consider the eight-month, eight-module medical assisting program at one large FPCU. Students can undertake any of the first seven modules in any order, but must complete all seven before taking the eighth module (externship). Of the forty-seven credit units offered in the program, there are no electives. All courses are designed to prepare students for employment; and this implies a highly specialized and prespecified course of instruction, one that differs from those at TCUs.

Instruction at FPCUs: Teaching Demonstrable Skills as Well as Formal Knowledge

It is entirely natural to think of the programs of FPCUs as career-oriented analogues to majors or concentrations at TCUs. Instead of art history, biochemistry, classics, economics, and fine arts, for example, FPCUs offer aviation systems/avionics maintenance technology, blood bank technology/technician, computer and information systems security, dental assistant, elder care provider/companion, and financial planning. One might logically presume that, while the content is different, the overall framework is fairly similar. Such a straightforward comparison might seem reasonable but is unduly simplistic and ultimately misleading.

The curriculum at FPCUs differs not only in content, with its strict focus on career preparation (the rather obvious difference) but also in the degree of application. At FPCUs, students have to learn how to *do* something, the acquisition of "know-how" knowledge in addition to largely "know-what" or "know-why" knowledge. "Know-what" refers to knowledge about "facts," and "know-why" refers to knowledge about "principles and laws of motion in nature, in the human mind and in society" (Center for Educational Research and Innovation 2000, p.14). "Know-how" refers to skills, or the ability to do something. Such knowledge may be related to the skills of production workers, but it plays a key role in all kinds of work. FPCUs place greater emphasis on preparing a student to *perform* as distinct from preparing a student to *know*.

TABLE 6.3

Comparing knowledge transmission at TCUs and FPCUs:
"Doing school" vs. "Doing a job"

At TCU, knowledge is . . .	At FPCUs, knowledge is . . .
Declarative (facts about . . .)	Procedural (how to . . .)
Usually explicit	Often tacit
Abstract	Concrete
Logical	Intuitive
"In the mind"	"Embedded in action"
An end in itself	A means to an end
Remote from application	Close to application
Forgotten quickly	Forgotten slowly
Rehearsed during revision	Rehearsed through practice
Tested by examination	Tested by performance
A process of acquisition	A process of engagement
Weakly related to identity	Strongly related to identity
Linked–being taught	Linked–being coached
Learned sequentially	Learned piecemeal
"Hooked" to a text	"Hooked" to persons/events
Stored in semantic memory	Stored in episodic memory
Usually fragmented	Ususally integrated
A stack of information	A stock of experience
Something to be remembered	Something to be understood

This is a sweeping generalization to make about two enormously variable sets of content. Indeed, there are exceptions to be found at both types of institutions, including, for example, highly career-oriented programs at TCUs. Liberal studies at FPCUs are prohibited, an issue we take up in later chapters. In general, however, the distinction holds up. But what precisely is the distinction? It is not unlike the distinctions that human capital theorists make about knowledge associated with "doing school" and "doing a job." In both environments knowledge is acquired, but the qualities of knowledge differ in degree and sometimes in kind, as portrayed in table 6.3 (Center for Educational Research and Innovation 2000, p. 55). The "doing school" attributes are generally characteristic of traditional postsecondary schooling—taking course experiences, such as being tested by examination, remembering information until that exam, and then moving onto the next subject. The "doing a job" (more correctly *going to school to learn to do a job*) attributes are more characteristic of many FPCU programs, such as being tested by performance and gaining a growing base of intuitive experience.

The two lists form a continuum rather than categories of mutually exclusive descriptors. Knowledge conveyed at TCUs is closer to the "doing school" side of the continuum, whereas knowledge conveyed at FPCUs is closer to the "doing a job" side of the continuum. As an illustration, consider some of the elements of the medical assisting program offered by Corinthian Colleges. The program consists of six modules totaling 560 clock hours (42 credit units) followed by an externship of 160 hours (5 credit units). The externship constitutes "a supervised, practical in-service in a medical office or clinic in which the student practices direct applications of all administrative and clinical functions as a medical assistant" (Corinthian Colleges 2004, Module A, p. ix). The prominent role of the externship as a culminating practical experience reflects the FPCU's emphasis on acquiring knowledge by doing a job, but performance through practice is evident throughout the entire curriculum.

The program objectives in the medical assisting program tilt heavily toward the right side of the continuum in table 6.3, requiring that, at least in part, students must be able to perform the skills at a given level of proficiency. Beyond merely demonstrating test-taking abilities, students must "demonstrate professionalism and ethical behavior"; "perform clinical responsibilities, including preparing patients for examination and procedures, preparing and administering medications as directed, collecting and processing specimens, recognizing emergencies, and performing CPR and first aid"; "identify minor surgical procedures and demonstrate the ability to assist with those procedures"; "maintain accurate patient records"; "perform administrative procedures that include telephone techniques, appointment scheduling, record management, and insurance billing procedures"; "apply principles of infection control and use appropriate aseptic technique"; and "accurately complete bookkeeping, banking, and financial procedures" (Corinthian Colleges 2004).

Such performance-based skills can be described as specifically job-related and technical, but FPCUs also extend their emphasis on doing job skills to include general workplace skills. These include getting along with different people, teamwork, and professional behavior, as well as a grammar and math review. Basic self-awareness understandings, such as dealing with success and failure, telephone etiquette, and handling criticism,

TABLE 6.4
Distribution of undergraduates at private for-profit institutions with a declared major, by field of study, 1999–2000

Field of Study	%
Arts and humanities	10.3
Computer science/IT	18.9
Engineering	7.2
Education	0.4
Business/management	16.5
Health	12.9
Vocational/technical	1.8
Other professional or technical majors	31.4

SOURCE: National Center for Education Statistics, Profile of Undergraduates in U.S. Postsecondary Institutions, 1999–2000 (table 2.2).
    NOTE: Majors with less than 0.4% enrollment are not represented; therefore, percentages do not add up to 100.

are also valued. These topics include both knowledge and performance elements.

Indeed, most of these performance competencies also require "doing school" knowledge; the end-of-module exams and end-of-program certification exams have extensive pencil-and-paper components. Throughout the program, however, and particularly in the externship, there is a heavy emphasis on "doing a job." The practice and performance elements of schooling at FPCUs constitute a much larger part of the overall program and are more uniformly present throughout the curriculum than is the case at TCUs.

This "doing a job" orientation is reflected across the spectrum of program specialties at FPCUs, especially when they are weighted by student enrollments. The eight broad categories of fields of study portrayed in table 6.4 are almost entirely career focused with one notable exception— arts and humanities. Even if we assumed that virtually none of the FPCU arts and humanities programs are career focused, enrollments in these programs constitute only about 10% of all undergraduate enrollments.

Placement for Well-Paid Employment:
The Embodiment of "Success"

Internal FPCU incentives generally align with external regulations that stipulate acceptable levels of placement. The higher the placement rate, the more successful an institution can claim to be. Regulations spell out in legally vetted detail the criteria for successful employment: "Employment usually means full-time employment for at least 32 hours per week for a period of at least 60 days in the occupations or job titles to which the program of instruction is represented to lead" (Maxine Waters School Reform and Student Protection Act 1989, 94854(k)(2)(A)); such employment must commence within six months from completion of the program. Graduates must be "available for placement," a mandate that implies that all graduates are counted except those who "are continuing their education, are in active military service or are deceased or disabled, and foreign students who are ineligible to work in the U.S. after graduation" (Corinthian Colleges 2004, p. 3). Extensive record keeping and ex-ante verification procedures are required of FPCUs to enable them to report placements and also allow external agencies to monitor them.

The 70% minimum placement rates are often exceeded by most FPCUs. In a recent year, for example, Strayer Education placed 79% successfully; Corinthian, 82%; Education Management, 87%; ITT Educational Services, 90%; and DeVry University, 96% (Ruch 2001; Corinthian Colleges 2004). Variations in placement rates can be the result of a wide variety of institutional and labor-market factors, including changes in employment demand, general economic conditions, and regional factors. Some students are already employed part-time at the relevant job (as often the case for students at University of Phoenix).

The first employment position does not always last. At one FPCU, approximately one-third of its diploma graduates require second and third jobs before a lasting employment match is made (Corinthian Colleges, personal communication, September 21, 2004). If FPCUs do not maintain placement rates comfortably above the required minimums, the consequences are material. FPCUs correspondingly align internal organizational accountability with these measures. To improve the odds of high placement performance, one FPCU requires its campuses to verify graduate employment early at ninety-one days. With this timeline, the institution can still take steps, if necessary, to ensure continuing employment, well before the six-month window closes. Further, that same FPCU uses the ninety-one-day verified employment rate to evaluate and reward its career services staff performance (Corinthian Colleges, personal communication, September 21, 2004).

Less visible but no less important than the placement rates of these and other FPCUs are the average salaries secured by graduates in these positions. Tuition at FPCUs is more expensive than at public institutions, so the payoff for students must be reasonably commensurate with their investment. No comparable regulatory parameters exist that stipulate how much a graduate must be earning, and publicly reported earnings data are not readily available. Both the student and the FPCU have an incentive to seek a high salary. But does a student's (relatively high) investment in a given FPCU program generate worthwhile returns?

Consider two perspectives on this question, that of the student and the public. Ruch's application of return on education investment (figure 6.2) seems to suggest an affirmative answer from the student perspective, although the logic and assumptions behind these numbers, such as assumptions about different salary levels before and after training, need to be scrutinized in greater detail than is possible here. On the surface, the estimated financial return a graduating student in the United States can expect after paying for his or her education is 18.7% for an average recipient of a TCU bachelor's degree, compared with 28.0% for a recipient of an FPCU bachelor's degree. The difference between TCU and FPCU returns on education investment is likely to increase in the future as FPCUs disproportionately add computer-related programs to their array of programs, which as a separate group generate a return of about 35%. (Fully half of the ten most frequently added programs at FPCUs in 2003 were computer-centric or computer-related.)

What about the *public's* perspective on returns to FPCU schooling? If the comparison is limited to taxpayer's subsidies for two years of full-time (public) community college schooling, the Career College Association estimates the differentials to be $7,722 (FPCU) compared to $18,069 (community college) (Career College Association 2003, p. 26). From that

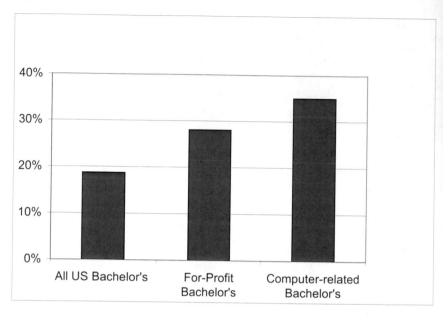

Figure 6.2. Return on Education Investment: Estimate of Average Financial Return for Various Bachelor's Degrees after Subtracting Education Expenses. *Source:* Ruch 2001

difference, earnings data may be utilized to derive how long it would theoretically take the average FPCU graduate (from a two-year program) to repay the public cost through taxes of his or her schooling (three and a half years) compared to a community college graduate (eight years). The public return on investment for each public dollar spent would then be 12% per community college graduate versus 29% per comparable FPCU graduate (p. 26).

As was true with student returns data, these taxpayer returns data require much greater scrutiny than is possible here. Given the high student and taxpayer stakes associated with postsecondary education, however, more thoroughly documented estimates of returns will likely surface in the future to influence definitions of success.

The defining characteristic of FPCUs may be summed up in one word—focus. FPCUs focus on students who would benefit most from some college. They focus largely on cues from local employers as they develop and grow programs. They also focus most of their recruiting emphasis on *correct* program placement, and focus on instruction that will most likely yield successful job placement. Finally, for-profits focus on successful placement. This orientation toward employment stands in sharp contrast to the more comprehensive nature of TCUs, suggesting that there are fundamental differences between the two types of institutions, which we consider in chapter 8. Before doing so, however, we turn to a discussion of the raison d'être for all colleges—the student. Do for-profits view students differently than TCUs?

CHAPTER SEVEN

Students and Other Priorities

A great deal has been made about how faculty at traditional colleges and universities prefers research over teaching; in reality, at the vast majority of postsecondary institutions, the faculty has always focused on teaching undergraduate students, often to the exclusion of other activities. Research did not become important in any systematic way until the late nineteenth century, and even then only for a minority of faculty. As we noted in chapter 5, by the early twentieth century, some institutions emphasized graduate education and research, but these institutions were then, and remain today, a tiny microcosm of the postsecondary universe. Johns Hopkins, Stanford, Harvard, Princeton, Caltech, MIT, and other similar institutions have garnered the most notoriety and resources, but to claim that they are representative of the postsecondary system is a bit like claiming that the New York Yankees (or the Boston Red Sox) are like all other baseball teams in the major and minor leagues.

Half of the institutions in the traditional postsecondary system are community colleges, where research as a function of faculty work is irrelevant. Public state colleges and universities educate 70% of all full-time students (National Center for Education Statistics 2003a). Although increasingly important, research remains a distant second in terms of institutional priorities for many of these institutions. That is, for every University of Michigan, there are multiple Fitchburg States. Small liberal arts colleges, professional schools, and religious institutions emphasize instruction in the humanities, a profession, or a religion more than research. Only at research universities (about 100 of the most prestigious in the country) is research pervasive and of primary importance.

The conundrum has always been that institutions that produce the greatest amount of research and have the best graduate programs seem to be the most admired by the general public—or at least by many educators. At research universities, faculty teaches less and does more research, and senior faculty is more likely to teach graduate students than undergraduates. Salaries are apt to be higher than at other institutions. Status is likely to be higher as well; historically, professors at research universities have received more honors and awards than their counterparts at other institutions. Thus, within the current system, teaching undergraduates is the more prevalent focus, but doing research is accorded greater respect. Not surprisingly, professors continuously endeavor to secure more time for research in exchange for less time teaching.

Perhaps one of the most confusing elements in the system of postsecondary education is that the individuals who are to become future faculty members are trained and socialized in graduate schools at research universities. At these institutions, graduate students learn and internalize the academic values of their professors, which generally give prominence to research rather than teaching. When they complete their studies, these graduate students go on to other institutions; as new faculty members, they discover that the institutions do not value research, or value it less than at the institutions where they received their training. Is it any wonder that those who work in the postsecondary system have encountered an ideological schizophrenia where everyone seemingly wants to do research even though the system needs people more to teach undergraduates? Nor is it surprising that the faculty metrics of research institutions increasingly are being incorporated into the faculty metrics at teaching institutions, such that grant dollars awarded and publication history are becoming a larger part of tenure and promotion decisions.

To be sure, this incongruence between the values of the faculty and the culture of the institution has created problems that have yet to be rectified. However, over the past generation, an understanding of the problem has become clearer, and a desire (if not a demand) to resolve it has increased. Students have asked why they have teaching assistants rather than *the real thing* in their classrooms. State legislators have wondered why they are paying faculty to conduct research when they really want them to teach undergraduates. Faculty have proposed the development of a reward system that is more in sync with the priorities of the institution. The large lecture class is no longer seen as the best way to teach all classes for all students. And for-profit colleges and universities have presented a competitive model that focuses exclusively on teaching (Lechuga 2005). Faculty at FPCUs do not conduct research as part of their contract and, for the most part, do not focus their teaching on graduate students. Even at FPCUs that offer graduate degrees, the faculty are not required to do research as part of their contract and instead are expected to focus exclusively on graduate education.

Part of the problem resides in misconceptions of the postsecondary system—including who attends, and who might or should attend, a postsecondary institution. While no longer accurate, the popular perception remains that most students are 18- to 22-year-olds who are full-time residents of a campus where football is played in the fall, graduation occurs in May, and the summer is a lull where everyone goes home or to Europe. The preponderance of research is about these students, and most studies have used the research university as the unit of analysis. Although research on traditional students at traditional campuses is worthwhile, and the merits of lifelong learning have been touted for decades, our purpose here is decidedly different.

In this chapter, we delineate in broad terms the students of the twenty-first century and consider how they might best be served. The uses of such data are twofold. On the one hand, the landscape we describe provides a more detailed portrait of today's students than those studies that concentrate on the small and decreasing percentage of students who attend residential institutions on a full-time basis. On the other hand, the data will reiterate a critical point we made earlier: rather than be in competition with one another, for-profit and traditional institutions are frequently reaching out to different, including older, constituencies—albeit with significant overlapping markets. Accordingly, once we have outlined the data, our intent is to demonstrate how both sectors might benefit from the strengths of the other with regard to how best to serve students.

The Instability of the Term "Student"

The definition of a student, the student's expectations, and the institution's and society's expectations of the student have never been stable concepts. At one time, postsecondary education was assumed to be primarily for the rich; following the creation of land-grant institutions, members of the working class were afforded access to college. In the past, a student attended college to become cultivated and well rounded; only in the nineteenth century did a student begin to go to college to be trained for a profession and, still later, for a job. Before the twentieth century, a college student was most likely white and male. The few women students who attended college earned degrees that were largely different from men. They were as likely to attend college to prepare themselves for marriage. If black students went to college, most went to institutions created specifically for them. For these students, the conferral of a degree largely meant that they would put their learning to use within the black community.

Students at one time were primarily full time; summer break in an agrarian society meant that the students—again, primarily young men—would return home to work on the family farm. Students from the upper classes had the summer to themselves. The assumption that summer was somehow connected to college was absent other than that it provided students with a chance to do something different from their studies.

After World War II, the definition of a student continued to evolve, and this new type resonates in what exists today. The GI Bill allowed returning veterans, all of whom were adults, to study for a college degree. One result of the GI Bill was that professors were forced to rethink their lectures to accommodate a changed student body. Women and minorities gained greater presence throughout all sectors of academia, and they were free to major in whatever they desired. To be a student no longer meant full-time enrollment. Part-time students, especially in community colleges, grew in number. The labor market forces described in chapter 2 increased the value of added schooling, but they also increased the opportunity cost of dropping out of the employment market to attend school full-time.

At the same time, full-time students expected more services from postsecondary institutions. Students arrived on campus with their children and needed daycare facilities. If someone had a disability or a special need, the assumption was that the individual had a legal right to equal access. Students factored in out-of-class experiences such as the quality of the fitness center in their determination of whether they would attend an institution. The result was that by the twenty-first century, the meaning of *student* and its various permutations was much more protean than it was when students first entered Harvard College in 1636 to study Latin, Greek, and theology

Who Are the Students Today?

In the fall of 2002, approximately 17 million students attended post-secondary institutions that were eligible for Title IV funding (see table 7.1). With some exceptions, these institutions comprise the bulk and mainstream of American higher education, across all sectors. To receive Title IV federal student financial aid (such as Pell Grants), all institutions, regardless of type, are required to collect certain data. To qualify for Title IV funding, an institution has to be accredited by an agency or an organization recognized by the U.S. Department of Education, have a program of more than 300 clock hours or 8 credit hours, have been in existence for at least two years, and signed an agreement with the U.S. Department of

TABLE 7.1
Enrollment in Title IV institutions by student level, attendance status, gender, and race/ethnicity, fall 2002

	Students	%
Student level		
Undergraduate	14,607,617	86.2
Graduate	2,036,421	12.0
First professional	318,989	1.9
Attendance status		
Full-time	10,272,256	60.3
Part-time	6,762,271	39.7
Gender		
Men	7,344,939	43.1
Women	9,690,091	56.9
Race/ethnicity		
White, non-Hispanic	10,593,759	62.2
Black, non-Hispanic	1,950,905	11.5
Hispanic	1,624,726	9.5
Asian/Pacific Islander	999,739	5.9
American Indian/Alaska native	160,406	0.9
Race/ethnicity unknown	1,111,747	6.5
Nonresident alien	593,745	3.5
Total	17,035,027	100.0

SOURCE: Knapp et al. 2005.

TABLE 7.2

*Enrollment in Title IV institutions by degree-granting status, level,
and control of institution, attendance status, gender, race/ethnicity, fall 2002*

	All Institutions		Degree-Granting		Non-Degree-Granting	
	Total Students	%	Total Students	%	Total Students	%
Level of institution						
4-year	10,083,252	59.2	10,082,332	60.7	920	0.2
2-year	6,640,516	39.0	6,529,379	39.3	111,137	26.3
Less than 2-year	311,259	1.8	0	0.0	311,259	73.5
Control of institution						
Public	12,883,071	75.6	12,751,993	76.8	131,078	31.0
Private not-for-profit	3,299,094	19.4	3,265,476	76.8	33,618	7.9
Private for-profit	852,862	5.0	594,242	3.6	258,620	61.1
Attendance status						
Full-time	10,272,746	60.3	9,946,359	59.9	326,397	77.1
Part-time	6,762,271	39.7	66,665,352	40.1	96,919	22.9
Gender						
Male	7,344,936	43.1	7,202,116	43.4	142,820	33.7
Female	9,690,091	56.9	9,409,595	56.6	280,469	66.3
Race/ethnicity						
White, non-Hispanic	10,593,759	62.2	10,390,157	62.5	203,602	48.1
Black, non-Hispanic	1,950,905	11.5	1,865,660	11.2	85,245	20.1
Hispanic	1,624,726	9.5	1,545,166	9.3	79,560	18.8
Asian/Pacific Islander	999,739	5.9	982,108	5.9	17,631	4.2
American Indian/ Alaska native	160,406	0.9	156,225	0.9	4,181	1.0
Race/ethnicity unknown	1,111,747	6.5	1,082,789	6.5	28,958	6.8
Nonresident alien	593,745	3.5	589,606	3.5	4,139	1.0
Total students	17,035,027	100.0	16,611,711	100.0	423,316	100.0

SOURCE: Knapp et al. 2005.

Education. In 1999–2000, about 38% of those institutions eligible to receive Title IV funding were FPCUs; as requirements change, the number
of institutions that qualify for financial aid is likely to increase (see chapter 8). Among the qualifying institutions are those with the largest enrollments, such as the University of Phoenix and DeVry.

Of these approximately 17 million students, close to 90% are undergraduates, and about 60% are full-time students; 57% of the students are
women and 62% are White, non-Hispanic. Slightly less than 60% of all
students attend a four-year institution and slightly less than 40% attend
a two-year college (see table 7.2). The remaining students, about 2%, go
to an institution of less than two years and more than likely a non-degree-

granting institution (one that awards a certificate such as cosmetology, law enforcement, etc.). Three-quarters of all students attend a public institution and another 20% attend a private not-for-profit. Somewhere between 5% and 10% of all students attend a private for-profit institution.

Of the 17 million students, only about 400,000 attend a non-degree-granting institution. A majority of the students at degree- and non-degree-granting institutions are full-time students and women. However, minority students account for 27% of the degree-granting population, whereas they constitute 44% of the non-degree-granting population.

Who Are For-Profit Students?

The profile of students at for-profit institutions differs from the overall population of students at traditional colleges and universities, but it is not significantly different from that of students who attend community colleges. As table 7.3 demonstrates, more women than men attend for-profit institutions of less than four years, as compared with their traditional counterparts. For-profits of less than four years have fewer white students and a greater percentage of students of color than their two-year counterparts. The average age of students is not particularly different, but the students who attend FPCUs are likely to be more financially independent and about 61% of attendees at for-profits work either part time or full time. Fewer students who attend a for-profit institution have a high school diploma, although fully 78% of the attendees have graduated from high school. FPCUs recruit and enroll students who do not have high school diplomas when it appears that the students have an "ability to benefit" from a particular FPCU program. Some FPCU students, then, come from the ranks of high school dropouts. Not unrelated, these students are among the most vulnerable and most at risk of dropping out and defaulting on federal loans. The fine line that FPCUs walk here is between "unprecedented access" (a good thing) and "overzealous sales pressure" (a bad thing).

Students who attend four-year FPCUs differ from their counterparts at two-year for-profits and four-year TCUs. Slightly more than 55% of students who attend four-year for-profits are men, as compared with 47% at

TABLE 7.3
Distribution of undergraduates enrolled in less-than-four-year institutions, according to selected characteristics and by level and control of institutions, 1995–1996
(%)

	Private, For-Profit			Public 2-Year	Total 2-Year Public and Private Nonprofits	Total
	Less than 2-year	2-Year	Total			
Gender						
Male	27.5	40.3	32.9	43.1	43.2	42.2
Female	72.5	59.7	67.1	56.9	56.8	57.8
Age						
23 years or younger	43.7	48.9	45.9	43.9	43.5	43.7
24–29 years	20.9	23.2	21.8	20.8	20.8	20.9
30 years or older	35.4	28.0	32.3	35.3	35.8	35.5
Race/ethnicity						
White, non-Hispanic	54.6	62.9	58.1	69.6	69.4	68.4
Black, non-Hispanic	22.9	18.8	21.2	12.4	12.6	13.4
Hispanic	18.3	14.1	16.5	12.5	12.4	12.7
Asian/Pacific Islander	3.1	3.7	3.4	4.4	4.4	4.3
American Indian/ Alaska native	1.1	0.5	0.9	1.1	1.1	1.1
Dependency status						
Dependent	25.1	34.9	29.2	38.4	37.9	37.1
Independent	74.9	65.1	70.8	61.6	62.1	62.9
Average hours worked per week while enrolled						
Not employed	45.9	29.8	39.1	16.4	17.2	19.2
1–20 hours	15.8	18.1	16.7	17.5	17.6	17.5
21–34 hours	14.0	18.6	15.9	16.9	17.0	16.9
35 hours or more	24.4	33.5	28.3	49.2	48.3	46.5
High school degree						
High school diploma	74.1	83.0	77.8	89.2	89.0	87.9
Diploma through GED or equivalent	15.4	13.6	14.7	6.7	6.9	7.6
Certificate of high school completion	0.6	0.2	0.4	0.6	0.6	0.6
No high school equivalent	9.9	3.2	7.1	3.6	3.6	3.9

SOURCE: Knapp et al. 2005.

two-year for-profits and 44% at traditional four-year institutions. More Black and Hispanic students attend two-year for-profit institutions than four-year for-profits—32% and 26%, respectively—but when compared with 16.6 % at four-year public institutions, one can easily surmise that students of color tend to find for-profit institutions an attractive possibility (see table 7.4).

TABLE 7.4
Distribution of students enrolled in for-profit and public degree-granting institutions according to selected characteristics and by level of institution, fall 2000
(%)

	For-profit Institutions		Public Institutions	
	2-Year	4-year	2-year	4-Year
Gender				
Male	47.5	55.3	42.8	44.5
Female	44.7	43.2	57.2	55.5
Race/ethnicity				
White, non-Hispanic	55.3	47.3	61.0	68.3
Black, non-Hispanic	18.0	15.8	11.7	10.1
Hispanic	14.0	10.4	13.4	6.5
Asian/Pacific Islander	3.8	6.8	6.4	5.9
American Indian/Alaska native	0.8	0.9	1.2	0.9

SOURCE: Knapp et al. 2003, p. 186.

TABLE 7.5
Distribution of undergraduates enrolled in for-profit institutions according to selected characteristics by level of institution, 1995–1996
(%)

	For-Profit Institutions		Public Institutions	
	Less than 4-Year	4-Year	2-Year	4-Year
Age distribution				
24 years of younger	45.9	37.1	43.9	62.8
25–29 years of age	21.8	23.1	20.8	15.0
30 years or older	32.3	39.8	35.3	21.7
Dependency				
Dependent	29.2	30.2	38.4	61.7
Independent	70.8	69.8	61.6	38.2
Attendance status				
Full-time	80.3	65.1	29.1	76.0
Part-time	19.7	34.9	70.9	24.0

SOURCE: Horn et al. 1998, p. 324.

As table 7.5 shows, students who attend a four-year for-profit institution tend to be older than their peers at for-profit institutions of less than four years and at traditional baccalaureate institutions. The four-year FPCUs and their counterparts of less than four years have an equal percentage of independent students at 70%, which is considerably higher than the 38% at traditional four-year institutions.

What Does Today's Student Want (or Need) from College?

The answer to such a question may have been easier in the past insofar as students were a more homogeneous group. Defining the wants and desires of a group of 18- to 22-year-olds, primarily white males from the middle and upper classes, may have been a challenge, but answers surely existed. Interestingly, however, the question was not often considered in the past—in large part because administrators, faculty, and parents deemed the homogeneous clientele of 18- to 22-year-olds unable to give a reasoned answer to the question, despite surveys that presumed the contrary.

The same question, posed to adults, was also fraught with difficulties, but answers also emerged. The faculty was able to define the curriculum that it believed students needed. Even though issues such as general education and distribution requirements were debated from time to time, during most of the twentieth century, the curriculum was a stable entity. The curriculum was aimed at transmitting knowledge that would lead individuals either to become more valuable citizens or to be better trained for a job—or, preferably, both. At the same time, many college curricula increasingly included greater proportions of highly specialized courses, which reflected faculty research interests and expertise. The structure and delivery of the curriculum was also left to the faculty, with assistance from administrators such as the registrar. As we noted in chapter 5, a class was more similar than different irrespective of campus or locale, as were credits, semesters, and graduation requirements. The ways teachers taught and the ways students learned at postsecondary institutions were also more alike than different. Yes, a Socratic seminar of ten students and a professor at St. John's College was certainly different from a large lecture in a hall filled with a thousand students at UC-Berkeley, but even those two disparate examples shared similarities; they were two ends of a relatively short continuum.

Postsecondary institutions themselves were also a well-defined entity. There were basically four-year institutions and institutions that were not for four years (less than or more than four years). If a student said he or she was going to go to "college," then the experience would eventually be more alike than different. The same could be said if an individual were to attend a community college or trade school. Obviously, we do not wish to overdraw the similarities. Students who attended UCLA had a different experience from those who attended Southern Oregon State College. The student who became an auto mechanic differed from the student who studied refrigeration at a community college. Yet, when one looks back at the landscape of higher education in the twentieth century until about 1970, the terrain looks much more similar than different, even after acknowledging the smaller fraction of the general population who became college students back then.

Parents, for their part, wanted to know that their children were safe and were being prepared for a career and for life. Although campuses did not legally act *in loco parentis,* they frequently assumed that role with regard to behavior because the students were young; such a phrase makes little sense if the age of the students is the same as the faculty. Further, parents who graduated from Columbia University and sent their children to their alma mater had different expectations than parents who had never attended college and sent their child to Northern Arizona University. Yet, both sets of parents shared similar beliefs regarding faculty knowledge and ability. The trust in the faculty's ability to undertake the training of their children in part had to do with the faculty's status as intellectuals and educators. Just as faith in medical doctors rose in the twentieth century, so too did the belief that faculty knew what was best for educating adolescents and preparing them for adulthood.

The late twentieth century provided a diversity of curricular options that were previously unavailable. When combined with a now radically heterogeneous population of students and a marketplace full of choices, the question of what students wanted (or needed) was no longer a simple matter. Along with curricular options, the structure and delivery of classes had the potential of being radically rethought. The technological enhancement of higher education may be seen as folly by some (Noble 1997) and a savior by others (Allen and Seaman 2004), but the fact of the matter is that many "consumers" have been quite happy with its use and potential, despite its flaws. In an age when the speed and intensity of interaction become more common, courses no longer exclusively meander through a term of fifteen weeks and instead now come in a range of frameworks and temporal sequences.

Faculty members, like medical doctors, are no longer the unquestioned arbiters of what gets offered when and to whom. Parents, legislators, and students demand to have a voice. To be sure, some parents are content to send their child to college in a traditional manner, as many students of previous generations experienced, but parents now expect quality service. Holland (2003, p. 3), for example, writes of "the outrageous extent to which modern universities are providing expensive amenities that they rationalize as necessary to recruit top students and faculty." He lists as evidence the University of Houston's $53 million Wellness Center, the largest Jacuzzi on the West Coast (seating fifty-three people) housed at Washington State University, and Penn State University's 500-gallon saltwater aquarium with a live coral reef. Cases can always be made that organizational accoutrements such as an aquarium have pedagogical benefits and a wellness center produces healthy students (although the pedagogical purposes of a large Jacuzzi may be a stretch—students can study together?). Virtually everyone recognizes, however, that these out-of-class innovations are geared more toward attracting a particular clientele. In a market where universities must compete with one another for students, such examples are now common.

That market is also much more complex. The question with which we began this section—what do students want?—is now accepted, albeit begrudgingly, as an important question. Students, as consumers, have a plethora of choices. Although a particular clientele may desire a wellness center, a rugby field, or vegan fare at the dining hall, a significant swatch of students care little about such amenities. They want evening classes, weekend classes, or short intensive classes that fit their work schedule. Others want to take classes from their home computer. Still others have little desire for out-of-class experiences with their professors. They want to know what is required of them and what they need to do to master the material.

A fair criticism of the notion that students are consumers is not simply that the faculty has been cast aside in determining pedagogical outcomes. Rather, faculty advice about what is good for a student is increasingly weighed along with other information when students decide. However, if one is concerned with providing a quality education, faculty input and research on education are useful. The analogy of education with business is apt but only goes so far. Simply because a consumer/student wants a medical degree in twelve months from the date the person is admitted to an institution does not necessarily suggest that such a time frame is an appropriate one.

Students know what they want, but they do not always know what they need. A patient who walks into a doctor's office and says, "I have a sore throat. I need an antibiotic," may well be correct. Or the patient might have the correct diagnosis, but the wrong treatment, or have the wrong diagnosis and wrong treatment and actually have an infectious disease or need an emergency operation. Similarly, a student who claims that online learning is the best way to take a course may be correct given his or her situation. At the same time, there is a great deal of research that points to the critical importance of student engagement and involvement not only in defining the quality of the educational experience but also in enabling a student to complete his or her education. It would certainly be ironic that, at a time when age-old pedagogies such as the lecture or seminar are being buttressed with ways to engage students more fully in and out of class, a new pedagogy (Internet-based instruction) adheres to a view of the student as passive recipient. Thus, if the previous question—what do students need?—appeared arrogant because it did not take into account the interests and concerns of other constituencies, we are simply pointing out that a new question—what do students want?—is similarly foolhardy if it is the only question asked. Learning is a multifaceted task that demands input from multiple parties (including public policy officials who heavily subsidize it) if it is to be successful.

Learning is also chiefly contextual. What an 18-year-old majoring in English at Swarthmore College needs and wants will be dramatically different from what the 35-year-old who takes evening courses in business administration at a University of Phoenix classroom in a shopping mall near her workplace is seeking. The English major would likely find Phoenix entirely unacceptable, just as the adult student would find much of what occurs at Swarthmore irrelevant and a waste of time. Nevertheless, both institutions undoubtedly have lessons to learn from each other. Swarthmore may benefit from Phoenix's use of distributed learning in its classes. The goal is not to mimic what Phoenix has done, but to consider how such a tool might be made contextually relevant to Swarthmore's students. Phoenix may call upon the wealth of knowledge Swarthmore has accumulated with regard to student learning to think about ways to enhance the quality of its course offerings.

It is incumbent on both types of institutions, however, to ensure that they have aligned the needs and wants of their students with the mission of their institution. Indeed, most institutions pursue students who most closely reflect their mission: in an increasingly competitive and differentiated higher education market, it would be foolhardy to do otherwise. The current lingo of *brand* is simply a business term that traditional postsecondary institutions have long employed by using the concept of *mission*. Many traditional institutions have been unsuccessful in clarifying and articulating their mission in demonstrable ways, whereas for-profit institutions depend largely on their ability to define their focus to attract clientele. Our assumption, which we will expand on in the conclusion, is that in the American postsecondary education market, if one's mission or brand is clear, there will be room for multiple providers. One challenge, however, revolves around the resources used to enable the institution to function and/or to turn a profit.

How Do Students Pay for College?

In a section on student payment for college, our purpose is not to make an extensive detour into the fiscal resources that an institution calls upon from year to year to meet costs and, for some, to realize a profit. Nevertheless, some gross averages are useful to highlight the importance of tuition for *all* institutions. Public four-year institutions, for example, in fiscal year 2000, received about a third of their current fund revenues from the state government, whereas public two-year institutions received more than 50% of their income from government coffers. Public two- and four-year institutions received about 20% of their funds from revenues and fees. Obviously, these numbers vary wildly based on state and institutional type. California, for example, provides a greater contribution to its public institutions than does Colorado. The reliance on state revenue for the University of Colorado at Boulder differs from that of Fort Lewis

College in Durango. Both are state public four-year institutions, but one is a research university with additional revenue streams and the other is not. Nevertheless, the trend is clear: for the vast majority of institutions in all sectors, the proportion of total revenues from tuition sources is growing. State appropriations to public institutions, still large as a fraction of total revenues, are declining as a share of total revenues.

As might be anticipated, private nonprofit institutions derive significantly less income from state appropriations (if at all) and considerably more from return on their investments, gifts and grants, and tuition. Again, for the sake of simplicity, we have grouped together all private institutions, but their revenue streams vary considerably. Tuition will play a larger role at a small liberal arts college than it does at a major research university such as Johns Hopkins that receives significant income from federal and private sources. A university with a medical school has vastly different revenues streams than one with virtually no auxiliary enterprises. Nevertheless, tuition plays a significant role at private nonprofits.

At for-profit institutions, tuition is an overwhelming source of revenue that dwarfs all other revenue streams. For-profit institutions generate more than 86% of their income from tuition, with government appropriations, grants, and contracts in a distant second place at 6%. For-profits do not have state support; they do not conduct research or write grants to support funding; they do not undertake capital campaigns to raise gifts, and their auxiliary enterprises are meager. Tuition is the name of their revenue-seeking game. A focus on the customer at for-profit institutions should come as no surprise. Just as a public or private institution's president may pay extensive attention to a wealthy donor who might give a donation, for-profits are diligent with their key "donors"—students.

What Students and Curricula Do Public Policy Makers Want to Subsidize?

This topic is intimately intertwined with, but quite separate from, the previous student tuition question. We shall further explore the question of tuition in the next chapter, but we note here that tuition is intimately tied to financial aid. Based on the U.S. Department of Education, as seen in table 7.6 data, 69% of all students receive some form of financial aid.

TABLE 7.6

*Fall enrollment of first-time, full-time degree/certificate-seeking undergraduates
and those with financial aid in Title IV degree-granting institutions, by control
and level of institution, academic year 1999–2000*

Level and Control of Institution	Fall Enrollment	Financial Aid Recipients	
		No.	%
Total	1,815,469	1,253,022	69.0
Public 4-year	770,443	538,883	69.6
Public 2-year	522,892	290,815	55.6
Private not-for-profit 4-year	405,426	333,179	82.2
Private not-for-profit 2-year	17,402	11,561	66.4
Private for-profit 4-year	38,931	28,894	74.2
Private for-profit 2-year	60,375	49,690	82.3

SOURCE: Knapp et al. 2003.

Public two-year institutions have the lowest percentage of students who receive financial aid (56%) and private not-for-profit and for-profit institutions have the highest percentage at 82%. Obviously, if the financial aid "well" were bottomless, and whoever wanted to dip into it could, then whether students applied for financial aid would not necessarily increase the competitive nature of different organizations. However, the allotment of public moneys available to students is tied to the vagaries of state and federal budget demands, changes in the performance of the economies in these jurisdictions, and changing tax yields from year to year. Over time, these vagaries line up into a trend.

A Pell Grant, for example, covered 84% of a student's tuition at a four-year institution in 1975; today, it covers less than 40%. The result is that, as subsidies to public institutions shrink and tuition prices rise to make up the difference, who is able to get government moneys has become even more important. The entry into the market of for-profit providers, then, presents not merely a philosophical issue regarding the quality of its curricular offerings and other elements; the more successful for-profits are suggesting that they will be taking financial aid money from public and private institutions that until recently have enjoyed a relative monopoly on that funding source.

The federal government is the most significant provider of financial aid to students who attend for-profit institutions. As for-profits have increased in size and enhanced their capabilities, they also have been able to tap into additional resources for their students. Thus, between 1993 and 1996, the percentage of students who received aid from nonfederal sources increased from 12% to 27% (National Center for Education Statistics 1999, p. 57). One fact has remained stable: students who attend for-profit institutions expect, and receive, financial aid to fund their education.

Not surprisingly, borrowers are less well off than those who do not borrow money for their education. Similarly, insofar as a four-year for-profit curriculum takes longer to complete and leads to an enhanced degree, tuition is much more than at a two-year for-profit institution. Accordingly, students tend to borrow more at four-year for-profits than for two-year or nondegree programs.

Loan default is a major problem, not only for the student, but also for the institution the student attends and for the ultimate provider of the loan (such as the federal government). When a student defaults on a loan, he or she obviously faces potential penalties. To varying extents, the institution is also held accountable. Thus, institutions need to be a bit like a bank when someone comes to take out a loan. Who is a good risk? Research has pointed out that risk factors associated with loan default include financial independence (the student is no longer a dependent of financially better off parents), lack of a traditional high school diploma, low-income status, and a black racial background. Poor black students who are financially independent have been found to be at the highest risk of defaulting on a loan (National Center for Education Statistics 1999). Students who attend for-profit institutions, especially institutions of less than four years, tend to be more at risk of loan default than students at traditional institutions. At less than four-year for-profit institutions, for example, 64% of all students who borrowed the maximum Stafford amount had two or more risk factors for default, and only 15% had zero risk factors (National Center for Education Statistics 2003b). Given the circumstances and characteristics of student markets for these programs, this is almost axiomatic.

The information on students at for-profit institutions and their propensity for being at risk for defaulting on a loan only compounds a complex problem. On the one hand, one should not be surprised that students who do not have wealthy parents and who come from the lower-income quartile are more likely to default on a loan than those students who come from the middle class with parents who are able to help with tuition. (They are also less well prepared educationally to succeed.) On the other hand, as we shall discuss in chapter 8, allegations have been made that for-profit institutions use students who do not appear to have a good chance of graduating or completing their studies. Such students are at risk of loan default. One likely result is that the student loses because he or she faces penalties and fines; the government loses because its loan is not repaid; but the for-profit institution wins because it has already received funding for tuition. (Actually, current regulations greatly reduce these benefits and any incentives for pursuing them. Institutions now have to repay the tuition for the proportion of the program already paid for but not taken by the student before dropping out.) Thus, as new entrants claim financial aid that was once intended for traditional institutions, the response is that these new entrants will not only use money that was intended primarily for public nonprofit institutions, but that the money will not be well spent. All of these points raise questions about how to judge the quality of institutions, their effects on the education on our populace, and the nature of government oversight.

What Criteria Might Be Employed to Determine Whether Students Are Well Served?

Although the criteria we discussed in chapter 6 are certainly pertinent here, the focus is different. In chapter 6, we considered how the institution judged success; here, we consider whether the student (rather than the institution) is well served. The question encompasses the notion that, if the students are well served, the larger society is also well served. Education is not a self-encapsulated activity that is strictly a private good to the individual. The broader public is somehow supposed to benefit from an individual's postsecondary education. If that were not the case, the government presumably would not have a role in financing any aspect of postsecondary education. If obtaining a postsecondary education were the equivalent of buying a car, then the borrower (i.e., the student) would seek a loan from a bank, rather than from the federal or state government. And borrowers surely never get a grant to buy a car.

Thus, four touchstones exist for determining whether students are well served:

(1) effective demand for the good;
(2) retention, graduation rates, and placement;
(3) the private return on public and private investments, and
(4) the public return on private and public investments.

The easiest element to judge is the demand for the good. If consumers do not buy the good, there is presumably little demand. Perhaps the cost is out of reach, the quality of the product is poor, or the product itself is unnecessary or simply not desirable. (We ignore here the critical problem of highly valued goods that are very expensive to provide and for which there is little demand or for which the private investment is difficult to recoup, such as primary care physicians serving in rural areas and developing countries or fully certified teachers serving in inner-city communities.)

Higher education, however, is a growth industry. Of all the woes traditional institutions claim to have, enrollment is not one of them at this time, especially as greater proportions of older students continue to enter the system. True, some institutions experience enrollment decline, and a handful of institutions either have gone out of business, been bought up, or merged over the past decade. However, a case might be made that such actions are more the result of declining regional demographics and aggressive acquisition practices by FPCUs rather than overall declines in demand. Between the fall of 2000 and the fall of 2002, enrollment in postsecondary education increased from 15.7 million to 17 million students (National Center for Education Statistics 2002b, 2005). Growth occurred in all sectors, including for-profit colleges and universities. For-profit enrollments grew from slightly less than 700,000 to more than 852,000 students, a 22% increase. Thus, one might reasonably conclude that, based on demand, postsecondary education—as a sector—is relatively healthy. Some students/consumers may not like one or another *service* (a particular college or university), but ultimately they can find a service that they will buy. The point could also be made that as public institutions become more private, the sector is being transformed. But such an observation has less to do with the overall health of the industry and more to do with its fiscal and governance structures.

The remaining criteria for determining the quality of student services are much harder to identify. The retention, graduation, and placement rates of FPCUs are now aggressively monitored and enforced, such as the 60% rule for retention/graduation, and the 70% rule for placement. The government has only recently begun collecting graduation data for *all* postsecondary institutions; of course, some TCUs are way above and others way below the 60% graduation metric. For example, community colleges are on average at about 36%. On the face of it, one might conclude that a great deal of work needs to be accomplished: less than 47% of all students who begin a bachelor's degree will graduate within a five-year period (National Center for Education Statistics 2004a). Obviously, an end point indicates that retention rates across the board are not good, with most students departing within fifteen weeks after they have started.

Such gross judgments, however, are inappropriate for numerous reasons. Simply because a consumer leaves and departs a particular institution does not necessarily mean that the system is failing. Recent work points out that numerous students reenter the system and eventually graduate, albeit from a different institution (Adelman 2004). It is also not entirely appropriate to lay blame on an institution for all student departures. Some students determine that a postsecondary education is not what they want or need. Other students are content to have received a portion of an education and do not need a terminal degree; others fail regardless of the attempts of the institution. Students also may have personal reasons for dropping out and may return at a later date.

The point here is that conclusions to be drawn from retention/graduation data are not always clear, regardless of institution type. Although one might reasonably conclude that the postsecondary system does an adequate job at present, one might simultaneously conclude that changes in the system might increase its *overall* reach and effectiveness. Despite major shortfalls recorded in numerous fields (e.g., engineering and emerging languages), the system is not entirely in chaos. To be sure, a great deal of work could be done to improve graduation rates and field-specific production rates. (Proposals to shift the basis for appropriations to public institutions from *pay on attendance* to *pay on completion* are but one reflection of this search.) Clearly, if students enter a process with the aim of completing a task, the ultimate goal should be to ensure that as many students as possible meet these goals. Of course, like other humans, students are influenced by all sorts of information, including public higher education policies, and make decisions accordingly.

If graduation rates are hard to determine, then simple answers to whether college provides a private or public return on investment is even more difficult, if not naive. Gross numbers are known, of course. As we pointed out in chapters 2 and 3, a college graduate earns more than someone without a college degree, and students in some fields and from some colleges do better than their peers. Forgone earnings when a student is in college are more easily recovered once the individual enters the job market in some fields than in others. A more highly educated society has a higher per capita income and a higher standard of living (Leslie and Brinkman 1988; Heller 1997). However, in a book on for-profit higher education, the question should be about for-profits. How do their graduates do? Few comprehensive or reliable data exist that say anything about the quality of jobs students assume when they graduate from an FPCU, or the comparability of jobs one acquires in the for-profit sector versus the nonprofit sector.

Similarly, the social return on investment is hard to gauge for traditional institutions, much less the for-profits. Does attendance in college make a person a more engaged citizen in a democracy? We know that individuals with bachelor's degrees have higher voting patterns, but no data exist that indicate that if an individual attends a for-profit college as opposed to a traditional institution, he or she will be more or less likely to be involved in social issues related to the improvement of a democracy. There are those, of course, who criticize for-profit institutions for their focus on training and bemoan the lack of discussions that frequently occur in humanities and other related classes. Although there are no data to back up such an assertion, even if the argument is true—on its face value, it seems logical insofar as the for-profits are more geared toward job employment—such a point has less to do with for-profits and more to do with types of education. Community colleges, for example, or the more focused professional schools within nonprofit institutions such as engineering could also be criticized on the same grounds.

The high rate of default on student loans by some FPCU institutions, though decreasing steadily over the past thirty years and especially since about 1998, is a worrisome feature that we will elaborate on in chapter 8. As we note in the next chapter, federal regulations came into play in large part because of the exceedingly high loan defaults of for-profit institutions. Due to increased regulation, many FPCU's that defaulted on loans have gone out of business, but it still remains a topic of concern for Congress. At the same time, banks would find a particular set of borrowers a bad investment if they continuously did not repay their loans. Why should the government come to any different conclusion? Although loans are taken out by individuals, if the rate of default is higher at a particular type of institution, then those institutions also will be suspect, which is why FPCU's have come under increased scrutiny—their defaults have been of a greater magnitude than TCU's.

The conclusion, then, is that the final determination of how best to serve students is in fact a dynamic concept that will never be fully realized. What students want and what they need changes over time. What students want will differ based on their backgrounds and career goals. Rather than assume that one sector or type of institution is better than another, what needs to take place is a more thorough investigation of how to produce the conditions for quality across and within sectors. Higher education is a growth industry and there is room for new entrants. As space is made for new players, one key action that should take place not only for these new entrants but also for the traditional sector is to develop benchmark data on issues such as retention, graduation, and private and social returns on investment.

CHAPTER EIGHT

Clashes of Cultures, Sectors, and Purposes

All organizations face challenges and hurdles. Institutions also have a life cycle: from birth to middle age, eventual old age for most, and either death or rebirth and transformation. Indeed, noted economists have argued that organizations and their work are destroyed in order to create new organizations and work. The challenges for organizations in emerging industries such as biogenetics differ from those that enter a mature industry such as postsecondary education with time-honored institutions and firmly established procedures. To be sure, well-established colleges and universities currently face a turbulent environment that has forced them to rethink how they function, but these challenges are quite different from those being confronted by the relatively new for-profit institutions, which have few formalized rules and procedures and literally invent business operations as they grow and evolve.

We noted in chapter 1 that some inventions may be conceptualized as sustainable technologies and others as disruptive. From the perspective of higher education, FPCUs utilize a technology that is disruptive and has the potential to revolutionize not simply their work but also that of the postsecondary sector. But no technology remains consistently disruptive. Consider the major inventions and new industries that came about in the twentieth century. Either they experienced tremendous growth, could not handle the related challenges, and died, or they burst onto the scene in a dramatic fashion and then went about establishing rules and procedures for how they were to conduct business. Many of the companies that made up the dot.com boom of the late 1990s are examples of the former; Apple Computer is an example of the latter.

Organizational growth is also not entirely dependent on leadership or internally driven processes and procedures. Some individuals may be brilliant innovators but are unable to move from a small-scale, hands-on focus to a larger bureaucratic organization. In such a scenario, a promising idea or technology never takes off. Other organizations may end up constrained by an initial culture that mediates against growth—an entrepreneurial culture cannot be assumed for all start-up companies. Cultures have to be determined and nurtured; they do not simply arise autonomously.

The environment also plays a critical role. Markets and consumers do not exist in isolation in the external environment. Multiple factors drive demand for specific goods and services, down as well as up. Local, state, and federal governments and agencies have the power to create, regulate, and mitigate markets. Legislators can make markets more efficient so that an organization has the potential for enormous growth, but markets can also become more constrained by rules and laws that seek to contain market transactions for one reason or another. Nonprofit companies and organizations that receive support from the citizenry through governmental funding, tax exemption, or philanthropic status are likely to face particular scrutiny because they receive these special advantages in exchange for contributing to the public good.

For-profit companies are also regulated for overlapping, yet slightly different, sets of reasons that are largely focused around a host of consumer protection issues and, for some, in addition, a range of public-sector contracting and accountability issues. A private corporation that seeks to make a profit by manufacturing mattresses, for example, will face less governmental oversight than a defense contractor whose sole purpose is to provide missiles for public defense. Both face a broad range of consumer protection regulations, for example, truth in advertising. Defense contractors will also face an additional array of regulations, for example, bidding and subcontracting requirements, associated with the fact that they are seeking to sell to government bodies. Our simple point here is that, although all for-profit companies face various forms of oversight and regulation, they face obligations and controls and enjoy advantages that are quite different from their public and private nonprofit counterparts. When for-profit firms enter the public-goods business, especially in those fields where governments and not-for-profits already have a long history of direct provision, both kinds of rules tend to apply. Private company boards have obligations to their shareholders; public boards are beholden to the citizenry. For-profit companies are subjected to unique oversight regulations stipulated by law. Due to their unique access to tax coffers, public institutions have rules that do not apply to private companies. An unusual challenge arises when organizations in multiple sectors compete to provide similar services. This is particularly true when one sector is the new kid on the block.

For-profit colleges and universities have come under a great deal of scrutiny and criticism. They predictably claim that they have been the object of unfair burden and regulation. In many respects, the problems and concerns that have emerged pertain to any profit-seeking company operating in a field that has traditionally been thought of as a (largely publicly provided) public good; the conflict will eventually be reconciled through the regulatory give-and-take typical of other fields. But today, FPCUs and TCUs face a clash of cultures. For-profits think of themselves as retail, consumer-service businesses, and their culture operates in that manner. Those in traditional higher education think of the behavior of for-profits as aberrant or odd because they do not mirror an academic culture.

Some problems that have arisen also may be attributed to the challenge of rapid growth. Others are simply violations that should not have occurred. The U.S. Department of Justice, the Securities and Exchange Commission, the U.S. Department of Education, and various accreditation agencies all have investigated the practices of different for-profit companies (as well as TCUs). Whereas in the past the charges have been made against fly-by-night proprietary institutions, the current allegations frequently include major companies such as ITT Educational Services, Corinthian Colleges, Career Education Corporation, and the University of Phoenix. Collectively, these corporations serve more than 450,000 students. The charges that have been brought against them relate to fraud, recruitment violations, noncompliance in the administration of Title IV funds, violation of student aid laws, false claims and noncompliance pertaining to federal student aid, tampering with student records, ineffective governance and oversight procedures, unethical practices related to payment of admissions counselors, and cover-up activities to avoid scrutiny.

As this book goes to press, ITT's issues with the Department of Justice, Corinthian's with the SEC and Department of Education, and Apollo's program review have all been resolved, but new problems continue to arise.

Inevitable comparisons are made by some between these "scandals" and the notorious noneducation examples such as Enron and WorldCom. Among many material differences that distinguish the two sets of events, the single most telling difference is that the noneducation examples focused on malfeasance by senior management at the very top of the organizations, whereas virtually all of the verifiable FPCU issues of malfeasance occurred at one or more of an FPCU's individual campuses. No matter how interpreted, however, the laundry list of allegations can neither be ignored nor taken as fact. Some charges have been dismissed, others have been proved and sanctions levied, and others remain unresolved. Further, just as one does not jump from a singular event to a generalization, one ought not to assume that all for-profit institutions act in ways consistent with these accusations. One response should be to question how well founded and widespread the allegations are and what regulatory responses, if any, are needed to reduce the occurrence of these practices to tolerable levels. Were the scandals that erupted over Enron and WorldCom examples of a few rotten apples in a barrel, or were they indicative of wholesale corporate corruption? Was the creation of the Sarbanes-Oxley Act of 2002 the correct remedy? (Because one of the central goals of "SOX" was to move business processes and controls to an acceptable level and to require the CEO to attest personally to their quality, it is likely that the larger FPCUs are devoting more effort to improving the quality and detail of their academic/financial record keeping.) Are the periodic athletic scandals that have emerged at an NCAA institution emblematic of college sports in general, or simply the behavior of a rogue university bent on winning at any cost, or even merely an uncovered conspiracy among several enthusiasts from the coaching staff and alumni support groups? Another response is to ensure that regardless of whether the scandals are incidental or widespread, they do not happen again. Hence, regulations and laws come about not only to guarantee that the market works as intended but to ensure that organizations, whether they are profit making or not, act in a minimally ethical and transparent manner.

For-profits, however, face a particular conundrum with regard to public policy and oversight. FPCUs are like other for-profit firms; they seek to enlarge their market share and increase the wealth of their shareholders or owners. Yet the product of an FPCU has traditionally been thought of as a public good—education, broadly defined, not unlike public safety, health, and social welfare. A firm that manufactures mattresses competes with other mattress makers. They may seek government support and/or protection in the form of trade agreements and/or restrictions if mattresses are made more cheaply abroad, but such support is fundamentally about manipulating the market in one way or another to provide some local or domestic firms a competitive advantage or reduce the disadvantage vis-à-vis foreign firms. At the same time, mattress companies must abide by a wide variety of labor, health, fair-trade, and consumer protection rules, each with its own procedures for monitoring and applying sanctions.

A growing number of for-profit institutions, however, have now entered a mature but growing market of older nonprofit and public institutions. What is the government's role here? Leveling the intersector playing field, of course, is not a new issue in society. But due to the sector's novelty and growing visibility in higher education, it is important to raise the question here. Should the government see a for-profit college, a public community college, and a private university as equals? Also, is equality to be achieved by creating the same rules for all institutions, regardless of type, or different rules for each? If the same rules are to apply for all institutions, then the legislative and regulatory purpose is to permit competition with the assumption that the market will take care of the rest. But if nonprofit and for-profit organizations are fundamentally different, with conflicting comparative advantages, then a differentiated stance that acknowledges the comparative advantages (and disadvantages) of each may be required.

Those who look at education as a market for services that produces largely private benefits with little positive spillovers for others are likely to find the organizational type irrelevant. If the goal is to provide a product (education) to consumers, then the form of the organization should not matter much. Indeed, for-profits should be providing it. Let the government get out of the way, enable the market to function like markets in other sectors, and the country will be better off. The underlying premise is that education is defined as training, which in turn is defined as a private benefit. Whoever provides the best product will thrive; those who provide second-rate products will not. Surely, second-rate mattress manufacturers should not be provided with governmental largesse, but they should be protected from unethical mattress providers. Even more certainly, first-rate manufacturers should not be constrained by bureaucratic red tape.

Those who look at education as a purely public good have a different interpretation. For them, for-profit companies are inherently incapable of providing public goods and services. The economic sector of organizations, they claim, is critical insofar as education is more than personal skill enhancement and the resulting increases in private benefits. Only organizations chartered as public and private nonprofits are structurally capable of providing public goods and services. Ideas that we discussed in chapter 5, such as academic freedom, come into play. A for-profit company will not do what is best for the country any more than a mattress manufacturer would. Its purpose is to increase profit, so why should it act in ways similar to nonprofit organizations? The notion that "What is good for General Motors is good for the country" was questionable at the time it was raised, and such an assumption is even more arguable when it concerns a public good such as education. Following this perspective, of course, the government should differentiate among nonprofit, public, and for-profit institutions. Sector location of organizations matters a great deal, because such location fundamentally shapes organizational purposes and behaviors, both "public" and "private."

We raise these ideas here because the several public-policy issues that have prompted much disagreement are fundamentally philosophical in nature. We discussed in chapter 6 how states regulate FPCUs; we focus now on the role of the federal government. The Higher Education Act, which Congress has yet to reauthorize, will not simply help for-profit institutions and harm public and private institutions because of the policies that have been proposed. The act provided an indication of philosophical assumptions about the nature of postsecondary education. Our purpose here is neither to enter into the fray and celebrate or bemoan how the environment is treating FPCUs or their public and nonprofit counterparts, nor to assess the specific allegations that have been brought against several FPCUs. Instead, we seek to delineate the underlying philosophies that guide the debate and suggest that these differences are a clash of cultures fueled by their respective economic sectors, which ultimately need to be (and we think will be) resolved. We then turn to two recent examples that have brought FPCU's and TCU's into the public eye. We use these examples as ways to demonstrate the very different cultures of the two entities and consider what the public wants of its postsecondary institutions.

Education and the Market
How to Define a Postsecondary Institution

The Higher Education Act (HEA) of 1965 has gone through periodic revision and adjustment since its inception and, of course, will continue to do so. In 1998 the HEA amendments moved toward a single definition of a postsecondary institution to enable all institutions access to Title IV programs. Previously the Higher Education Act had defined a postsecondary institution in four different sections. Congress combined those definitions into two sections of a new Title I. However, a distinction between nonprofit and for-profit institutions remained in Section 101 of the act such that nonprofit institutions were defined as having assets irrevocably dedicated to the public interest (Wolanin 2003).

The shift that began in 1998 signaled that Congress believed postsecondary institutions were more alike than different, regardless of their funding source or purpose. The House Committee that penned the bill eventually wrote: "No institutional sector will be guaranteed priority under the law; institutions will only be provided with the ability to compete on an equal basis for federal funding" (U.S. House of Representatives 2004, p. 5). Such an assertion assumes that nonprofit and for-profit institutions are sufficiently similar; that the sector-specific advantages should not drive the distinction; and that interorganizational competition for students should decide who should receive federal funds for student financial aid. As David Moore (2004, p. 12), chief executive of Corinthian Colleges, stated:

Consolidation recognized that the purpose of all institutions is to provide students access to higher education. Furthermore, it made plain that the same core requirements apply to all institutions—authorization by a state in which the institution operates, accreditation by an agency recognized by the U.S. secretary of education, and certification of eligibility to participate in student financial-assistance programs authorized in Title IV of the act by the Department of Education.

His final point is critical for FPCUs—the ability to tap into federal funds for financial aid. The majority of federal support for higher education comes from student aid programs that are outlined in Title IV.

However, in Section 101 of the act, the dual definition preserved a distinction between for-profit and nonprofit institutions. The difference enabled nonprofit *institutions* (as opposed to students) to receive federal support from Title III, Title V, and Title VI of HEA, whereas for-profits were forbidden from doing so. Title III provided institutional support for developing institutions that enrolled large numbers of low-income students. Tribal colleges and Historically Black Colleges and Universities (HBCUs) also received financial support from Title III. Institutions that had at least a 25% Hispanic population where more than 50% came from low-income backgrounds were able to receive Title V funds. (These student demographic characteristics are mirrored in many FPCUs.)

Proponents of a single definition of postsecondary education appear to argue from two different sides. They suggest that "fewer than 10 percent of all Title IV eligible for-profit institutions would be able to file competitive grant applications. . . . It is unlikely that more than a fraction of these relatively few institutions would apply" (Moore 2004). The implication, of course, is that a single definition would not lead to significant changes for how the funding currently gets appropriated. Yet the Career College Association (CCA), the trade association for FPCUs, has made the change to a single definition one of its top five agenda items. One wonders why a trade group would place such a priority on an item that supposedly is irrelevant for more than 90% of its members. Very possibly it may be because the real issue is not access to Title III or Title V funds, but the right of FPCUs to offer liberal arts degrees, a goal that several FPCUs have publicly asserted. That would affect interinstitutional competition, and the change of the 90–10 rule would be relevant for much more than 10% of its members. It would also explain why analogous TCU "associations" (read trade groups) are also so anxious about this issue.

Opponents of the change have suggested one reason why a single definition will be significant. The American Council on Education (ACE) issued a brief endorsed by forty-five higher education associations. They noted that a single definition "will make a large number of short-term proprietary schools eligible for scores of federal programs run by other agencies that are linked to the current definition of HEA. . . . The impact will be considerable, spreading across a variety of agencies, including the Departments of Defense, Health and Human Services, Homeland Security, and Agriculture, as well as the National Science Foundation" (ACE 2004, p. 10). The potential also exists for many states to mirror what the federal government has done and to move toward single definitions.

ACE also has been quite clear about the consequences. Previously, Title V provided funding to 165 institutions; a single definition enables another 110 schools to become instantly eligible. Insofar as federal funding was not increased, and in many cases was cut, the result will be that more institutions will compete for fewer dollars. Proponents of a single definition say there are no negative consequences. They suggest that federal funds should be based solely on whether an individual benefits from the education an institution provides. Federal funding, they argue, should be geared toward providing fiscal resources for students to attend a postsecondary institution. Insofar as for-profits primarily have a different kind of student (older, lower socioeconomic status, part-time, and heretofore not college-bound), supporters suggest that a growing number of individuals are being discriminated against. Many students in the twenty-first century have family and work responsibilities. They increasingly turn to for-profit institutions for their education because these colleges cater to their needs with regard to location, time of classes, and other factors. Why should such students be denied aid for an institution, if it is their institution of choice? Further, these students may be unable to attend another institution, even if the institution qualifies for funding based on an archaic definition of the term *student*. Thus, funding turns on characteristics of the individual, with institutional *attributes* (as opposed to institutional *performance*) appearing less relevant.

Title III is geared toward the funding of *institutions*, not individuals. The initial impetus for such funding was to help institutions that primarily focused on underrepresented minorities. Title III also focused on specific institutions—tribally controlled colleges and HBCUs. Simply because the University of New Mexico or the University of Oklahoma had a significant percentage of Native American students did not mean that it qualified for Title III funding. The assumption was that the mission of these public institutions was somehow worthy of federal largesse. "Developing" institutions (fiscally struggling institutions created by and for selected language, cultural, and racial minority populations) received Title III funds under the assumption that institutions with a special mission of reaching out to underrepresented populations deserved funds to help them get started. Once these institutions were developed, they presumably would no longer need Title III funds. Opponents of a single definition also argue that institution-based grants should not be made available to private for-profit institutions. Why, they ask, should taxpayer funds be channeled to private companies whose sole purpose is to turn a profit?

Opponents also make a distinction between Title IV funds that focus on the individual and other funds that focus on the institution. All institutions will have some students who qualify for Title IV moneys because the funding is targeted to the individual. But only certain institutions will receive other kinds of funding because the funding is intended for institutions with particular missions. Are the public purposes and goals of higher education advanced more through aid to individuals with priority characteristics (low socioeconomic or minority status) or to institutions with priority characteristics (primary characteristics of student bodies)?

Opponents of a single definition argue that public nonprofit institutions have a special mission and a public responsibility and charter. Nonprofit colleges and universities "serve society in a variety of ways," Donald Heller (2003, p. 2) argues, "through their education, research, and service missions. They are important members of their communities; they offer not only classes, but also free arts, cultural, recreational, social-service, business, and extension programs." Heller goes on to argue that research universities also play a critical role in advancing knowledge through applied and basic research and that no proprietary institutions are research focused. Arguably FPCUs also contribute to the public good, but by a different means—increased tax revenues to governments that in turn fund public services. FPCUs provide directly through corporate income taxes as well as from their graduates' contribution of higher individual taxes through their higher earning potential.

Public institutions are responsible to the public, whereas for-profits are responsible to a profit-seeking board of individuals, including investors. Public boards operate in the open, where information about them is freely received. Even private nonprofit institutions have obligations to provide services that promote the public good. Proprietary institutions have no such obligations. Indeed, because they operate as a business, and thus seek to protect proprietary information from competitors, FPCUs (except for the publicly traded FPCUs) are extremely closemouthed about information. Public information is not readily available, and FPCUs act in a way that is consistent with their mission: they have no obligation to share information with the public other than what is demanded by federal and state regulations. Due to these regulations from the Securities and Exchange Commission, as well as various education agencies, one could argue that publicly traded FPCUs are much more transparent than the average TCU. But the more general point is that FPCUs have a greater proprietary interest in their operating information and are less inclined than TCUs to share what they have. On the basis of this difference, opponents argue that dual definitions are appropriate.

The response by those who seek a single definition is that for-profit institutions provide a great deal of information to the federal government and to investors (and, if they are publicly traded, to the public at large) that nonprofits do not have to submit. For-profit companies have disclosure obligations in accordance with securities laws, which nonprofits do not have. Nonprofits have similar financial reporting obligations (e.g., independent annual financial audits) to gain and retain their nonprofit status. Public TCUs face governmental disclosure obligations. The financial health of TCUs and FPCUs is also independently rated and publicly reported by firms such as Moody's and Standard and Poor's in order to facilitate access to lenders. As mentioned earlier, for-profits also pay taxes and contribute to the public good by preparing students for the work force—students who in turn earn larger salaries as a result of their education and, as a consequence, also pay more taxes. While such responses are certainly true, by any measurable standards, public institutions are more open with information than for-profit institutions and have public service functions that for-profits do not have, or are not eager to provide. The point has less to do with whether for-profits provide information that is required of them and do what they are expected to do, and more to do with what one thinks about the public good and the role of public institutions in advancing it.

In sum, the movement toward a single definition of a postsecondary institution turns on two key premises. One assumption is that public and private nonprofit institutions are materially and consequentially different in mission and scope than for-profit institutions. The second assumption is that students and society are better served by having an array of choices of providers, regardless of institutional type and control. The resolution of which assumption is correct has implications for those who receive hundreds of millions of dollars in federal and state funding, who pay hundreds of millions of dollars in corporate income, property, and other taxes, who receive tax exemptions, and who can grant tax deductions.

How to Structure Relationships between Institutions

One of the more sensitive issues among all institutions, nonprofits and for-profits alike, is whether to accept transfer credits from one institution to another. Professors frequently prefer that students study their curricula, with the assumption that their institution has unique and better curricula than another institution. Administrators see lost revenue in allowing transfer credits. Public policy makers see improved articulation as a student and social benefit. Each argument is strong.

If an individual transfers in thirty credits, then the institution will generate thirty fewer credits of tuition. Institutional reputation also comes into play. Students who transfer from a community college to a major research university, for example, do nothing to enhance the reputation of the institution, at least in the short run. Thus, relatively few institutional incentives exist to accept transfer credit, even if they constitute a positive spillover to society. The result is that students frequently suffer when they complete coursework at one institution only to discover that they cannot transfer those units to another institution. Institutions also suffer—some more than others. Although accreditation serves as one form of institutional legitimation, if that same institution does not have its credits honored by other institutions, then the college suffers fiscally and its prestige is tarnished.

The problem is only increasing. More than 50% of all students attend multiple postsecondary institutions. The increase in distance learning will only exacerbate the articulation issue as students become more likely to take basic general education courses on line and then seek to transfer the credit to a campus or to move across regions for work-related reasons while trying to pursue a degree. The expectation is also that prototypical attendance patterns, where students spent a full four years on a single campus, will decrease. Students and their learning experiences will be in multiple areas over a longer period of time, which suggests that transfers will increase as well.

Some steps have been taken to alleviate the problem, but they are primarily contained to a state's system of higher education; a widespread solution has proved elusive. The University of California and the California Community College System, for example, have articulation agreements that allow for the automatic transfer of similar courses (such as English 101) between institutions. Florida has a common numeric for its courses that makes comparability easier to assess. Tribal colleges frequently have articulation agreements with public state universities in the states where they are situated. Such examples are increasingly typical, but they are generally contained by state or region.

Frequently, one initial indicator of the possibility for accepting transfer credits has been whether the institution from which the student is trying to transfer the credit is accredited. However, a more common situation is for regionally accredited institutions to recognize credit from one another and reject credit from institutions accredited by national accrediting bodies. For-profits, like their nonprofit counterparts, see many benefits to accreditation, not the least of which is the ability to access Title IV funding. Most for-profit institutions, however, have found national accreditation an easier hurdle to jump than regional accreditation.

A lawsuit was brought against some associations for not having a policy for transferring credit other than to summarily reject any request. The U.S. Department of Justice targeted the American Bar Association and the Southern Association for Colleges and Schools. The former prohibited law schools that wanted accreditation from accepting any transfer credit from for-profits. The latter placed a significant burden of review on accepting any credit from institutions that were nationally rather than regionally accredited. The settlement that was reached placed the responsibility on the specific institution to have a policy in place. There could be no blanket policy related to the nature of the institution from which the credit was being transferred or from where the institution was accredited (Wolanin 2003, p. 134).

FPCUs sought in the HEA to stipulate that criterion as a basis for policy. They argued that students who tried to transfer from a for-profit college encountered blanket refusals from nonprofits, even to evaluate the courses. Students met with arbitrary refusals to accept validly earned credits. The lack of an acceptable route to transfer credits from one institution to another obviously makes a degree less worthwhile. FPCUs did not seek a blanket acceptance but instead sought policies that prohibited outright refusals. Parenthetically, it is worth noting that transfer is generally a one-way street; FPCU students transfer to the nonprofits, but not vice versa. Arguably, current low levels of interinstitutional articulation will pose increasing social and economic costs for increasingly mobile students.

The opponents of the change used much of the same data FPCUs employed, but interpreted it in a different light. Insofar as close to 50% of students attended more than one institution during their academic career, transfer apparently was functioning in a satisfactory manner. As ACE (2004) wrote, "This does not mean that transfer of credit works perfectly—it does not. But for huge numbers of students the process works well." By basic numbers, the statement is correct: huge numbers of students are able to transfer their credits from one institution to another. The question, however, remains—for how many students should the process not "work well" before a solution is proposed?

The proposed solution was a multitude of provisions for the transfer of credits that stipulated in great detail that institutions must outline *objective criteria* upon which transfer credits would be accepted, course by course. The reporting requirements demanded by the changes may have seemed useful to those outside of academia, but within the academy, they were deemed onerous. In effect, every institution would have to develop criteria on a course-by-course basis that stipulated the general level of consensus about what a required level of proficiency was in each course, based on objective criteria.

Assume, for example, that an English department develops a curriculum with an intense focus on writing in introductory courses, and a focus on literature in later courses. Assume also that an English department at another institution does the opposite. The student who transfers from institution A to institution B may have his or her transfer credits rejected. Such a rejection may make sense to some individuals insofar as there are no objective criteria for how to sequence introductory English classes; the assessment of writing is also always partially subjective. However, with the stipulations advocated by the for-profits, the institutions must either have common curricula or face a lawsuit. Regardless of progress on the articulation front, current levels of articulation will increasingly play into the hands of multicampus and distance-learning programs where a student can move and remain enrolled.

The difference of opinion revolves around two issues. Nonprofit institutions have traditionally allowed faculty the autonomy to develop curricula; the assumption has been that the determination of curricular standards is an intellectual undertaking that is resistant to cookie-cutter models. The result is that curricula may vary from institution to institution. For-profit institutions have a different approach to curricula, as we discussed in chapter 5. Faculty play a less critical role in curricular development; for a given course title, curricula are standard from instructor to instructor, and programs with the same title are standard from campus to campus. Tension erupts when one group wishes to transfer its English 101 to another institution. The approaches to curricula and who determines curricula are two issues where the for-profits and nonprofits have a fundamental disagreement, or rather have yet to imagine a common interest.

How an Institution Should Support Itself

Public and private postsecondary institutions have utilized multiple funding streams to support themselves. Whereas public universities in the past received substantial support from the state, support from that revenue source has declined as a proportion of all revenues in recent decades, such that public and private nonprofit university funding streams are today looking more alike than different. Tuition revenue still accounts for the majority of income on most campuses, but as we discussed in chapter 4, income from research, donors, entrepreneurial activities, and foundations also account for significant support. Some leaders of public institutions have initiated discussions with their states about the possibility of changing their status from a public to a private university or college since state support has declined dramatically and no turnaround is foreseen.

Students and their families who can afford tuition and are willing to pay rely on their own household resources, including income from concurrent employment. Some students will receive scholarships either from moneys the institution has received from donors or directly from the donor. State grants are also available. Significant amounts of grants and loans come from the federal government. Finally, employers now constitute a small but rapidly growing source of tuition support, especially for work-related education.

The operation of for-profit institutions is dramatically different, as we already have detailed. They conduct no research so they have negligible income from grant-related activities or foundations. They have not embarked on capital campaigns with the exception of some campaigns for donor dollars to nonlocal philanthropies to fund student aid at FPCUs. Noninstructional entrepreneurial activities are minuscule. As with their private nonprofit counterparts, they generally do not receive direct state support. Students typically do not receive scholarships from the institution or from private donors. State grants are usually unavailable to students who attend a for-profit. The result is that virtually all of the income for an FPCU is derived from tuition, but much of this tuition is derived from grants or loans from federal coffers. A lesser portion comes either directly out of the pockets of the students or their employers. Hence, for-profits depend heavily on federal support mediated through student choice. If the federal government forbade grants and loans to students who attended for-profits, the vast majority of FPCUs would face a rocky future, indeed. Likewise, of course, many TCUs would face an unsure future if governments pulled their tax-related advantages.

To obtain federal funding, a proprietary institution has to meet three

broad criteria: the institution has to have been in business for two con-
secutive years; the institution has to either be a candidate for accreditation or accredited, and the institution cannot derive more than 90% of its
revenues from federal grants and loans, commonly referred to as the 90–
10 rule. The rationale for these rules is to protect the federal government
from fraud and misuse of funds. Two years has been deemed a reasonable time for an institution to prove that it is up and running and not going to perish and/or abscond with federal moneys. Candidacy for accreditation, or accreditation, is common to all postsecondary institutions.
However, the 90–10 rule was implemented specifically because some for-
profit institutions have been charged with significant instances of fraud;
initially, the rule was 85–15, and in the previous reauthorization of the
HEA, Congress changed it to 90–10. How an institution configures the
10% of its income that does not come from the federal government is a
specific formula developed and refined by the Department of Education.

First, the institution must examine Title IV program funds used by students to satisfy tuition, fees, and other institutional charges. Second, it
must assess the total sum of revenues (including Title IV funds) generated from tuition, fees, and other institutional charges that are necessary
for education or training of its students. A majority of for-profit institutions relies on students' out-of-pocket costs for tuition and fees. To a lesser
extent, FPCUs rely on revenue generated from activities conducted that
are directly related to students' education and training as well as scholar-
ship funds derived from outside sources and income generated from such
funds. To be sure, the U.S. Department of Education (2003b) is somewhat
vague about how FPCUs should generate the 10% non-Title IV revenue.
It speaks in very general terms. What the regulation explicitly states are
the types of revenue that *cannot* be counted in the 10% minimum. The
way most FPCUs try to generate the 10% is through income derived from
tuition and fees directly paid by the students. Income from items such as
books and supplies, state tuition saving plans, and certain federal contracts cannot be counted.

The CCA has fought the 90–10 rule on the grounds that it is biased
against for-profits and harms low-income students. Opponents of the
90–10 rule have argued from two different perspectives for its elimina-

tion. John McKernan, a former governor of Maine and CEO of Education Management Corporation, spoke out against the 90–10 rule because he claimed it unfairly constrained for-profit companies and denied access to students. While McKernan acknowledged that the rule had been implemented in the early 1990s to combat fraud and abuse, he pointed out that "such abuses have largely been cleaned up" (Pulley 2004, p. 1). However, as the CCA (2005) notes, "there is little evidence the rule has done anything but hurt students." The CCA suggests that fraud and abuse have declined not because of the 90–10 rule, but because FPCUs have become more professional and have consistently met the gate-keeping tools provided by Congress.

The sole argument that CCA and its supporters put forward for the repeal of the 90–10 rule is based on a concern for low-income students. "The rule," states CCA (2005), "often forces institutions to take actions that are not in the best interest of students, such as raising tuition, locating campuses away from center city neighborhoods, and discouraging high need students from applying." In a "Dear Colleague" letter, Republican Congressmen Boehner and McKeon (2004) used the exact same language as the CCA with the addition: "There is little evidence that the rule has done anything but hurt students." They particularly objected to the rule being applied only to for-profit companies insofar as they enrolled a disproportionate number of "needy, high-risk, and minority students." David Moore (2004) also noted, "The 90/10 rule thus creates disincentives for institutions to serve those most in need of student financial assistance, especially the poor, minorities, and women."

The only alternative for institutions that fall under the 90–10 rule, apparently, is "to reorient their missions and programs away from students who are most in need of assistance" or to meet the criterion "by raising tuition and fees" (Moore 2004). The result is that rather than have a program in the inner city, for example, a for-profit is likely to move to the suburbs where there are students who can afford the tuition so that the institution can reach the 10% quota. Indirect data also exist to prove this assertion. A decade ago, almost two-thirds of proprietary students attended classes in central urban areas. Less than five years later, the percentage had dropped to 50%; the increase occurred in suburban-urban fringe areas (Boehner and McKeon 2004). At the same time default rates also dropped at FPCUs.

Supporters of the 90–10 rule have a different argument. They suggest that 90–10 has played a role in safeguarding Title IV programs from fraud and abuse. As ACE (2004) has written, "Schools that cannot clearly and convincingly demonstrate that they can pass a very modest market test should not be judged eligible to participate in the federal student aid program in the first place." David Warren, president of the National Association of Independent Colleges and Universities, stated:

> The 90–10 rule was meant to ensure that an educational institution offered a product that consumers were willing to pay for, instead of avoiding the discipline of the marketplace by being totally reliant on student-aid funds. Since for-profit entities, by definition, set their prices above their costs, we are particularly concerned that student-aid funds will be used to pay the profit margin of business. (Personal communication, May 26, 2004)

In its response to the proposed HEA bill, ACE noted that the 90–10 rule was one of several gate-keeping measures that had enabled the student loan default rate to drop from 20.4% in 1990 to 5.4% in 2002. They also noted the irony that companies in the private sector were unwilling to demonstrate "that there is at least a miniscule private sector market for their service" (ACE 2004).

Two arguments are at work here. First, the creation of the 90–10 rule (and its predecessors) was an attempt to implement a host of regulations to avoid fraud and abuse of federal financial aid funds. Second, the specific 90–10 rule assumed that if an institution could not generate one-tenth of its support from nonfederal sources, then it did not deserve federal funding. The rule applied only to proprietary institutions for two reasons. The rampant fraud and abuse of taxpayer money fell within the realm of for-profit institutions; although irregularities happen in any system, nothing close to what occurred with FPCUs has ever occurred with TCUs in their use of Title IV moneys. Of course, it is not clear how well low-income students have really been served by either type of institution.

Again, public institutions are supposed to have a different role. They serve the public. The assumption has long been, for example, that the uniformly low tuition at public universities has been preserved because "the public" benefits when students attend the institution. (Others have argued that the "low-tuition, low-financial aid" strategy of many public TCUs has provided inherent subsidies to middle- and upper-income families at the expense of low-income families.) No one will deny that when a student attends a for-profit institution, the individual benefits, and, by extension, the public benefits through the creation of a more educated work force. But no one should overlook the fact that for-profit institutions intend to make a profit. Their purpose is less to serve the public good than to make money. Such an observation neither obscures the fact that public institutions often fall short of their goals and can be self-serving nor assumes that making a profit in an economic system based on private enterprise ought to be in any way suspect or in no way contribute to the public good. However, at a time when definitions are in flux, the distinction between nonprofits and for-profits ought to be made and analyzed.

Neither the opponents nor the supporters of the 90 10 rule have shown demonstrably that the rule has led to the lowering of default rates. The rule was one of a host of actions Congress took to stem fraud. It is disingenuous for FPCUs to claim that the rule has been ineffective since they have no proof other than their own assertions; at least the supporters of the rule point out that the rule is one of a series of actions that have been taken. It is equally disingenuous to suggest that a causal relationship exists between the rule and the inability of for-profits to hold classes in low-income neighborhoods. Although strict formulas exist with regard to how a for-profit might account for the 10% of the income needed to demonstrate viability, as noted earlier, an array of options exists, including tuition and fee charges paid directly to the institution by the student, and specific charges related to educational activities that directly support a student's education and training.

FPCUs also should point out that the overriding concern with this rule is not that students are disadvantaged but that the companies and institutions are. In effect, FPCUs claim that because of the rule they cannot sell their product in certain areas, and if they did, they would experience a smaller profit margin. Similarly, while supporters of the rule may wish to help government agencies avoid fraud, they are also protecting those who already receive the money from having their shares reduced by denying some institutions the ability to claim federal moneys.

The debate over the 90–10 rule highlights three points. First, it was not very long ago that institutions within this sector had a major credibility problem. Thus, the continued allegations of fraud and misconduct allow the perception of a tainted industry to linger. Second, the massive reliance on federal funds to survive comes at the same time that public institutions are moving away from public support. The fluidity of degrees of *privateness* and *publicness* is far from settled and will undoubtedly create tension for the foreseeable future. Third, because FPCUs are a hybrid—private companies that think of themselves as similar to other businesses but offer a product that has been considered a public good—the culture of the industry will continue to engender conflict and suspicion among some. We return to this point in the conclusion.

How to Define Pedagogy and Curricula

Any student of higher education knows that for more than a decade distance learning has been held up as having a great deal of promise that has yet to be realized. More ventures have failed than succeeded, and the prophecies of an impending revolution have yet to fully materialize. True, the work environment has been radically altered as individuals use the Internet to augment, even restructure, their jobs, but despite very recent encouraging signs, the process of teaching and learning has remained largely a face-to-face enterprise both in the nonprofit and for-profit sectors.

The need for alternative learning environments certainly exists. By 2008 there will be more than 3.2 million high school graduates. Space for a large fraction of those graduates and college-aspiring adults to attend a nonprofit or for-profit institution does not currently exist. There are no existing plans that will provide a spatial solution (Wolanin 2003, p. 95). When one factors in the need for adult learning, the demand for some form of a postsecondary education (e.g., with certificate-based courses, A.A. and B.A. degrees) will only increase. However, distance learning has yet to be the solution to this problem. Courseware development and teaching have proved to be labor intensive, costly, and frequently inferior to the standard modes of teaching and learning. Many believe that as with any new technology, there will be a major breakthrough at some point that will transform the delivery of education, but that day has not yet arrived.

Another provision of the HEA was that for students to be eligible for Title IV financial aid, they needed to attend an institution that did not offer more than half of its courses on line or as correspondence courses, or have more than half of its students involved in distance education or correspondence courses. Known as the 50 – 50 rule, the rationale behind its implementation was yet again to constrain proprietary institutions who sought to tap into Title IV moneys. By requiring institutions to have face-to-face instruction, the law sought to ensure some measure of academic quality. Proponents of the law sought to avoid the emergence of companies that offered virtual courses or mail-order courses that had negligible value and consumed federal moneys, hoping in the process that valuable cost-effective innovations in teaching would continue to be explored and pursued by all institutions.

Opponents of the rule argued that multiple safeguards were already in place and that, while such a rule may have been useful at one point, the time had long since passed when virtual learning should be seen as second rate. Rather than restrict access to distance learning, argued the opponents, ways should be found to increase opportunities for virtual education. Repeal of the 50% telecommunications rule had the potential to increase the use of technology in delivering education and to provide an increase in the number of students with postsecondary options. Although nonprofit institutions also stood to benefit from repeal of the rule, the assumption was that the major beneficiary would be FPCUs.

Even those who opposed the change acknowledged that "the vast expansion of distance education means that the 50% rule might need to be revisited" (ACE 2004, p. 9). However, opponents of the change suggested that anyone who met the 50% threshold should simply ask for a waiver from the U.S. secretary of education. The hesitancy in repealing the rule stemmed from a desire to maintain some authority over quality and, again, over who had access to Title IV moneys. An alternative suggestion was that an institution would be exempt from the rule if its loan default rate had fallen below 10% during the previous three years (Wolanin 2003, p. 99).

The 50% provision highlighted yet again a variety of underlying tensions (often resource-related) between the TCUs and FPCUs. Clearly, one motivating rationale for the repeal of the rule was the ability of new entrants to claim a share of a fixed pot of money—Title IV funds. Those who were already at the table did not want to invite newcomers. A concern about fraud existed that was related to educational quality. Everyone acknowledges that substandard teaching and learning took place at numerous fly-by-night institutions, either through distance learning or correspondence courses; one way to stem the flow of such courses was through the 50–50 provision. Yet, such a draconian solution simultaneously depressed a technological innovation that appeared to hold much promise and was undergoing rapid change. Those best able to make use of the changes were not the traditional nonprofits, but the upstart (start-up) companies found in the for-profit sector.

The Clash of Cultures

In early 2005 two scandals erupted, each evoking the perceived nominal culture of higher education institutions in their respective sectors. One was reported by CBS's *60 Minutes* in a program that detailed allegations of fraud at several for-profit institutions owned by Career Education Corporation. The second pertained to a tenured professor at the University of Colorado at Boulder who had written provocative comments that portrayed the United States as an aggressor nation where terrorists were justified in bombing the World Trade Center. He labeled individuals who died in the World Trade Center as "little Eichmanns" (Churchill 2001). The scandals and their institutional responses reflect the different cultures and economic sectors in which the organizations reside. Our purpose here is to underscore that it is not only legislatively that these institutions differ from one another. They enact different stances because they have different organizational cultures, which serve to highlight the tensions that exist between the two sectors.

"Asses in Classes"

The *60 Minutes* story was a quintessential exposé complete with hidden cameras and senior officials declining comment. The reporter interviewed students on camera who said that the for-profit college they attended promised a 98% job placement rate, but the students eventually learned that the claim was entirely false. Many of the students were unemployed. Admissions officers reported that their job was little more than sales.

One said: "We're telling you that you're gonna have a 95% chance that you are gonna have a job paying $35,000 to $40,000 a year by the time they are done in 18 months. We later found out it's not true at all" (Fager 2005). An accreditation report detailed that roughly only one-third of the students even finished the program and that the graduates earned less than $11 per hour.

Other admissions counselors pointed out that a quota system existed to get new students enrolled. A former student placement manager at one of the for-profits explained the rationale: "I don't believe that they would be a $1 billion company in 10 years, if it weren't for the federal government loan programs." The corporate culture, explained the individual, "was all about the numbers. Getting students enrolled, getting students in the seats. Keeping students in the seats, getting them passed enough to graduate, and then trying to get them any job we could" (Fager 2005).

The interviews reflected what many had claimed normally took place at for-profit institutions. A report by the U.S. Department of Education made the same allegations against the University of Phoenix. Admissions officers' salaries were based on how many students they recruited. In direct violation of Sections 487 (a) and 487 (a) (20) of the Higher Education Act, individuals who brought in a high head-count received significant raises, free trips, bonuses, and awards (U.S. Department of Education 2003a, p. 27). The report also pointed out that "72 percent of the recruiters interviewed stated that it was always about the numbers—all about 'butts in seats' or 'asses in classes'—to use the vernacular commonly heard at UOP" (Blumenstyk 2004, p. 3). Individuals who did not meet their quota received little or no raise and were disciplined. The matter was eventually settled with no admission of wrongdoing by University of Phoenix, which contested this characterization in the Department of Education report.

The response by the for-profits after the *60 Minutes* report mirrored their culture. The day after the exposé, Merrill Lynch issued a report, which noted: "While the piece is clearly a negative, it does remove the overhang of what was always expected to be a negative report, and we believe that some of the impact was already built into the stocks which were down on Friday in anticipation of the piece airing this weekend." The stocks actually shot up on the Monday after *60 Minutes* aired (Gubins and Fine 2005, p. 1).

In the *60 Minutes* piece, the president of CCA stated, "This is not an industry-wide problem. And let me address the whole question of being under investigation. Allegations from a legal standpoint are not facts and are not evidence" (Fager 2005). He then went on to point out how for-profits cater to working adults and minorities. The Merrill Lynch report, in a section headed "Political Risk," stated, "Another potential concern is any potential political risk related to the piece. . . . The Career College Association is launching an advertising campaign in Washington to promote career colleges in reaction to the *60 Minutes* piece. . . . This is a particularly important time as the Higher Education Act is up for reauthorization. However, the political environment is more favorable for for-profit institutions than it has been in the past" (Gubins and Fine 2005, p. 2).

Confirmation that the CCA was launching an ad campaign could not be immediately verified; portions of the CCA Web site are closed to outside (nonmember) scrutiny. The public cannot view CCA's perspective on the exposé or numerous other controversial topics. No comments were made by the institutions that had been highlighted in the *60 Minutes* piece other than to deny the accusations or to assert that they were in compliance with government regulations. All of the employees who had been interviewed on the television program were former employees; no current employees were willing to make a public comment and feared dismissal if they did.

Little Eichmanns

Ward Churchill, a self-identified Native American, a tenured professor, and chair of Ethnic Studies at the University of Colorado at Boulder, has always been an outspoken critic of American foreign policy. He frequently used words such as *genocide* and *atrocity* in relation to how Americans had acted in relation to people who were different from Anglo-Americans. Over the years, he had been invited frequently to speak on college campuses; in February 2005 he was set to give a speech at Hamilton College in upstate New York.

A few weeks prior to his visit, a report on Fox TV's *The Factor with Bill O'Reilly* quoted an article that Churchill had written shortly after 9/11. In the article, Churchill wrote, "If there was a better, more effective, or in fact any other way of visiting some penalty befitting their participation upon the little Eichmanns inhabiting the sterile sanctuary of the twin towers, I'd really be interested in hearing about it" (Churchill 2001). The ensuing brouhaha rippled not only throughout the university campus but also throughout the state and country. Subsequent reports outlined that Professor Churchill also had accused the U.S. military of creating a smallpox epidemic among the Mandan people, a Native American tribe, in 1837. Churchill wrote, "At Fort Clark on the upper Missouri River . . . the U.S. Army distributed smallpox-laden blankets as gifts among the Mandan. The blankets had been gathered from a military infirmary in St. Louis where troops infected with the disease were quarantined" (Brown 2005).

Churchill was unapologetic with regard to his remarks about the 9/11 attacks. In the midst of the public debate, he (2005a) stated:

> The bottom line of my argument is that the best and perhaps only way to prevent a 9/11-style attack on the U.S. is for American citizens to compel their government to comply with the rule of law. . . . To the extent we shirk this responsibility, we, like the "Good Germans" of the 1930's and '40s, are complicit in its actions and have no legitimate basis for complaint when we suffer the consequences.

He also gave a public speech at the University of Colorado, where he (2005b) said, "I don't answer to [Governor] Bill Owens; I don't answer to the Board of Regents. The Board of Regents should do its job and let me do mine." The audience, composed mostly of college students, was a mixture of individuals who cheered him and others who found his views repugnant. Although he subsequently stepped down as chair of the ethnic studies department, he vowed to sue the university if he was fired.

The public outcry was equally severe. The chancellor of the university stated, "Like many people in Colorado and around the country, I personally, found the essay to be profoundly repugnant and hurtful to everyone touched by the tragedy of September 11, 2001" (Smallwood 2005, p. A36).

The faculty senate stated,

> If we stand for the dissemination of knowledge, of the freedom to question, and of freedom of expression, then we must protect all, including Professor Churchill and others, expressing the most unpopular sentiments. Anything less than an affirmation of academic freedom for all the University's faculty is an admission that we are not truly committed to the University's mission and philosophy. (Dodge 2005)

Jerry Rutledge, chair of University Board of Regents stated, "Let me reiterate my very, very strong belief that Professor Churchill's essay and subsequent remarks are outrageous, egregious and patently offensive. Those incendiary remarks are an embarrassment to a tremendously strong teaching and research university such as CU" (Smallwood 2005). Even the governor of Colorado got into the fray. In a press release issued by the Office of the Governor, Governor Owens stated, "No one wants to infringe on Mr. Churchill's right to express himself. But we are not compelled to accept his pro-terrorist views at state taxpayer subsidy nor under the banner of the University of Colorado" (Dodge 2005). Eventually, the University of Colorado System hired a public relations firm to "repair its public image" (Selingo 2005, p. A27). At the same time, the head of the University of Colorado system resigned, the faculty and administration initiated a full-blown investigation that resulted in a public report, and a vigorous debate occurred on and off campus about Professor Churchill's comments. A faculty investigative committee recommended that Churchill be sanctioned and possibly fired.

Round Pegs in Square Holes

These two admittedly disparate examples highlight how different the cultures are of both institutions, not in terms of the problems they face, but the manner in which they face them. An individual at one institution makes controversial and repugnant statements and provokes an outcry. Public officials feel compelled to respond, and various levels of the administration, faculty, and board open investigations. Faculty members at the institution argue for and against what the professor has stated. In the process some allege that he achieved tenure by falsely asserting on his resume that he was a member of an Indian tribe, a charge that was supported by several members of that tribe. Even as inquiries into his credentials are underway, the professor feels free to speak out and threatens a lawsuit against the university if they remove his tenure.

In the first example, no one at the institutions speaks out; the administration states that it is in compliance with federal regulations, and an analysis is done about how the negative publicity will impact the stocks of the company. Public officials do not make any statement, and the lobbying arm of the trade organization in which the institutions are situated initiates a public relations campaign.

The manner in which the institutions respond seems to be in conflict with which topic really matters. On the one hand, an individual seemed to have made inane and repugnant comments. However obnoxious his ideas may be, no one claims that he participated in violent acts against anyone or that his words physically harmed anyone. Indeed, what he did may well have been technically *legal* under the rules of tenure and free speech within that system. On the other hand, some institutions are purported to be involved in a series of ongoing activities that shortchange students and make ill use of public moneys. To what extent are these individual incidents reflective of the broader differences in TCU and FPCU governance discussed earlier, *shared* versus *traditional?*

By now, it should be clear that we are neither fire-breathing critics of FPCUs, nor their uncritical apologists. We have outlined the multitude of useful functions they have undertaken and the ways in which they have been innovative and resourceful in creating new markets. We also have detailed what we believe to be a fact: they are not going away. We recognize that FPCUs and nonprofits have different tasks, different ways of approaching their work, different advantages, different constraints, and different incentives, and, no surprise, they behave differently, even as they both educate postsecondary students. We neither envision in a generation's time that FPCUs will have morphed into traditional colleges and universities any more than TCUs will morph into FPCUs—nor do we believe they should. Indeed, as argued earlier, it is easier to imagine increased differentiation within FPCUs and TCUs. However, the examples we have outlined in this chapter highlight a clash of cultures. We could enter into a critique of the foibles of traditional postsecondary institutions, but that is not the purpose of this book, and we have done so elsewhere (Tierney 2003, 2004). Our concern is that for-profits are currently the proverbial round peg trying to fit into a square hole. Insofar as many of them are turning a healthy profit, they appear to have captured the ideology of the corporate cultures of which they are a part. We wish to suggest, however, that more thought needs to be given to how they also might adapt to the best aspects of academia's culture while retaining the distinctive strengths they already possess. It is this topic that we turn to in the final chapter.

Growth, Demand, and Purpose in Postsecondary Education

We have attempted to sketch the trajectory of a moving target, a dynamic organizational type in a continually shifting environment. The shift has not been caused by for-profits—more the opposite—but the energy and determination of FPCUs have nevertheless contributed to the changed environment. In what follows, we synthesize the argument we have made in the previous chapters and suggest five overarching themes that are likely to frame postsecondary education in the coming decades.

We began by suggesting that FPCUs may be the most significant organizational innovation in postsecondary education since the growth of American higher education in the early twentieth century. We observed that even though the 1960s was seen as a time of experiment and reform, organizational frameworks and formats were never questioned or altered in a manner akin to what for-profits are doing now. We likened the changes to what Christensen (1997) has defined as disruptive technologies—changes that are not merely improving the way a system operates but instead are reconfiguring the system itself with new technologies and new services for new students. Typically, such changes are much more likely to occur outside of the institutions in the traditional system, and FPCUs are a strong example of why and how.

Although FPCUs have been in existence for more than a century, their real growth has occurred over the past twenty years. As with their traditional counterparts, FPCUs are hard to characterize because they defy a one-size-fits-all format, as each FPCU pursues its unique place in the market. "Mom and pop" proprietary institutions that provide training in how to be a travel agent or a beautician exist alongside multicampus behemoths such as the University of Phoenix. Some for-profits are owned by one or two individuals and others are publicly traded on the stock market. Many institutions are accredited; many more are not. Fly-by-night organizations that are eventually hounded out of business are lumped together with organizations such as Strayer, whose image is squeaky clean. So even as large FPCUs continue to acquire smaller ones, FPCUs are as a group characterized by their organizational diversity, rather than similarity.

Where the FPCUs are more similar than different, however, is the manner in which they function as profit-seeking enterprises. While we noted in chapter 2 the various ways in which FPCUs govern themselves, their similarities are greater than their differences. At each FPCU, senior management and investor boards make all the strategic decisions; faculty and students are missing partners in governance. A hierarchical model exists that, nevertheless, actively seeks input from external constituencies such as regional employers and national occupational specialty associations. Senior administrators and the board not only set the direction of the institution, but they also keep a constant eye on the ability of the organization to make a profit. Investments in learning are worthwhile only to the extent that those investments at some point turn a profit for the company. For these reasons, for-profits are not full-service providers; they do not provide programs with low demand and high costs relative to prices.

Success for FPCUs ultimately turns on profitability, but there are three primary indirect indicators. Students have morphed into customers; customers need to believe that the product they are buying (a set of skills symbolized by a degree or certificate) is worthwhile. Rather than abstract notions of citizenship or general learning for the public good, FPCUs focus on training. Just as customers need to believe they have invested in a good product, so too do employers. However, for employers, students *are* the product. If students are not productive employees, then clearly the programs where they earned their degree or certificate are not worthwhile. Just as a customer will not continue to patronize a store that sells defective goods, so too will employers refrain from hiring graduates from an FPCU that provides faulty training. Students, in turn, will not attend the for-profit if it cannot offer training that will be valued in the marketplace.

Whereas TCUs have been quite internally focused in the creation of their curricula (groups from the faculty come together to decide requirements, electives, and other elements), FPCUs have done the opposite. Faculty members are irrelevant except for their role in delivering the curriculum that has been predesigned by specialized curriculum developers in consort with employers. Employers help decide what should be learned, and the students determine when courses are offered, in what format, and, to a certain extent, at what price. Employers ostensibly know the skills they want imparted to existing and potential employees; the assumption is that in a host of curricular areas, learning objectives and certification examinations provide a better means for measuring skills than faculty assessments.

However, any well-designed course is irrelevant if the customers are unable to take the classes because they are offered at inconvenient times or locations. When the constituency is primarily working adults, course offerings during the day and at distant campuses are likely to be problematic. Similarly, long summer breaks are inefficient for a population that cannot afford to take a summer vacation and instead wants to earn a degree as quickly as possible.

Customers are also price sensitive. If the goal is a job, and the entry point to that job is a piece of paper that states that the individual has passed a particular exam or taken a set of skill-related courses, then it is often deemed irrelevant where the person gets the training. Unlike at TCUs, where a degree from Harvard is likely to open more doors than a degree from Boise State (although even that is now questionable), the determiner of where a customer buys a degree is likely to turn on convenience and price sensitivity—at least to the extent that program quality differences are not discernable. Why pay more for a course if the employer has no reason to value where the course was taken?

FPCUs are not only aware of what customers will pay for a degree; they are also aware that the organization has to be able to facilitate access to financial aid for students. If FPCUs are able to address price sensitivity by way of aggressive cost controls and government grants and loans, then they have created a significant incentive for more students to take their classes. Just as for-profits must be sure that they offer skills that will enable students to get a job when they exit an FPCU, when students enter a for-profit, they need to be able to tap into Title IV and other moneys made available by the Higher Education Act or by employer tuition subsidies. Ensuring that students have access to loans and grants creates the possibility for a vastly expanded market pool for FPCUs, more than if all students had to use their own income to pay for an education.

Profit-making companies employ lobbyists and make donations to political officials to ensure that the regulatory environment is favorable to their product; this is not unlike what TCUs have been doing for years. Insofar as FPCUs are profit-making companies, they behave in a manner akin to other companies when significant legislation appears before Congress (and other legislative bodies) that will impact them. As the stakes in education for all players (including students, providers, and governments) have increased, the regulatory environment is more consequential today than it was a generation ago for FPCUs and TCUs. Despite their private, profit-seeking status, FPCUs are affected by public policies and appropriations in ways not dissimilar from TCUs. What does this foretell? We do not wish to make predictions about the future, but we do suggest that five touchstones are likely to remain critical topics of conversation for FPCUs and for their traditional counterparts in the future: the changing environment within which all institutions of higher education operate, the prominence of and problems associated with innovation in higher education, specific issues of delivery and content, an increased amalgamation of cultures resulting from a blurring of borders between FPCUs and TCUs as sectors, and growing differentiation and distinctiveness among individual institutions.

The Environment for FPCUs

Bold statements have been made about the future of traditional and for-profit institutions. The management guru Peter Drucker (1997, p. 127) predicted a decade ago that traditional colleges and universities would soon be a thing of the past: "Thirty years from now the big university campuses will be relics. Universities won't survive. It's as large a change as when we first got the printed book." On the other hand, for-profits have been likened to "diploma mills" that provide "McEducation" (Strosnider 1997).

We are much less apocalyptic and condemnatory. In a globalized economy, knowledge is a growth industry. As we argued in chapter 3, more, not fewer, individuals will need some form of a postsecondary education. Increasing demand suggests that different consumers will want different goods and services. The suggestion that many parents a generation from now will not want to send their teenagers somewhere safe and get them out of the house during their early adulthood is far-fetched. And for those students, they are likely to want the kind of experience that many of us had when we attended college, complete with a campus, dorms, a student center, athletics, and a faculty. Many other students will want a different kind of education, and we suspect that many of them will find that education at FPCUs.

We are reminded that as early as 1925 individuals bemoaned the increasing corporatization of the academy. In her novel *The Professor's House,* for example, Willa Cather (1990, p. 120) wrote of two faculty members who stood arm in arm against the Visigoths:

> Both, with all their might, had resisted the new commercialism, the aim to "show results" that was undermining and vulgarizing education. The state legislature and the board of regents seemed determined to make a trade school of the university. Candidates for the degree of Bachelor of Arts were allowed credits for commercial studies, courses in book-keeping, experimental farming, domestic science, dress-making, and what not.

Undoubtedly, Cather and others would look askance at what is taking place in academia today. We point this out here, however, to highlight that the tension in views about what should be offered in college, who should offer the courses, who should be able to take them, who should pay for them, and how should it all be evaluated are healthy, perennial, enduring questions that deserve vigorous debate. Cather's villains in 1925 were not the FPCUs, but the legislatures. Today, the hall of infamy is full of nominees, and FPCUs are one prominent example for some critics. At the same time, the regulatory environment has become increasingly supportive of for-profits and will likely not impede their growth in any substantial measure. After all, colleges and universities that create jobs, educate the work force, and pay rather than require taxes deserve some policy consideration. We anticipate, however, that the skeptical questioning that has been directed at FPCUs will continue, because such scrutiny is central to the life of a healthy citizenry and society. Yet, we also suggest that FPCUs will be able to participate in the debate more fully if they, well, *participate* in the debate. Is this likely?

We think that FPCUs and TCUs will increasingly find themselves interacting—*read* debating, dialoguing, competing, and cooperating—with each other more in the future than has been the case in the past, in large part because they all will be affected (in different ways) by common environment factors. Education is increasingly seen as an investment commodity (Bassett 2005; Altbach 2002) that can yield favorable returns. As the perceived and real value and price of postsecondary degrees continue to grow, consumers will more critically examine all schooling alternatives, regardless of sector, and competition will increase (Society for College and University Planning 2006, p. 8). Much of the recent historical growth of FPCUs has not come at the expense of TCUs, due in large part to the growth in number of high school graduates and the growth of nontraditional students in postsecondary education (Blumenstyk 2003). As FPCUs continue to grow and expand from certificates to degrees and from vocational trades into traditional programs (e.g., teacher education), they may well be "bumping up" against TCUs to a greater degree than has been the case (Blumenstyk 2003).

Similarly, the role of public actors—accrediting bodies, governments at all levels, regulatory agencies, student aid intermediaries, and the like—will continue to shape the opportunities for growth and development of both FPCUs and TCUs (Blumenstyk 2006a). Frustration with fraud and abuse at FPCUs will compete with frustration over high prices and mission drift in TCUs, and inherent desires to control will compete with inherent desires to foster and grow an educated citizenry, at both regional and national levels. Regulatory and control bodies partially have functioned as barriers to entry of new and expanding FPCUs. They have not had the same effect on TCU growth in part because in recent decades relatively few TCUs have come into existence and/or expanded across regulatory borders.

Forces for efficiency and consolidation are affecting all of higher education. Many businesses outside of higher education are "slimming down"—outsourcing, offshoring, eliminating pensions, increasing employee contributions for medical insurance, and in some cases slashing jobs and pay" (Society for College and University Planning 2006, p. 3). FPCUs are not immune from this—nor are TCUs. The relentless search for efficiencies will in some cases affect both FPCUs and TCUs; in some other cases, it will further push TCUs to behave like FPCUs, by reducing costs, increasing focus, and innovating. At the same time, FPCUs will continue to consolidate through mergers and acquisitions, further commodifying schooling, capturing scale economies, and focusing public policy issues on the behavior of large FPCUs. Analogous behavior among TCUs is reflected not in mergers and acquisitions but in a growing number of TCU partnerships and alliances, such as the one reported last year among Yale, UC-Berkeley, Australian National University, National University of Singapore, Peking University, the Swiss Federal Institute of Technology Zurich, the University of Copenhagen, and the University of Tokyo (Society for College and University Planning 2006, p. 5). Incentives to consolidate exist across higher education.

Finally, pervasive changes in information technology will continue to provide opportunities and threats to all higher education institutions— opportunities to create more productive forms of academic work, increasing the scope, scale, and reach of programs and threats from the inabilities to invest in sufficient IT infrastructure in order to capture those opportunities. Given the combination of all of these environmental factors, technological changes being not the least of them, the capability and incentives to innovate emerge as a central theme in the future of FPCUs and TCUs.

Innovation in a Maturing Industry

Industries and the organizations within them are not in a state of perpetual revolution; they go through life cycles and learn how to adapt to those life cycles—or they die. Apple Computer started in a garage where no rules and regulations existed, but there was a great deal of creativity and insight. For Apple to grow and thrive, the company could not have continued to work out of a garage. The idea that generated the computer revolution eventually settled down into a company where creativity was still possible, but an organizational frame could take hold. FPCUs will mature as well. The for-profit postsecondary education industry will eventually define a niche for itself, and what today seems radical and suspect will most likely settle into a stable phase that receives widespread acceptance as a plausible alternative, compliment, or supplement to traditional forms of postsecondary education.

We are reminded that innovation in American higher education has not had an entirely successful history. Experiments such as Black Mountain College became fiscally, if not intellectually, implausible and went out of business. The experiments at TCUs in the 1960s that we touched on in chapter 1 regressed to the norm, so that today those changes are largely overlooked and forgotten. Over the same period, the forces touched on in chapter 2 have driven up the value of schooling to individuals and societies. Some organizational forms have taken hold—community colleges, to name one example. The United States continues for the time being to remain the most schooled country on earth. Whether FPCUs are the Black Mountains of the twenty-first century or are akin to community colleges remains to be seen, of course. The outcome has to do with how FPCUs mature as a growing part of the postsecondary education industry, how the environment regards for-profit institutions, and how new technologies shape teaching and learning.

Within this broad context of a maturing industry lies the unfolding stories of individual FPCUs, each pursuing survival, success, and renewal through innovation broadly defined. Certainly it includes the pursuit of distinctive niches and markets through new goods and services, such as Apollo Group's goal of creating what would be recognized as *the* "national online community college" (Gubins 2006, p. 4), or Laureate's "unique strategy" of focusing on the interaction of international higher education markets and U.S. online programs (p. 9). Lincoln Educational Services' aggressive pursuit of instructional programs in construction and auto-related skilled trades is yet another example (p. 10). A slightly broader definition of innovation, however, would also include change strategies in which FPCUs also shifted out of markets and initiatives when their future became unduly problematic. These "innovations" would include, for example, considerations by DeVry to pull out of its "big-box" campuses (p. 8), or the decisions of Sylvan Learning Systems and Kaplan slightly more than a decade ago to enter and a few years later to pull out of the business of providing remedial education on college campuses (Blumenstyk 2006b). The internal capacity to get out of programs or lines of business may continue to distinguish FPCUs from many TCUs.

Innovations tend not to occur without the organizational capacity to innovate. In a sense, the precursor to visible, programmatic innovations in most FPCUs (and TCUs) lies in the capacity for those organizations to create and sustain their internal infrastructure in order to be able to innovate, improve quality, and grow. To illustrate, Career Education Corporation's current strategic emphasis on infrastructure includes "adding more controls, increased training, and a legal and compliance structure" (Gubins 2006, p. 5). Corinthian's focus on "improving its systems and execution" is similar, born in this instance out of a recognition that in order to innovate in the future, it needs to get better control of a variety of internal operating systems, ranging from student acquisition to facilities utilization (p. 6).

Throughout the book we have focused on organizations that currently fall unambiguously into a broad definition of FPCU. As implied in earlier chapters, right alongside FPCUs exist many non-FPCU for-profit postsecondary education businesses. Although they were not the subject of our work, inevitable innovations in some of those non-FPCU firms will move them more squarely into the FPCU space with all of the attendant implications for current FPCUs and TCUs. One illustration, drawn almost at random from a wide array of candidates, is Productivity Point, a firm specializing in custom software and IT training. Its current scope of educational services include:

> learning solutions for customers in *technology, energy, pharmaceutical / healthcare, financial, manufacturing, government and education.* Our solutions provide services that bring value to our customers. That's why we don't impose a one-size-fits-all solution for your organization. Instead, we tailor the approach to fit your needs, based on our discussions with you. As we collaborate with you to design your program, we can combine any of a number of education products and services.(www.propoint.com; emphasis in original)

One of the fundamental features that currently distinguish FPCUs from TCUs is their relatively close working relationship with employers. What differentiates non-FPCU Productivity Point from FPCUs like, say,

DeVry or ITT beyond size and corporate form (publicly traded vs. privately held)? How relevant is that distinction? What would cause that distinction to vanish? The challenge of categorizing FPCUs, especially vis-à-vis TCUs, is actually small compared to identifying and categorizing the growing numbers of other "learning solutions" organizations. The basic point here is that "FPCU innovation" takes place in businesses other than those currently labeled as FPCUs.

The Unsettled Question of Delivery

Distance learning was to have become the great postsecondary savior (or demon) by now. That is, some predicted that distance learning would have had such a significant impact by the first decade of the twenty-first century that teaching and learning was sure to have been transformed. Those who were wedded to the past, primarily faculty at TCUs, viewed such a transformation with alarm, whereas those who wanted to create dramatic change welcomed such predictions. The result, of course, has been well short of revolutionary. A modest impact has been felt in some areas, but the vast landscape of postsecondary education—both traditional and for-profit—has been left largely unchanged, leaving still open the issue of which institutions will most likely capitalize on the learning technologies that are emerging in society.

As we mentioned earlier, the majority of discussion about distance learning has been focused on scale. Obviously, if students are able to take courses from their laptops, then a great many more students (customers) in more diverse locations can be reached. The issues of personalization and multiple learning styles will be market tested as new distance-learning products and services emerge. Although such development is surely useful to students-cum-customers in elusive markets, we suspect that the dialogue surrounding distance learning is likely to change, and with it a modestly disruptive technology will enable significant change. Rather than an increase in markets, the discussion will focus on pedagogical improvements that will enable vastly improved learning. The technology has not been brought to any scale yet, but will be sometime soon. The question is not if but when. Indications are that for-profits will be well represented among those institutions seeking prominently to employ learning technologies as an integral component of its offerings.

For our purposes here, however, the point has less to do with distance learning as a learning tool, and more to do with how FPCUs and, by inference, TCUs will address such developments. Who is better situated to take advantage of a disruptive technology—the traditional organization with a defined system for how to conduct activities, with a significant portion of the organization believing how it operates is satisfactory, or the investor-backed start-up company that has no set procedures and whose leadership seeks to expand markets in as aggressive manner as possible? Conceivably, FPCUs could be held back by a provider and/or consumer environment that is not receptive to their product or manner of doing business for one reason or another. But that perspective by itself is probably too simplistic. So far the opposite seems to have been the case.

Pursuit of online delivery of programs by FPCUs continues to outpace adoptions by TCUs. At many individual FPCUs online learning is a leading growth and profitable line of business. Consider as an illustration Kaplan University's online performance in 2004. It was the fastest-growing business within Kaplan, and part of Kaplan Higher Education, which was the largest profit producer among the four divisions of Kaplan, which in turn was the largest contributor to operating revenue increases among the four business divisions of the Washington Post Company (2005, pp. 3, 9), the ultimate owner of Kaplan University online. More broadly, FPCUs as a group are currently growing overall enrollments at about 8% per annum in contrast to 2% for higher education as a whole (Blumenstyk 2005). Much of that FPCU growth comes from students who take courses online. More than one-third of online enrollments occur at FPCUs like Kaplan University online, and of the $5 billion generated by all higher education institutions in online education in 2004, $2 out of every $5 went to FPCUs (Blumenstyk 2005). On an international level, however, the rapid proliferation of public (governmental) and private nonprofit, as well as for-profit, e-learning providers, partners, e-learning content specialists, and IT-related e-learning support organizations suggests that alliances and partnerships of organizations rather than stand-alone FPCUs, even big ones, may be currently in the lead on distance learning (Learning

Business 2004). Indeed, a form of "common ground" around distance-learning standards and methods may draw FPCUs and TCUs into additional conversations with each other.

Beyond Sectors: The Amalgamation of Cultures

An underlying assumption in this book has been that neither sector (the traditional or the for-profit) is strictly nonprofit or strictly for-profit, just as within the traditional sector a public university such as Penn State is not entirely different from a private university such as the University of Pennsylvania. Although the world is changing abroad as well, it is much easier to find dichotomies such as public/private, for-profit/not-for-profit in countries such as Australia and Malaysia than in the United States. Instead, what is taking place is a quasi-fiscal amalgamation so that, rather than dichotomies, we think of organizations in the postsecondary sector as lying along a continuum of varying degrees of privateness and publicness. Such institutions involve variations in funding, governance, control, and programmatic offerings. Indeed, in the examples we pointed out in chapter 8, there is no small irony that the for-profit institutions featured on *60 Minutes* earn up to 90% of their income from publicly subsidized tuition revenues, and the State of Colorado provides less than ten cents on the dollar to the operating budget for the University of Colorado at Boulder. Which is public and which is private?

Although less visible than sector share of annual operating revenues, access to financial capital to innovate (however defined) is also a fundamental issue that will shape the futures of FPCUs and TCUs. Most growth and innovation initiatives of any importance in higher education ultimately require significant infusions of cash, accessed through debt or equity. Investment capital can find its way to individual FPCUs, but it can also dry up and/or go elsewhere. Stock prices for publicly traded FPCUs can fall dramatically as well as rise, as they did between January 2004 and January 2005 (Blumenstyk 2006c). Access by TCUs to debt (subsidized or market rate) is less "fickle" (the good news) but at the same time provides fewer options at generally smaller scale (the bad news). Future growth and change for both FPCUs and TCUs will hinge on individual institutional access to financial capital. Characteristic "big ticket" behaviors among FPCUs—major capital expenditures, mergers, acquisitions, initial public offerings, private buyouts—all require access to capital usually beyond that which is available in an operating budget. The recent purchase of Education Management Corporation for $3.4 billion by two private equity firms illustrates the scale of the issue (Blumenstyk 2006c).

Our larger point, however, has less to do with fiscal amalgamations than with cultural ones. Many in the private sector will bemoan the inept, or absent, management strategies at TCUs. "Higher education needs to be more like a business" has become a common refrain for more than a generation. Again, in a book on for-profit colleges and universities, our purpose is not to debate such an assertion. Instead, we wish to suggest that if FPCUs are to thrive, then the adage needs to be turned around: the FPCU business needs to adopt some parts of traditional higher education. We do not suggest that FPCUs become traditional institutions—to make such a proclamation defeats much of the potential they have. But, at present, a counterproductive Cold War exists.

We concede that FPCUs govern themselves differently and that TCUs frequently have different curricular purposes. In the future, however, TCUs are likely to look and act in much the same way that they look and act today, and FPCUs are likely to cater largely to the same kind of clientele they currently seek. Students will face a widening array of schooling choices. It behooves both FPCUs and TCUs to explore how the comparative advantages of each model can be incorporated with those of the other.

We also suggest that, insofar as there is room for both institutional types to grow, they need to (and, we think, will) figure out ways to get along—indeed, to actively collaborate rather than to sit apart or to try to ignore one another. While TCUs have gotten the *education* part of the equation down better than the *business* side, FPCUs have learned their business lessons much better than their education lessons. It seems mistaken, for example, that those at for-profits often do not know about, and hence do not capitalize on, the advances in learning that have become standard practice in the higher education arena. A robust literature exists on topics such as cooperative learning, student engagement, retention, attrition, service learning, and others. Yet, all too frequently, we have found at FPCUs a complete unawareness of these topics. The point, of course, is not that FPCUs should simplemindedly adopt strategies utilized by one organization for their own, but at the same time, to willfully ignore such literature and experience seems foolhardy. We have attended FPCU meetings, for example, where individuals discussed the need to develop ways to better engage students out of class; a discussion ensued that basically reinvented a wheel that the TCUs had created a generation earlier. Further, there is a defensiveness and secretiveness about FPCUs that may be understandable but must be overcome. We appreciate that businesses do not share business plans with one another, and the degree of openness in public institutions would be unthinkable in the corporate world. But the reflexive posture that FPCUs often take with regard to deniability will place them at odds in a business that pertains to free and open access to knowledge. Rather than adopt a posture that says "we are different from you and want nothing to do with you and, in fact, hope to eat your lunch," for-profits would be well advised to pursue détente and seek possible synergies, rather than settle for disdain. When the not-too-distant future of global competition in postsecondary education arrives, FPCUs and TCUs will increasingly look to each other as partners.

Amalgamation will also be accelerated by third parties. One of the important categories of players at that future table will be leaders from (noneducation) business, government, and nongovernmental organizations who have personal experience working with FPCUs in contractor relationships and with TCUs as members of governing boards, as individual donors, and as supporters—as well as in contractor relationships. As an illustration, a number of middle and upper managers at the following corporations are inevitably associated with a wide variety of TCUs in voluntary (nonpaid) capacities: AT&T, Verizon, General Motors, PEPCO, SallieMae, Northrop Grumman Information Technology, EDS, UPS, Lockheed Martin, Raytheon, the National Guard, the District of Columbia, the General Services Administration, the United States Navy, and the U.S. Department of Energy. With every one of these (plus seventy additional) organizations, Strayer Education (2005, p. 9) has in place "sponsorship and reimbursement arrangements of varying sorts." Other FPCUs cultivate other employer networks of business leaders. Over time, more and more business leaders are gaining firsthand, if anecdotal, knowledge of both FPCUs and TCUs.

A Focus on Mission, Brand, and Overarching Themes

We have suggested that FPCUs and TCUs should and will engage in an armistice. To a certain extent, the broad distinctions associated with economic sector location will increasingly blur, and the two institutions will become more alike, at least by borrowing what is best in each organization. Traditional colleges and universities are more likely to talk about the *mission* of their organization, and for-profits will use the business lingo of *brand*. Regardless of the jargon employed by each group, the future lies with those in educational organizations who can delineate a plausible story line about what they do and then follow through with it.

As we discussed in chapter 4, not all for-profit institutions are alike, but they have become framed in the public's eye as similar. Not only will multiple for-profits not want to be consigned to the same domain as their disreputable counterparts, but FPCUs will have multiple roles and capacities. Just as some TCUs are small liberal arts colleges and others are large research universities, we suspect that in the future, some FPCUs will remain small single-campus, single-focus institutions and others will go global with campuses throughout the world. Beyond the number of campuses, we anticipate that FPCUs will seek to create distinctive brands among themselves, perhaps more successfully than TCUs have distinguished their individual missions from each other.

The challenge for educational institutions remains one of definition and distinction. What are those commonalities that extend across all institutional types, and what are the unique positive attributes of an organization that enable it to stand out from the rest? We have focused here on an emerging organizational type that is not without problems and challenges, as any new entrant to a settled market is likely to face. The promise they hold has yet to be fully realized; the question remains open as to whether it will be realized or what shape it will eventually take. After all, who would have predicted in the late nineteenth century that a bunch of largely mediocre colleges and universities would eventually become the envy of the world?

We conclude, then, not with a prediction, but with a sense of the possibilities that for-profit colleges and universities hold in a dynamic environment where knowledge dissemination and production play a key role to economic well-being and security. At the beginning of the introduction to this book we made the distinction between "lumpers" and "splitters" in social science research: we raised the question of whether FPCUs ultimately represented variations within a unitary, broader arena of postsecondary education (lumpers), or whether FPCUs instead represented a unique and singular departure from that broader area (splitters). Despite all of the differences between FPCUs and TCUs that we have examined here, ultimately they represent variations on a common theme more than they represent two distinct entities, and this should become more evident in the future.

Adelman, C. 2000. A parallel universe: Certification in the information technology guild. *Change, 32*(3): 20–29.

———. 2004. *Principle indicators of student academic histories in postsecondary education, 1972–2000.* Washington, DC: U.S. Department of Education, Institute of Education Sciences.

Allen, I. E., and J. Seaman. 2004. *Entering the mainstream: The quality and extent of online education in the Unite d States, 2003 and 2004.* Sloan Consortium. www.sloanc.org/resources/entering_mainstream.pdf.

Altbach, P. G. 2002. Knowledge and education as international commodities: The collapse of the common good. *International Higher Education, 28*(3). Retrieved August 14, 2006, from www.bc.edu/bc_org/avp/soe/cihe/newsletter/News28/textoo1.htm.

American Council on Education. 2004. *Letter on behalf of 45 higher education associations.* Washington, DC: David Ward.

Autor, D. H. 2001. Wiring the labor market. *Journal of Economic Perspectives, 15*(1): 25–40.

Autor, D. H., R. Levy, and R. J. Murnane. 2002. *The skill content of recent technological change: An empirical exploration.* MIT Department of Economics Working Paper No. 01-22, September. Cambridge, MA.

Bassett, R. M. 2005. The high profile of trade in higher education services. *International Higher Education, 40*(3). Retrieved August 14, 2006, from www.bc .edu/bc_org/avp/soe/cihe/newsletter/Number40/p5_Bassett.htm.

Becker, G. S. 1975. *Human capital* (2nd ed.). Chicago: University of Chicago Press.

Berg, G. A. 2005. *Lessons from the edge: For-profit and nontraditional higher education in America.* New York: Praeger.

Birnbaum, R. 2005. Review of *The innovator's dilemma: When new technologies cause great firms to fail* and *The innovator's solution: Creating and sustaining successful growth. Academe, 91*(1): 80–84.

Blumenstyk, G. 2003. Financial outlook 2004: For-profit colleges; Growth at home and abroad. *Chronicle of Higher Education, 50*(17): A12. Retrieved August 14, 2006, from http://chronicle.com/weekly/v50/i17/17a01201.htm.

———. 2004. U. of Phoenix pressure in recruiting, report says. *Chronicle of Higher Education, 51*(7): A1. Retrieved August 14, 2006, from http://chronicle.com/weekly/v51/i07/07a00101.htm.

———. 2005. Outlook 2005: For-profit education; Online courses fuel growth. *Chronicle of Higher Education, 51*(18): A11. Retrieved August 18, 2006, from http://chronicle.com/weekly/v51/i18/18a01101.htm.

————. 2006a. New York regents adopt tougher restrictions on for-profit colleges. *Chronicle of Higher Education, 52*(39): A22. Retrieved August 14, 2006, from http://chronicle.com/weekly/v52/i39/39a02201.htm.

————. 2006b. Businesses have remedies for sale, but a cure is not guaranteed. *Chronicle of Higher Education, 52*(27): B30. Retrieved August 14, 2006, from http://chronicle.com/free/v52/i27/27b03001.htm.

————. 2006c. The chronicle index of for-profit higher education. *Chronicle of Higher Education, 52*(49): A24. Retrieved August 18, 2006, from http://chronicle.com/weekly/v52/i49/49a02401.htm.

Boehner, J., and H. P. McKean. 2005. *Outdated "90-10" higher education rule reduces college access for poor and minority students-and must be eliminated.* Retrieved January 21, 2005, from www.career.org/Template.cfm?Section=Home&CONTENTID=1697&TEMPLATE=/ContentManagement/ContentDisplay.cfm.

Bresnahan, T. F., E. Brynjolfsson, and L. M. Hitt. 2000. Information technology and recent changes in work organization increase the demand for skilled labor. In M. M. Blair and T. A. Kochan (Eds.), *The new relationship: Human capital in the American corporation* (pp. 145–84). Washington, DC.: Brookings Institution Press.

Brown, T. 2005. Assessing Ward Churchill's version of the 1837 smallpox epidemic. Retrieved February 24, 2005, from http://hal.lamar.edu/~browntf/Churchill1.htm.

Burton-Jones, A. 1999. *Knowledge capitalism.* Oxford: Oxford University Press.

Callan, P. M. 2002. Coping with recession: Public policy, economic downturns, and higher education. San Jose, CA: National Center for Public Policy and Higher Education. Retrieved February 2002, from www.highereducation.org/catreports/finance.shtml.

Career College Association. 2003. *Fact book 2003: A profile of career colleges and universities.* Washington, DC.: Career College Association.

Carnevale, A. P., and D. M. Descrochers. 2003. *Standards for what? The economic roots of K–16 reform.* Washington, DC: Educational Testing Service.

Cather, W. 1990. *The professor's house.* New York: Vintage Books.

Center for Educational Research and Innovation. 2000. *Knowledge management in the learning society.* Paris: Organisation for Economic Co-operation and Development.

Cervantes, M., and D. Guellec. 2002. The brain drain: Old myths, new realities. *OECD Observer,* May.

Childe, J. L., and A. Newell. 2004. *Education services: 2004 Post-secondary outlook.* New York: Bear Stearns Equity Research.

Christensen, C. M. 1997. *The innovator's dilemma: When new technologies cause great firms to fail.* Boston: Harvard Graduate Business School Press.

Christensen, C. M., and M. E. Raynor. 2003. *The innovator's solution: Creating and sustaining successful growth.* Boston: Harvard Graduate Business School Press.

Churchill, W. 2001. Some people push back: On the justice of roosting chickens. *Pockets of Resistance, 11* (September 11). Retrieved April 10, 2005, from www .darknightpress.org/index.php?i=news&c=recent&view=9.

———. 2005a. Ward Churchill responds to criticism of "Some people push back." Retrieved May 5, 2005, from www.kersplebedeb.com/mystuff/s11/ward_ churchill_reponds.html.

———. 2005b. What did I really say? And why did I say it? *Counterpunch.* Retrieved May 5, 2005, from www.counterpunch.org/churchill02212005.html.

Cohen, M., and J. March. 1974. *Leadership and ambiguity: The American college president.* New York: McGraw Hill.

Coombes, A. 2003. Trade schools graduate into big jobs, income producers. Retrieved July 22, 2005, from http://cbs.marketwatch.com.

Corinthian Colleges Inc. 2003. Corinthian colleges to expand into Canada. Santa Ana, CA: Corinthian Colleges Inc. Retrieved August 14, 2006, from http:// phx.corporate-ir.net/phoenix.zhtml?c=115380&p=irol-newsArticle&ID= 425150&highlight=.

———. 2004. *Medical assisting: Patient care and communication* (2nd ed.). Santa Ana, CA: Corinthian Colleges Inc.

———. 2005. Companyseek. Retrieved July 25, 2005, from www.companyseek .com/corinthiancolleges-COCO.htm.

Dodge, J. 2005. Regents respond to Churchill's essay at a meeting today. Retrieved May 5, 2005, from http://newmedia.colorado.edu/silverandgold/messages/ 4177.html.

Drucker, P. F. 1997. Seeing things as they really are. *Forbes, 159*(5): 122–29.

Fager, J. (Executive Producer). 2005. *60 Minutes.* January 30. Transcript of television broadcast. New York: Columbia Broadcasting System.

Finney, J. E., and P. Kelly. 2004. Affordability: Obtaining and making sense of information and how students, families, and states pay for higher education. *Change, 36*(4): 54–59.

Floyd. C. E. 2005. For-profit degree granting colleges: Who are these guys and what do they mean for students, traditional institutions, and public policy? In J. C. Smart (Ed.) *Higher education: Handbook of theory and research (Volume XX)* (pp. 539–90). Dordrecht: Springer.

Gabel, M., and H. Bruner. 2003. *Global, Inc.: An atlas of the multinational corporation.* New York: New Press.

Gallagher, S., and E. Bassett. 2004. *Postsecondary institutions learning markets and opportunities 2004: For-profit postsecondary education market overview.* Boston: Eduventures.

Gallagher, S., and B. Poroy. 2005. *For-profit postsecondary education sales and marketing overview 2005.* Boston: Eduventures.

Grant, G., and D. Riesman. 1978. *The perpetual dream: Reform and experiment in the American college.* Chicago: University of Chicago Press.

Gubins, S. 2006. Industry overview, ML conference highlights. *Education and Training Services Bi-Weekly.* Retrieved August 14, 2006, from www.ml.com/independent research.

Gubins, S., and L. R. Fine. 2005. Negative 60 minutes piece finally airs. *Education and Training Services Bi-Weekly,* January 31, p. 3. New York: Merrill Lynch.

Gubins, S., L. R. Fine, and H. Richey. 2006. ML conference highlights. *Education and Training Services Bi-Weekly,* March 3, p. 15. New York: Merrill Lynch.

Gubins, S., L. R. Fine, B. Rosen, and H. Chang. 2005. Postsecondary education primer. *Education and Training Services Bi-Weekly,* March 8, p. 18. New York: Merrill Lynch.

Halstead, K. 1998. *State profiles: Financing public higher education, 1978 to 1995.* Washington, DC: Research Associates of Washington.

Heller, D. E. 1997. Student price response in higher education: An update to Leslie and Brinkman. *Journal of Higher Education, 86*(6): 624–59.

———. 2003. Not all institutions are alike. *Chronicle of Higher Education, 50*(12): B7.

Henry, G. T., and R. Rubenstein. 2002. Paying for grades: Impact of merit-based aid on educational quality. *Journal of Policy Analysis and Management, 21*(1): 93–109.

Holland, E. 2003. The tale of two systems of delivering higher education. Arlington, VA: Lexington Institute.

Horn, L. J., J. Berktold, and A. G. Malizio. 1998. *Profile of undergraduates in U.S. postsecondary education institutions: 1995–96.* Washington, DC: National Center for Education Statistics.

Hughes, K. L., Bailey, T. R., and Mechur, M. J. 2001. School-to-work: Making a difference in education. New York: Institute on Education and the Economy, Teachers College Columbia University. www.tc.columbia.edu/iee/STWrelease .HTM.

Jencks, C., and D. Riesman. 1968. *The academic revolution.* Garden City, NY: Doubleday.

Karoly, L. A., and C. W. A. Panis. 2004. *The 21st century at work: Forces shaping the future workforce and workplace in the United States.* Santa Monica, CA: RAND Corporation.

Kinser, K. 2006. From Main Street to Wall Street: For-profit higher education. *ASHE Higher Education Report, 31*(5). J-B ASHE Higher Education Report Series (AEHE). San Francisco: Jossey-Bass.

Kirp, D. L. 2003. *Shakespeare, Einstein, and the bottom line: The marketing of higher education.* Cambridge, MA: Harvard University Press.

Knapp, L. G., J. E. Kelly, R. W. Whitmore, W. Shiying, and L. M. Gallego. 2003. Enrollment in postsecondary institutions, fall 2000 and financial statistics, fiscal year 2000. *Education Statistics Quarterly, 5*(2). Washington, DC: National Cen-

ter for Education Statistics. Retrieved October 10, 2003, from http://nces.ed
.gov/programs/quarterly/vol_5/5_2/q4_4.asp.

Knapp, L. G., J. E. Kelly-Reid, R. W. Whitmore, S. Wu, S. Huh, B. Levine, M. Berzof-
sky, and S. G. Broyles. 2005. *Enrollment in postsecondary institutions, fall 2002
and financial statistics, fiscal year 2002* (NCES 2005-168). U.S. Department of
Education. Washington, DC: National Center for Education Statistics.

Learning Business. 2004. "International Information Sources," Learning Busi-
ness.fi. Retrieved on July 25, 2005, from http://learningbusiness.fi/portal/
news/international_information_sources/.

Lechuga, V. M. 2005. *The changing landscape of the academic profession: Faculty culture at for-profit colleges and universities.* Ed.D. diss., University of Southern California.

Leslie, L. L., and P. T. Brinkman. 1988. *The economic value of higher education.* New
York: Macmillan.

Lexington Institute. 2003. *A tale of two systems of delivering higher education.* Arlington, VA: R. Holland.

Marchese, T. 1998. Not so distant competitors: How new providers are remaking
the postsecondary marketplace. *AAHE Bulletin,* May June, 24 35.

Maxine Waters School Reform and Student Protection Act. 1989. Education code:
Sections 94850–82.

Milken Institute. 2004. *Briefing book.* Milken Institute Global Conference (April
22–24). Los Angeles, CA.

Mishel, L., J. Berstein, and H. Boushey. 2003. *Working America, 2002/2003.* Ithaca,
NY: Cornell University Press.

Moore, D. 2004. Testimony of Mr. David Moore, Chairman and CEO, Corinthian
Colleges, Inc. Proceedings of the Committee on Education and the Workforce,
108th Congress, 2nd sess. Retrieved January 21, 2005, from http://edworkforce
.house.gov/hearings/108th/fc/heaprop061604/moore.htm.

Morgan, D. R., K. Kickham., and T. J. LaPlant. 2001. State support for higher education: A political economy approach. *Policy Studies Journal, 39*(3): 359–71.

National Center for Education Statistics. 1995. *Students at private for-profit institutions.* Washington, DC: U.S. Department of Education.

———. 1999. *Students at private, for-profit institutions.* Washington, DC: U.S. Department of Education.

———. 2001. *Digest for education statistics, 2001.* U.S. Department of Education:
Washington, DC.

———. 2002a. *Postsecondary institutions in the United States: Fall 2000 and degrees
and other awards conferred: 1999–2000.* Washington, DC: U.S. Department of
Education.

———. 2002b. *Enrollment in postsecondary institutions, fall 2000 and financial statistics, fiscal year 2000.* Washington, DC: U.S. Department of Education.

————. 2003a. *Digest of education statistics, 2003.* Washington, DC: U.S. Department of Education.

————. 2003b. *Characteristics of undergraduate borrowers: 1999–2000.* Washington, DC: U.S. Department of Education.

————. 2004a. *College persistence on the rise? Changes in 5-year degree completion and postsecondary persistence rates between 1999 and 2000.* Washington, DC: U.S. Department of Education.

————. 2004b. *Total expenditures of educational institutions related to the gross domestic product, by level of institution: Selected years, 1929–30 to 2003–04.* http://nces.ed.gov/programs/digest/d04/tables/dt04_029.asp.

————. 2005. *Enrollment in postsecondary institutions, fall 2003; Graduation rates 1997 and 2000 cohorts; and financial statistics, fiscal year 2003.* Washington, DC: U.S. Department of Education.

National Center for Public Policy and Higher Education. 2003. *Losing ground: A national status report on the affordability of American higher education.* San Jose, CA: NCPPHE.

Neumark, D., and D. Reed. 2002. *Employment relationships in the new economy.* Working Paper No. 8910. Cambridge, MA: National Bureau of Economic Research.

Noble, D. F. 1997. *Digital diploma mills, Part I: The automation of higher education.* Toronto: York University, National Coalition for Universities in the Public Interest.

Noone, L. P., and C. Swenson. 2001. Five dirty little secrets in higher education. *Educause Review, 36*(6): 20–31.

Osborne, D., and T. Gaebler. 1992. Catalytic government: Steering rather than rowing. In D. Osborne and T. Gaebler, *Reinventing government: How the entrepreneurial spirit is transforming the public sector* (pp. 25–48). Reading, MA: William Patrick.

Pak, R. 2005. Does Utah have a college graduate brain drain? Salt Lake City: Utah Foundation.

Peterson. 2006. *Online learning programs.* Retrieved August 15, 2006, from http://www.petersons.com/distancelearning/code/search.asp?path=ce.fas.distance.

Productivity Point. www.propoint.com.

Pulley, J. L. 2004. Federal rules hurt for-profit colleges and their students, conference speaker says. *Chronicle of Higher Education,* June 4. Retrieved June 4, 2004, from http://chronicle.com/daily/2004/06/2004060401n.htm.

Pusser, B,. and S. Turner. 2004. The challenge of convergence: Nonprofit and for-profit governance in higher education. In R. G. Ehrenberg (Ed.), *Governing academia* (pp. 235–57). Ithaca: Cornell University Press.

Readings, B. 1996. *The university in ruins.* Cambridge, MA: Harvard University Press.

Rosenau, P. V. (Ed.). 2000. *Public-private policy partnerships.* Cambridge, MA: MIT Press.

Ruch, R. S. 2001. *Higher ed, inc.: The rise of the for-profit university.* Baltimore: Johns Hopkins University Press.

Rudolph, F. 1962. *The American college and university: A history.* New York: Knopf.

Selingo, J. 2005. Facing down the e-maelstrom. *Chronicle of Higher Education,* 51(34): A27.

Silber, J. M. 2004. *Education and training.* New York: Harris Nesbitt Corp.

Smallwood, S. 2005. U. of Colorado will investigate allegations of misconduct against controversial professor. *Chronicle of Higher Education,* 51(30): A36.

Smith, P. 1990. *Killing the spirit: Higher education in America.* New York: Viking.

Society for College and University Planning. 2006. *Trends in Higher Education: February 2006.* Retrieved August 14, 2006, from www.scup.org.

Strayer Education. 2005. Securities and exchange commission form 10-k, annual report for fiscal year ending December 31, 2005. Retrieved August 16, 2006, from www.strayereducation.com/EdgarDetail.cfm?CompanyID=STRA&CIK=1013934&FID=950136–06–1965&SID=06–00.

Strosnider, K. 1997. For-profit university challenges traditional colleges. *Chronicle of Higher Education,* 43(39): A32.

Tierney, W. G. (Ed.). 2003. *Academic vantage points: Reflections on the university in the 21st century.* Los Angeles, CA: Center for Higher Education Policy Analysis.

———— (Ed.). 2004. *Competing conceptions of academic governance: Negotiating the perfect storm.* Baltimore: Johns Hopkins University Press.

U.S. Census Bureau. 2000. *Current population survey.* Washington, DC: U.S. Bureau of Labor Statistics.

U.S. Department of Education. 2003a. *Program review report: University of Phoenix* (PRCN 200340922254). Washington, DC.

————. 2003b. *Institutional and program eligibility.* 34 C.F.R.600.5. Washington, DC.

U.S. House of Representatives. 2004. H.R. 4283. To amend and extend the Higher Education Act of 1965. 108th Congress, 2nd Session.

Washington Post Company. 2005. *2004 annual report.* Retrieved August 14, 2006, from www.washpostco.com.

Wolanin, T. 2003. *Reauthorizing the Higher Education Act: Issues and options.* Washington, DC: Institute for Higher Education Policy.

INDEX

Page numbers in *italics* indicate figures and tables.